THE CARROT OR THE STICK
for School Desegregation Policy

The Carrot

or the Stick

for School Desegregation Policy

*Magnet Schools or
Forced Busing*

CHRISTINE H. ROSSELL

TEMPLE UNIVERSITY PRESS

Philadelphia

Temple University Press, Philadelphia 19122
Copyright © 1990 by Temple University. All rights reserved
Published 1990
Printed in the United States of America

The paper used in this publication meets the minimum requirements of American
National Standard for Information Sciences—Permanence of Paper for Printed
Library Materials, ANSI Z39.48-1984

Library of Congress Cataloging-in-Publication Data

Rossell, Christine H.
The carrot or the stick for school desegregation policy : magnet
schools or forced busing / Christine H. Rossell.
       p. cm.
Includes bibliographical references, p. 229
ISBN 0-87722-682-2
1. School integration—United States.   2. Magnet schools—United
States.   I. Title.
LC214.2.R66   1990
370.19′342—dc20
                                                                89-37634
                                                                     CIP

To
Jens and Elise,
Ann and Bob

Contents

Preface

THIS BOOK compares the desegregation effectiveness of voluntary plans with magnet schools to mandatory reassignment plans with magnet schools. In doing this it addresses a number of issues in the field of school desegregation and public policy. These issues include how school desegregation plans have evolved over time, how one measures the desegregation effectiveness of desegregation remedies, whether policies are more likely to achieve their goals and be more effective if citizens are commanded to obey or given incentives to do so, the characteristics of magnet schools that are attractive to white and black parents, the effect of magnet schools on the quality of education, the national school desegregation trends, and the relative merit of voluntary and mandatory plans as assessed by criteria commonly used by policy analysts. My analysis of these issues has generated some findings that, although surprising and contrary to three decades of school desegregation research, make sense given what we know about current racial attitudes and preferences and both big city and national demographic trends.

School desegregation plans, particularly court-approved desegregation plans, have changed dramatically from 1954 to the present and so has my thinking on what is an effective school desegregation plan. I am a liberal and a child of the sixties. I believed, as did many of my generation, that the civil rights movement was the embodiment of virtue and that racism and segregation were the embodiment of evil. School segregation was thus, like other forms of segregation, not only too important an issue to be left to the private actions of racist individuals, but if one wanted to actually eliminate segregation, it *could* not be left to individuals. As the Supreme Court observed in *Green v. New Kent County* (1968) some fourteen years after *Brown*, simply forbidding discrimination did not dismantle the dual system because whites and blacks did not transfer to opposite-race schools despite the repeal of segregation laws and the adoption of freedom of choice. The new information obtained from observing the outcome of the nondiscrimination remedies implemented from 1954 to 1968 served as the impetus for the court decisions that characterized the era of affirmative action school desegregation remedies—that is, remedies that forced blacks and whites to go to school together by requiring school districts to reassign students from their one-race schools to opposite-race schools.

Those of us doing research in the field of school desegregation believed in these affirmative action remedies. We had been convinced by the Coleman Report and by civil rights leaders that not only was "force" the morally correct position but that it was the most effective way to desegregate a school system. We believed this despite growing evidence in the mid-1970s that many school systems had or were experiencing what could only be described as massive white flight from desegregation. Only two academics, James Coleman and David Armor, were prescient enough during this period to conclude that white flight from mandatory reassignment plans was so extensive and long lasting that a voluntary plan might ultimately produce more desegregation. By contrast, I argued that, despite white flight, mandatory plans still produced more desegregation than voluntary plans, and equally as important, mandatory reassignment of whites was the only technique able to desegregate all-black schools. I think that I also believed that a desegregation technique that was preferred by blacks but not by whites must be the morally superior technique as well.

In general then, those of us who favored mandatory reassignment plans in the 1970s felt that the case for their superiority rested on both their greater effectiveness in desegregating school systems and their moral superiority over freedom of choice. In terms of the three criteria by which public policies are often evaluated—effectiveness, equity, and efficiency—mandatory reassignments were thus thought to be superior to freedom of choice on the first two.

This changed, however, with the advent of magnet–voluntary plans in the late 1970s, which for the first time gave whites an incentive to transfer voluntarily to black schools. Given the reputation of choice plans in the 1960s as "token desegregation," it is a little surprising how often in the 1980s judges have been convinced of the greater effectiveness and efficiency of the magnet–voluntary plans. As a result, I know of no mandatory reassignment plan implemented in the North since 1981 and of only two implemented in the South since 1981. This does not mean, however, that the adoption of a voluntary plan by a court is an easy decision. A recent federal district court order in June 1989 in Natchez, Mississippi, suggests that whereas in the 1960s it took courage for judges to order a mandatory reassignment plan although they believed it to be the more effective plan, it now takes courage for judges in the Fifth Circuit (currently Mississippi, Louisiana, and Texas; formerly Florida, Alabama, Mississippi, and Georgia) to order a voluntary magnet school plan although they believe it to be the more effective plan. In the 1960s judges feared the wrath of white citizens; in the 1980s judges fear the wrath of appellate courts whose decisions can be easily misinterpreted as forbidding voluntary plans. Perhaps this will change before the decade is over, and voluntary plans with incentives will become the conventional, preferred technique for southern courts in the same way that mandatory reassignment plans were in the 1970s. I can only hope that the publication of this book will contribute to this.

The writing of this book would not have been possible without the specific contributions and general support of numerous colleagues over the last decade and a half. Some of the findings with regard to parental opinion on magnet programs in Chapter 4 come from surveys conducted by David Armor and me in Yonkers, New York, and Savannah, Georgia. It was David Armor, however, who pioneered this technique and developed the instrument used to predict the actual behavior of parents in response to different kinds of desegregation plans. These surveys have proven to be remarkably accurate in forecasting not only the percentage of white students who will not show up at their assigned school if a mandatory reassignment plan is implemented, but also the percentage who will voluntarily transfer to an opposite-race school with or without magnet programs.

I am further indebted to both David Armor and James Coleman for having the courage to challenge the prevailing assumptions in school desegregation and educational research. They have caused many of us working in the field of school desegregation to clarify our thinking and improve our research.

My greatest obligation, however, is to Robert Crain who invited me to write my dissertation at Johns Hopkins University seventeen years ago using his data and working under his supervision. I have no doubt that his tutelage made a difference in the direction of my career. I am also indebted to Willis Hawley for giving me opportunities to grow and expand my research repertoire, culminating in several articles and our two books analyzing and synthesizing the findings of school desegregation research. These two gentlemen were the very finest role models for me. Finally, Jennifer Hochschild's very fine book, *The New American Dilemma*, has given me new ideas and a foil against which to play off my own work.

I have also learned a lot about the law and desegregation from the attorneys I have worked with from 1977 to 1989. These are William Gavin, Veronica Roeser, Mark Rosenbaum (ACLU), Bert Dougherty, Salliann Dougherty, Jeremiah Glassman, Franz Marshall, Gregg Meyers, Joseph Rich (Justice Department), and school district or city attorneys Michael Hoge (Seattle School District), Peter Collisson, Robert Post, and Celia Ruiz (San Jose Unified School District), John Dudley (Yonkers School District), Alfred Lindseth and Steve Scheer (Savannah School District), Holmes Adams and Cheri Green (Natchez School District), Richard Vernon (City of Laurel), Frank Hamsher, William

Werner (City of St. Louis), Tom Donovan (Berkeley Unified School District with Celia Ruiz), Gary Sams and Charles Weatherly (DeKalb County). The school district superintendents and deputies that I have worked with, Ramon Cortines (San Jose), Donald Batista and Joan Raymond (Yonkers), Ronald Etheridge and Cecil Carter (Savannah), Andrew Viscovich and Clifford Wong (Berkeley), Melvin Buckley (Natchez), and their staffs taught me how school districts are run and gave me confidence that they are administered by intelligent, decent men and women trying to do the best job possible in a world of limited resources.

Ruth Clarke was my graduate research assistant on this project. She supervised the data collection, assembled the data file, and generated the indices used in this analysis. Her expertise with computers and data assembly is unsurpassed, and I owe her a debt of gratitude. There is simply no one who understands these data and their construction the way she does. The project was funded by the National Institute of Education and the Department of Education over a period of four years by grants NIE-G-83-0019 and G008720232.

This report would not have been possible without the professional, competent, and helpful assistance of school personnel in each of the 119 school districts in this sample. Since 1974, Office for Civil Rights data have only been collected in the even-numbered years, and so the enrollment data for the odd years, as well as much of the desegregation plan information, have been obtained directly from the school districts. No matter how many times my staff and I wrote or called for further data and clarifications, no matter how many questions we asked, we were always treated in a manner which cheered us on and enabled us to complete this research. Indeed, this has been my experience for the last seventeen years of conducting school desegregation research.

The completion of this project to date has depended on the assistance of Keith Culbertson, Denise Flood, Diah Hamidjojo, Melinda Ho, Priscilla Lee, Aurora Martarell, Kim Nash, Patrick

Ng, and numerous others in the coding of these data. Keypunch-
ing and quality control were provided by Shannon MacDougall
and Dennis Ross. Word processing and Lotus 1-2-3 analysis
were provided by Jennifer Bump, Judy Carbone, Lisa Duchene,
Denise Flood, Pam Gueldner, Suzanne O'Connor, and Haeyoung
Sohn. I was assisted in the editing of this book by Judy Carbone,
Gretchen Lovas, and Scott Osberg.

I am grateful to Gary Orfield for comments on an earlier
draft of this manuscript and to Jane Barry for brilliant copy editing. I would also like to thank Michael Ames, editor-in-chief at
Temple University Press, for expediting a decision on this manuscript when I requested a quick turn-around. I thank Mary Ca-
pouya, my production editor at Temple, for her patience, alert-
ness, and intelligence. I take sole responsibility, however, for
errors and omissions.

Finally, I thank my parents for raising me to believe in the
baseness of racial and ethnic prejudice, and my husband Jens
Sorensen and our daughter Elise Sorensen Rossell for enriching
my life and for putting up with the many hours of work this
project has taken from our home life.

THE CARROT OR THE STICK
for School Desegregation Policy

1

The Past and the Future of School Desegregation Remedies

The Evolution of School Desegregation Remedies

FROM THE perspective of black Americans, the 1980s must appear to be a time of retrenchment and lack of momentum—even of loss of some hard-won gains of the 1960s. The civil rights conviction of the 1960s that "we shall overcome" has become in the minds of many "we shall hold our own."

The most obvious cause of this perception is the Reagan administration's conservative policies on welfare and civil rights. But even before Ronald Reagan was elected, there was a feeling among blacks, intellectuals, and others that in the wake of "forced busing" and affirmative action, the civil rights coalition had disintegrated. With the change in civil rights policies from the symbolic to the tangible, costs escalated for the middle-class white students and intellectuals who had made up the white contingent of the coalition. The coalition had been united in protesting government-enforced segregation of one group of Americans from another group, but this unity dissolved when confronted with government policies that, in the eyes of many, seemed to substitute one form of discrimination for another.

Even without a change in the nature of civil rights policies, it would be hard to recreate the moral fervor of the 1960s that culminated in the passage of the 1964 Civil Rights Act. Forty-five years have passed since Gunnar Myrdal, the Swedish social sci-

1

entist, shocked American intellectuals by documenting the condition of black Americans in *An American Dilemma: The Negro Problem and American Democracy*. The gap between the democratic creed of equality and the fact of racial inequality, between our words and our deeds, was an egregious but rarely articulated flaw in the fabric of American democracy. It was a flaw that would, Myrdal contended, become increasingly intolerable to white Americans and this discomfort would lead inevitably to improvement in the lot of black people. So long as the American creed—that all men are created equal—retained its legitimacy, change would come about because the moral conscience of white America would be unable to live with the contradiction between their high-minded beliefs and their actual behavior and they would begin to demand change. With the benefit of hindsight, it seems clear that black protest as much as white guilt was a catalyst for change. Nevertheless, there can be no doubt that the civil rights movement achieved its symbolic goals; the United States has made great strides toward being an egalitarian society.

From a legal standpoint, black Americans have voting rights and equal access to public accommodations. Discrimination in housing, employment, and education is illegal. Indeed, the entire framework of legalized discrimination has been swept away. At the very heart of this transition in the legal basis of American race relations and the status of black Americans is the *Brown v. Board of Education*[1] decision of 1954. It is hard to find an intellectual who does not revere the *Brown* decision. Even J. Harvie Wilkinson (1979:62), a leading conservative in the Reagan administration's Justice Department, writes, "No single decision has had more moral force than *Brown;* few struggles have been morally more significant than the one for racial integration of American life."

The impact of the *Brown* decision has been far wider than school desegregation. Indeed, shortly after this decree federal courts at all levels were citing *Brown* in cases challenging different forms of official segregation. Against segregated beaches in Baltimore, golf courses in Atlanta, and public housing in Michigan and Missouri, *Brown* was invoked again and again to show that state-sanctioned segregation must be expunged from the laws. *Brown* eliminated the status of black Americans as "official pariahs." It set forth, as a goal of the American people, the elimination of discrimination and thus of segregation.

The means by which this would be accomplished, however, continued to evolve over the next four decades. From 1954 to 1970 desegregation was largely token and voluntary throughout the United States. In the North, desegregation was accomplished through political rather than legal demands because no northern states had segregation laws—the few that had had them in the past had abolished them after the Civil War. The demand for school desegregation in the North, of course, generated serious political conflicts. In each case the outcome depended on the political power of the various groups involved: the black civil rights leaders, black and white elected officials, the school board, the school superintendent and administration, the mayor, the civic elite, and black and white "grass roots" organizations. The demand might be in the form of a letter, a demonstration at a school board meeting, or a lawsuit, and it could be made by black parents of children attending an overcrowded school, a civil rights group, or a group of white parents whose children attended a racially changing school.

In the early 1960s, when demands for school desegregation were first being made in the North, most "professional" school administrators believed that desegregation was not a proper or a necessary function of the schools. First, they argued that school segregation was a function of segregated neighborhoods "freely" chosen by whites and blacks. Second, they claimed that desegregation placed an unreasonable burden upon the schools because it was a purely social, not educational, program.

Thus, desegregation in the North began as a bitter conflict over the proper role of the schools, with both sides seeing themselves as advocates of moral right. The American school system had had a long history of pretending to resist the intrusion of politics and interest groups in the pursuit of a universal, high-quality public education in which all students are treated the same regardless of their community, class, or social origin. School administrators argued that the role of the schools was to educate, not to remedy social ills created by the private actions of individuals in the larger society. In response, civil rights leaders accused the school systems of narrow-mindedness and racism.

The outcome of this conflict in the North was the same as in the South—the school districts did nothing or at most instituted a freedom-of-choice plan voluntary in nature, small in scope, and burdensome only to the black children willing to travel long distances at their own expense in order to reap its benefits. In the North these plans were called "majority-to-minority" desegregation plans. A child could transfer from any school in which his or her race was in the majority to any school in which his or her race was in the minority. Significant numbers of black students—as much as 25 percent of the black student population in a school district—got on a bus at their own expense to go to a white school across town because their parents believed what most Americans believe: that education is a means of upward mobility.

Desegregation in the South during this period consisted of court-approved "choice" plans, some very similar in concept to the northern plans. They took three forms: pupil-placement laws, freedom-of-choice plans, and "incremental desegregation" plans. Pupil-placement laws initially assigned students to the schools designated for their race. Requests for transfers were then considered on an individual basis, in light of various "non-racial" factors. These included the "psychological effect" on the student of attending the requested school, the "psychological qualification" of the student for the curriculum at the requested school, the possibility of disruption within the school, and the possibility of protest or economic retaliation by whites against blacks in the community. Little desegregation was accomplished by these plans. Because the initial assignment was on the basis of race, the courts began in the early 1960s[2] to find them unconstitutional.

School authorities then replaced pupil-placement laws with freedom-of-choice plans. Most of these plans required every pupil to exercise a choice at the beginning of each school year, thus eliminating the automatic initial assignment of pupils to schools for their race. Although a pupil's choice could be denied only on grounds of overcrowding, the actual number of black students enrolling in desegregated schools was minuscule. A Student Non-Violent Coordinating Committee 1965 report explains why:

> One of the easiest ways for school boards to comply . . . is to adopt a so-called "freedom-of-choice" plan. The method is simple . . . get a few Negroes to sign up to attend white schools, and then let the local citizens "encourage" them to withdraw their applications. An even better way is to reject all Negro applicants because of overcrowding, bad character, improper registration, or any other excuses. . . . But, if by chance a few Negroes slip through—go directly to the parents' employers or the local welfare agent. (Cited in Orfield, 1969:128)

Virginia relied on its state pupil-placement board to keep integration to a minimum. The state board assigned all pupils to schools in accordance with three criteria that could be used to keep black students out of white schools:

1. Orderly administration of the public schools.
2. Competent instruction of the pupils enrolled.
3. Health, safety, education and general welfare of the pupils. (U.S. Commission on Civil Rights, 1962:163)

As a result of such tactics, almost 94 percent of southern black students were still in all-black schools in 1965. Consequently, the Office for Civil Rights (OCR) collaborated with the

Justice Department in tightening up guidelines for freedom-of-choice plans. The mechanics of the choice process were broken down into 25 "problem areas." One area involved the method of making choice forms available to black parents. Typically the forms were sent home with students. Parents were often afraid to have their child bring a form back to his or her principal that indicated that he or she wished to transfer to another school. In some districts black teachers were pressured to select black schools for their black students. In order to solve these problems, OCR created a new requirement that forms must be mailed to parents from school headquarters and parents must be permitted to return the forms by mail (see Orfield, 1969:137). Still the plans did not desegregate.

It was that fact that caused the Supreme Court finally to bite the bullet in 1968 in *Green v. County School Board of New Kent County, [Virginia]*.[3] Although *Green* is much less well known than *Brown*, current debates over race and schools probably owe their intellectual origins to *Green*, not *Brown*, because it was in *Green* that the Court finally decided that eliminating racial discrimination was not enough to establish a unitary system (that is, a system in which there were no white schools and no Negro schools, but "just schools"). The actual requirement was not "just schools," but schools that were racially mixed to a greater degree than would occur merely as a result of ending discrimination.

Green thus marked the end of the period of "nondiscrimination" remedies and began the period of "affirmative action" remedies. Plans were not only to be judged by their effects, but it was assumed a priori after *Green* that the most effective plan would be one that *required* black and white students to transfer from their formerly one-race schools to opposite-race schools. This conclusion was drawn on the basis of empirical observation by the Court that forbidding discrimination and allowing voluntary transfer plans had not dismantled the dual system of black and white schools. As the Court noted of the two-school New Kent County system:

The New Kent School Board's "freedom-of-choice" plan cannot be accepted as a sufficient step to "effectuate a transition" to a unitary system. In three years of operation not a single white child has chosen to attend Watkins school and although 115 Negro children enrolled in New Kent school in 1967 (up from 35 in 1965 and 111 in 1966) 85% of the Negro children in the system still attend the all-Negro Watkins school. In other words, the school system remains a dual system.

Green was followed by *Alexander v. Holmes*[4] which prohibited incremental desegregation, including grade-a-year plans and other proposals that delayed desegregation. Grade-a-year plans are phased so that one additional grade is added to the plan each year. For example, the first year's plan might begin by desegregating 12th grade; the second year's plan would add the 11th grade, so that 11th and 12th grades were desegregated; and so forth. A grade-a-year plan might also start with the lowest grade and work its way up. Regardless of the starting point, such plans could take up to 12 years to be fully implemented.

Alexander put an end to delayed desegregation plans, forcing the district courts to order immediate massive desegregation in the middle of the school year for all school boards in active litigation in the Fifth Circuit. Between 1970 and 1971 the public schools of the Deep South were substantially integrated by court orders based almost exclusively on segregation statistics.

The Fifth Circuit carefully avoided using loaded terms like "busing" and "racial balancing." Nevertheless, extensive transportation was required in most of these cases solely on a showing of insufficient racial mixing in the local schools. Although the court was silent on the extent of permissible remedies, these plans usually included the pairing or clustering of schools and the redrawing of attendance zones. In a typical pairing of a K–5 black school and a K–5 white school (that is, schools with kindergartens and grades one through five), all students would go to the white school for grades K to 2 and to the black school for grades 3 to 5. In a three-school clustering, all students would typically go to one school for grades K and 1, another school for grades 2 and 3, and a third school for grades 4 and 5. These plans also included the redrawing of attendance zones so that some schools were integrated while continuing to have contiguous attendance areas.

Plan characteristics were not specified in *Green* or *Alexander*. Nor was the degree of integration that would have to be achieved or any deviation that might be allowed in individual cases. The school districts simply did what was necessary to achieve court approval of their plans, and that usually meant adopting the plaintiff's plan. It was not until *Swann v. Charlotte–Mecklenburg Board of Education*[5] in 1971 that the Supreme Court specifically addressed the issue of permissible remedies. *Swann* represented an innovation in the determination of both violation and remedy. The Court found that a school board that had racially motivated institutional practices, such as locating black schools in the middle of black neighborhoods and creating segregated feeder patterns, was guilty of de jure segregation even when the state segregation law had long since been rescinded. This finding foreshadowed the beginning of findings of unconstitutional segregation in the North. The major permissible remedies discussed in *Swann* were: (1) racial balance; (2) nondiscriminatory one-race schools; (3) altering of attendance zones, and pairing, clustering, or grouping of schools; and (4) transportation of students out of their neighborhood to another school in the district.

With regard to racial balance—the extent to which each school must reflect the racial composition of the school district—the Supreme Court held that mathematical ratios were permissible but not required. It found no constitutional requirement to have every school in every community reflect the racial composition of the school system as a whole, although that was "a useful starting point in shaping a remedy."[6]

One-race schools are not unconstitutional per se, but the burden in a previously de jure segregated school system is on the school authorities to show that "such school assignments are genuinely nondiscriminatory."[7] With regard to the pairing of schools and altering of attendance zones, these and other techniques were to be judged by their results. They are permissible if they desegregate schools, even if they are "administratively awkward, inconvenient, and even bizarre in some situations and may impose burdens on some."[8]

Busing—the transportation of students from one part of the district to a school in another part of the district to achieve desegregation—was a permissible tool for dismantling a dual system where "feasible." Although the Court declined to provide any specific guidelines for future cases, it did state that busing was to be limited by considerations of time and distances, avoiding plans that would "either risk the health of the children or significantly impinge on the educational process."[9] In one court case the time limit was defined as anything over 45 minutes;[10] in another it was a bus ride of two and one-half hours per day for 1st- and 2nd-graders.[11] In 1977 the federal district court in Los Angeles, California, allowed busing distances taking an hour each way.

The principal question after *Swann* was whether—or, more realistically, when and how—the requirement of racial balance would be extended to racially imbalanced school systems outside the South. The question was answered in 1973 when, in *Keyes v. School District No. 1, Denver, Colorado*,[12] the first "northern" case to reach the Supreme Court, the Court found the requirement of racially balanced schools applicable to a school district that had never had a law mandating segregated schools. The Court still could not bring itself to state openly that it interpreted the Constitution as requiring integration. It continued to insist that the only requirement was the elimination of de jure segregation. However, de jure segregation was defined as encompassing almost any action a school board might take that resulted in racially imbalanced schools. Under *Keyes*, when intentionally segregative actions are found to have affected a "substantial portion of the schools," the burden of proof shifts to the defendant. The failure to desegregate a segregated school, even when that segregation results from neighborhood segregation and private acts of discrimination, is then seen as intentional segregation unless the school district can prove otherwise. In short, the concept of de jure segregation soon became so all-inclusive that it was almost impossible for a northern school district accused of de jure segregation to defend itself.

Attitudes Toward Desegregation

As a result of these decisions, mandatory reassignment or "forced busing" plans were implemented all over the United States between 1970 and 1976. They were accompanied by protest demonstrations, white flight, and, ironically, a reduction in racial prejudice. Indeed, if one focuses on racial attitudes, the end appears to justify the means. Figure 1.1 shows large reductions in school segregation in the South and similarly large reductions in racial intolerance in the same region from 1967 through 1976.[13] In the North, we find smaller reductions in school segregation and smaller reductions in racial intolerance. Although experiencing more attitudinal change and ultimately becoming more racially balanced, the South still exhibited more racial intolerance than the North in 1976.

There is nothing in these data that would suggest a causal relationship between desegregation and attitudes. What the data do show, however, is that the backlash predicted by opponents of government intervention simply did not appear in national polls.

Other polls show similar declines in racial prejudice and similar disparities between the South and the North during this period. As shown in Table 1.1, in 1959 the percentage of whites who would object to sending their child to a school with a "few" blacks was 72 percent in the South compared with 7 percent in the North (defined as nonsouthern states). By 1975 that proportion had declined to 15 percent in the South and 3 percent in the North. By 1980 there was no difference between the South and the North in the percentage objecting to sending a child to a

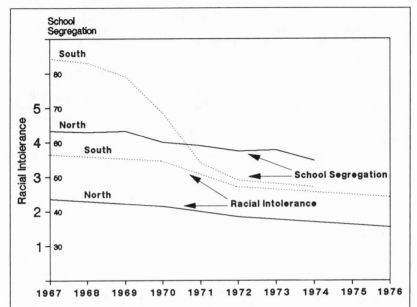

FIGURE 1.1   REDUCTIONS IN SCHOOL SEGREGATION AND REDUCTIONS IN RACIAL INTOLERANCE, 1967–1976

school where there were a few blacks. Only 5 percent said they would object.

Thus, these data suggest that the civil rights movement was extraordinarily successful in achieving its symbolic goals. Almost no one is upset if there are a few blacks in his or her child's school. The Little Rock crisis, and others like it, where angry white mobs protested against allowing a handful of black chil-

TABLE 1.1

ATTITUDE OF WHITE PARENTS TO SENDING CHILDREN TO SCHOOLS
WITH VARIOUS PROPORTIONS OF BLACK STUDENTS, 1959–1985

		Percentage of White Parents Objecting						
		Gallup					*NORC*	
Region	*Black Enrollment*	*1959*	*1965*	*1969*	*1975*	*1980*	*1983*	*1985*
South	"Few"	72	37	21	15	5		
	"Half"	83	68	46	38	27		
	"Majority"	86	78	64	61	66		
Outside	"Few"	7	7	7	3	5		
South	"Half"	34	28	28	24	22		
	"Majority"	58	52	54	47	51		
National	"Few"						5	4
	"Half"						18	16
	"Majority"						42	39

Sources: From a series of polls conducted by Gallup Poll from 1959 to 1980: *Gallup Opinion Index* (1976), no. 127, February, p. 9 (Princeton, N.J.: Gallup Poll); *The Gallup Poll: 1959–1971*, vol. 3 (Princeton, N.J.: Gallup Poll), pp. 1598, 1940–41, 2211; (1980), "Whites and Blacks in Sharp Disagreement on Busing: White Parents' Acceptance of Integrated Schools Has Grown Since 1958," no. 30, December 5–8, p. 4 (Princeton, N.J.: Gallup Poll); National Opinion Research Center (1972–1985), *General Social Surveys, 1972–85: Cumulative Codebook* (Chicago: NORC).

Note: Only parents who said they would not object to sending their children to school with a few blacks were asked the next question about a school whose enrollment was half black; only parents who would not object to those schools were asked the third question about predominantly black schools.

dren to enter their school, are in the past. Blacks are no longer "official pariahs."

Many whites are, however, still opposed to having a substantial number of blacks in their school. Opposition to a school that has a majority of black students has declined since 1959—from 86 percent of white southerners and 58 percent of white northerners to 39 percent of all whites by 1985—but this is still substantially higher than the 4 percent that would object to a school with a few blacks and the 7 percent who think that whites and blacks should go to separate schools (National Opinion Research Center, 1985).

At the same time that white racial intolerance was declining, white flight was increasing. With the advent of the post-*Swann* mandatory reassignment plans, white enrollment losses in the North grew from an average annual 2.4 percent loss before desegregation to a 10.0 percent loss with the implementation of a plan.[14] In the South, white enrollment losses went from an average 0.8 percent loss to a 7.5 percent loss (Rossell, 1978a: app. 1). The southern loss is even more dramatic because it occurred in the kinds of school districts once thought to be most immune to white flight—countywide districts already encompassing the suburban areas to which whites would normally be expected to flee.[15]

White flight is not inconsistent with white attitudes. Although whites support the principle of integration, they overwhelmingly oppose the most widely used method of desegregating schools—mandatory reassignment or "busing." In 1982, 77 percent of the white population opposed the busing of schoolchildren for the purpose of "racial balance," "school desegregation," or "school integration" (Gallup Poll, 1982). By 1988, this figure had declined only to 71 percent (National Opinion Research Center, 1988).[16] Overwhelming opposition is also found in local surveys. In 1986, 86 percent of white parents in Yonkers, New York, and 70 percent of white parents in Savannah, Georgia, were opposed to busing for school desegregation (Rossell, 1986b, 1986c). These findings contrast sharply with the mere 7 percent of whites who oppose the principle of school integration (National Opinion Research Center, 1985).

What accounts for the high level of rejection of busing? Two major theories of the determinants of political attitudes and behavior have been used to explain white opposition to busing. The first of these is that whites express attitudes and behave in ways that are in their own self-interest. In other words, white parents oppose busing because it entails real costs and burdens for them and their children. The second theory is that whites are motivated by diffuse attitudes formed in early childhood. In other words, racism explains white opposition to busing. Although white opposition to busing is undoubtedly more complex than these two theories would suggest, the utility of these competing models in explaining white opposition has been the center of a longstanding debate in political science and psychology (see, for example, McConahay, 1982; Sears et al., 1980; Sears, Hensler, and Speer, 1979).

The "self-interest" theory has been advanced by Buchanan and Tullock (1962), Downs (1957), Page (1977), Salem and Bowers (1972), and Stover and Brown (1975), who have argued that citizens express preferences or act on the basis of the relative costs and benefits of alternative preferences and actions. A self-interested attitude or action is usually defined as one that is instrumental to an individual's attainment of valued goals. Typically, in order to make the hypothesis falsifiable, the range of goals is restricted to those which bear directly on the material well-being of individuals' private lives—their financial status, health, shelter, family's well-being, and so on (McConahay, 1982; Sears et al., 1980; Sears, Hensler, and Speer, 1979).

The "diffuse attitudes" or "symbolic politics" research, by contrast, finds that attitudes acquired early in life are determinants of both general and specific support for political objects. The most important of these political objects are party identification, liberal or conservative ideology, nationalism, religious beliefs, and racial prejudice (Almond and Verba, 1963; Dennis, 1973; Easton, 1965; McConahay, 1982; Sears et al., 1980; Sears, Hensler, and Speer, 1979). When confronted with new policy issues later in life, individuals respond to them on the basis of longstanding beliefs about society and the polity rather than their current private needs.

In the case of busing, a symbolic politics perspective would suggest that whites acquire basic traditional social values, including racial prejudice, early in life. Although these attitudes may be modified later on by the social environment, they still persist. This combination of prejudice and traditional values inculcated in early childhood has been called "symbolic racism" by Kinder and Sears (1981) and "modern racism" by McConahay (1982). These authors argue that opposition to busing may be rationalized in terms of its negative or positive effects, but that it is in reality rooted in attitudes formed in early socialization.

On the other hand, some argue that opposition to busing is more influenced by self-interest than other areas of race relations that affect the private lives of white parents less directly and tangibly. Moreover, most opponents of busing have taken great pains to justify their positions on nonracial grounds. Both popular and scholarly opponents have asserted that busing harms education, causes great inconvenience and suffering to students and their parents, and violates the integrity of neighborhoods.

Most studies have found little evidence that self-interest has a significant influence on white opposition to busing. This was the finding of national surveys (Erbe, 1977; Kelley, 1974; Kinder and Rhodebeck, 1982; Sears et al., 1980; Sears, Hensler, and Speer, 1979; and Weidman, 1975); case studies of Los Angeles (Caditz, 1975, 1976; Kinder and Sears, 1981; Miller, 1981); Milwaukee, Wisconsin (Jacobson, 1978); Louisville, Kentucky (McConahay, 1982), and a case study of seven districts in Florida (Gatlin, Giles, and Cataldo, 1978). Nevertheless, there is some conflicting evidence on this issue. Armor's (1980) study of Los Angeles and Stinchcombe and Taylor's (1980) study of Boston, Massachusetts, controlling for attitudes toward racial integration, found greater opposition to busing among those whites who perceived busing as most costly. Sears and Allen (1984) found self-interest to have a significant effect on opposition toward busing in Los Angeles in the period between the court order and implementation. They hypothesize that periods like this one, characterized by a combination of high probability of desegregation and extreme anxiety and uncertainty over who will be affected, are most likely to produce the kind of attitudinal change that allows self-interest to dominate early socialization. They are also periods of maximum public protest and white flight (Rossell, 1983).

The phase during which self-interest might be related to opposition to busing could extend over a longer period than that identified by Sears and Allen, however; for example, McClendon and Pestello's (1982) study of Akron, Ohio, found self-interest to be significantly related to opposition to busing, explaining 16 percent of the variance. In contrast, opposition to desegregation and attitudes toward discrimination explained only 5 percent. This study was conducted in 1978 just after a school segregation trial had ended but before the court's decision. Similarly, Nicoletti and Patterson's (1974) study of Denver in 1969, conducted after a partial desegregation plan had been implemented, found self-interest to be significantly related to opposition to busing.

Self-Interest and Compliance

The studies discussed above involve attitudes or opinions. It is possible that self-interest may be even more important in predicting behavior. One type of behavior that is crucial to the outcome of any desegregation plan is white flight. My study of white flight in hundreds of individual schools in Los Angeles, Boston, and Baton Rouge, Louisiana, found that, on average, 55 percent of the white students reassigned to schools with minority enrollment above 90 percent did not show up at their assigned schools; the same was true of 47 percent of those reassigned to schools between 80 and 89 percent minority, and 43 percent of those reassigned to schools between 50 and 79 percent minority (Rossell, 1988). Across all minority schools, 50 percent of the whites reassigned did not show up at the minority schools they had been assigned to. On the other hand, of those white students who were allowed to remain at their neighborhood school, projected to be racially balanced at the same level as the formerly black schools, only 21 percent, on average, left the school system. This pattern alone suggests that self-interest is operating to some extent, since all schools were projected to have similar racial balances, but the loss was less than half as much when white students were allowed to stay at their neighborhood school as when they were transferred to another one.

The assumption that whites are acting on the basis of self-interest can be statistically tested. I hypothesized that whites were acting on the basis of self-interest if the relationship between the percentage of students who are minority and white flight disappeared when other important characteristics that affect the quality of education and quality of life were statistically controlled. The characteristics that capture self-interest are the social class and academic achievement of the students at the minority or white school, busing distance, and school characteristics. We would expect white parents to be acting in their self-interest if white flight is greater: (1) the lower the social class of the minority school whites are assigned to; (2) the higher the social class of the white school reassigned from; (3) the greater the busing distance; and (4) the larger the assigned school. Because these self-interest variables are also related to the percentage of students who are minority in a school, it is necessary to control for them to determine whether the relationship between percentage minority and white flight is spurious.

In Los Angeles, the relationship between the percentage of students who are minority and implementation-year white flight (a statistically significant correlation of .26) disappeared when these other variables were controlled, but in Baton Rouge it remained. Thus, in the implementation year, self-interested behavior appears to be less strong in Baton Rouge than in Los Angeles, where self-interest was evident in the relationships between white flight and the social class of the minority school and the busing distance to it. In Baton Rouge, the significant relationship between preimplementation percent black and white flight (r = .61) remained even when these other variables were controlled.

On the other hand, there was some evidence of self-interested behavior in Baton Rouge. There was more white flight in

both Baton Rouge and Los Angeles when the academic achievement of the white school was higher. This reflects self-interest
in that the higher the academic achievement of a white school,
the greater the likelihood that the minority school its pupils are
assigned to will be one with lower achievement. On the other
hand, the higher the academic achievement of a white school,
the higher the income and the greater the ability to leave. Thus,
if higher income is only a surrogate for ability to leave, it is not,
strictly speaking, a measure of self-interest.

Self-interested behavior was demonstrated in the post-implementation year in both districts. In Baton Rouge, the relationship between the percentage black and white flight disappeared, and there was more white flight when the achievement
of the formerly minority school was lower. On the other hand,
the percentage black in the white school the previous year became a significant predictor in Los Angeles. But so did the social
status of the minority students. The higher the social status of
the minority students, the less white flight.

Busing distance was not related to white flight in Baton
Rouge in the implementation year, although it was in Los Angeles. One possible explanation has to do with the salience of the
issue in each school district. With transportation taking up to an
hour in Los Angeles, the issue was highly publicized and very
important to white parents. With no bus ride over 20 minutes in
Baton Rouge, the issue was less controversial and salient there.

Busing distance is not the only issue on which Los Angeles
parents had more information than Baton Rouge parents. Los
Angeles went through a voluntary pairing stage in the year before desegregation. Parents in each school were asked to select a
school with enrollment of the opposite race to be paired with.
Accordingly, school administrators provided white parents with
extensive information on the characteristics of the minority
schools. This was not done in Baton Rouge and in fact appears to
be unique to Los Angeles.

Hence, one interpretation of this study is that where parents
are provided with accurate information on the achievement and

social class of minority schools, they will act rationally on that information, minimizing racial considerations. Where they are not provided with such information, racial composition may be perceived as a surrogate for quality of education. Indeed, the fact that the achievement of the minority school became important to parents in Baton Rouge only after a year of experience at such schools suggests that they had previously lacked sufficient information to perform the kind of self-interested cost–benefit analysis performed by Los Angeles parents. In short, the analysis of school-level white flight in Los Angeles and Baton Rouge suggests that the clearer and more reliable the information available to parents, the more they act in a rational, self-interested manner and the less they act on irrational, racial fears.

This does not mean, of course, that racial fears are not at all important. As suggested above, white behavior is probably more complicated than either theory suggests. Nor does this analysis mean that Baton Rouge parents were not acting on the basis of self-interest. It is possible that they were acting on the basis of misinformed self-interest. The analysis presented here cannot, unfortunately, test this. Nevertheless, if one has to choose one theory over the other, these data suggest that the self-interest theory more accurately describes the current behavior of most whites than the racism theory.

The Public Choice Model

The possible dominance of self-interest factors over racial factors in motivating compliance with desegregation plans has important implications for the direction of school desegregation policy. If racism is the cause of white opposition to busing, then there is little hope of designing plans that will both appeal to the interests of whites and desegregate school systems, since three-fourths or more of whites are opposed to busing and thus "racist" (see McConahay, 1982, on this point). On the other hand, if nonracial considerations, especially self-interest, are the strongest motivators of white flight, then political actors can modify school desegregation plans to accommodate the personal, economic, and educational demands of different groups.

One type of school desegregation plan that might harness self-interest is a voluntary "choice" plan in which superior magnet programs with higher per pupil expenditures and special curricula are placed in minority neighborhood schools. If self-interest is operant in the realm of school desegregation, then such plans might entice white parents to volunteer for magnet schools and thus produce more interracial exposure than mandatory plans that cause half the whites to leave the school system.

The use of magnet schools to attract students to desegregated schools is an alternative to "forced busing" that has its intellectual foundation in public choice theory. Public choice theory is the application of microeconomic theory to problems within the public domain. Like the self-interest theory of attitudes, public choice theory presumes that citizens will act in their own self-interest, as do consumers in the marketplace (Buchanan and Tollison, 1984; Downs, 1957; Friedman, 1962; Friedman and Friedman, 1981; Olson, 1965; Tiebout, 1956). This model assumes that it is more efficient for a government agency to seek to change the behavior of citizens by restructuring, rather than bluntly limiting, the environment of choice. The targeted population has the freedom to choose among a wide range of alternatives. They are expected to act in the manner that is economically most advantageous to them—as if they were operating in a marketplace—but they are encouraged through positive and negative incentives to pick actions that are consistent with the desired social goals.

In a magnet school plan, this model would operate in the following way. Most or all of the predominantly minority schools that need to be desegregated would be selected to have magnet programs. (If they already have good reputations in the community, white schools can often be desegregated solely by minority student transfers under a majority-to-minority transfer program, as long as students are given transportation.) More money would be spent on the magnet schools in order to attract white students, and their curricula would be altered so that each magnet school's curriculum has a special theme or focus. The magnet school themes would be widely publicized, and parents would be actively and aggressively recruited. The primary assumption behind the implementation of a magnet school program in a segregated neighborhood school system is that parents will evaluate the educational program of the neighborhood school and that of the desegregated magnet school in rational, programmatic terms. The corollary assumption is that the additional money spent on the magnet school and its special theme will be sufficient to induce large numbers of white parents to choose the magnet schools and thus desegregate both the individual schools and larger school system.

Although numerous scholars have recommended the use of incentives to induce voluntary desegregation (Armor, 1980; Bullock, 1976; Meadows, 1976; Orfield, 1976; Rossell and Hawley, 1982), the efficacy of the public choice model for desegregation has been questioned as much in the literature on desegregation remedies as it has been in the literature on racial attitudes. The general conclusion, even in writings as late as 1988, is that voluntary plans do not work (Orfield, 1978, 1988; Rossell, 1978a, 1978b, 1979, 1983; Rossell and Hawley, 1983; Royster, Baltzell, and Simmons, 1979). A review of the research by Hawley and Smylie (1986:282), for example, citing studies published through 1983, concludes:

> Wishful thinking to the contrary and occasional anecdotes notwithstanding, wholly voluntary strategies are only partially successful in reducing racial isolation. . . . Those based primarily on voluntary strategies . . . have limited impact on levels of racial isolation throughout the system, particularly in districts with substantial proportions of minority students.

Similarly, the Fifth Circuit Court of Appeals concluded that a voluntary plan with magnets proposed for the Hattiesburg, Mississippi, school district "did not meet the constitutional test for dismantling a long established dual system. Magnet schools should be a supplement to a mandatory desegregation plan based to a reasonable extent on mandatory reassignment and pairing and clustering of schools."[17]

Thus, the dominant model of policymaking in the school desegregation literature and in the courts is the "command and control" model. In this model citizens are assumed to be recalcitrant, so that compliance must be mandated. Directions and prohibitions are drafted with a limited, specific range of actions in mind. For school desegregation policy, this principle takes the form of specific assignments of specific students to schools that their attendance will desegregate. The command and control model is assumed to be more effective in achieving the goal of desegregating a school system because citizens are either too consumed by racial prejudice to act in their own self-interest, or because no school district can afford the kind of incentives that would be necessary for benefits to outweigh costs in the minds of parents whose early childhood socialization weights the costs of desegregation heavily. Even if evasion (that is, white flight) occurs, the model assumes that the net benefit from a command and control approach will still be greater than if one relied on voluntary transfers.

The public choice model and the command and control model each suggest a model of individual decisionmaking. The public choice model assumes that sufficient numbers of parents are rational enough on issues of desegregation and race that they will embrace the socially desirable goal of school integration when incentives are provided. Rationality, of course, is a function of the way that costs and benefits are perceived by parents. Schwartz (1976), for example, distinguishes between accurate and inaccurate perception of benefits and suggests that motivation that depends on some expectation of benefits should be considered rational, whether or not the expectation is accurate.

This distinction applies to school desegregation plans as well. If parents volunteer for a magnet school because they believe their child will receive a better education in one, they should be considered rational regardless of the accuracy of that belief. If parents withdraw their child from the school system because he or she is mandatorily reassigned to a formerly black school that they consider educationally inferior, they should be considered rational whether that school is educationally inferior or not. Unfortunately, because there is usually no information on parental beliefs, we have to depend on aggregate analyses of school characteristics that assume accurate information. These analyses can demonstrate that most parents are rational because they appear to be considering objective information on school quality, but not that parents are "irrational" when they appear not to be considering such information.

Nevertheless, if the command and control model of policymaking is more effective than the incentive model, this implies that most citizens are primarily motivated by attitudes formed in early socialization; incentives (at least as presently structured) will not lure them out of their neighborhood schools to desegregated magnet schools. They have to be "forced" to go to desegregated schools.

Of course, neither model describes all behavior in this area. It is always possible that people are more rational on these issues than the extent of volunteering for magnet schools would suggest, but that for most people the incentives are not yet great enough to overcome their lingering racial fears. Aggregate analysis is fraught with uncertainty over causality, hence in the analysis that I present in this book, I frequently use modifiers such as "most" or "sufficient numbers" when I am comparing parental volunteering for desegregated magnet schools to parental compliance with mandatory reassignment, the command and control approach.

Magnet School Plans

It is possible to assess to a degree the competing models of policymaking and individual behavior described above because there are now a number of voluntary magnet school plans with which to compare the mandatory plans. In 1976, four years prior to the Reagan administration, two federal district courts simultaneously approved plans that relied primarily on incentives to motivate voluntary transfers. In *Arthur v. Nyquist*,[18] the federal district court found the school board of Buffalo, New York, guilty of intentional segregation. In a second, unpublished decision, the court approved implementation of a plan that relied primarily on magnet schools in black neighborhoods and on majority-to-minority transfers to white schools to desegregate the elementary schools (grades K–8). In *Amos v. Board of Directors of the City of Milwaukee*,[19] the federal district court found the Milwaukee school board guilty of intentional segregation and, in a series of subsequent decisions,[20] approved a plan similar to Buffalo's that relied primarily on magnet schools to desegregate black schools and on majority-to-minority transfers to desegregate white schools. This decision was followed by court-approved magnet school plans in other school districts, such as San Diego, California, Houston, Texas, and San Bernardino, California, and was preceded by modest magnet school plans adopted by school boards in predominantly white school systems in the West, such as Tacoma, Washington, and Portland, Oregon.

The courts have also allowed mandatory plans to be dismantled and replaced with magnet school plans. In 1988 in Savannah–Chatham County, Georgia, a federal district court approved the dismantling of the mandatory assignment plan implemented in 1970 and 1971 after *Alexander*. The court opinion gave the following reason:

> During the first year [of the 1971 mandatory reassignment plan], approximately forty-two percent of all white students assigned to a black receiving school failed to enroll in the school to which they had been assigned mandatorily. This "white flight" continued over the years as the school district, which had been a majority white district prior to the 1971 plan, became predominantly black. It became increasingly clear that the mandatory plan under which the school system had been operating since 1971 was unsuccessful in eliminating the last vestiges of the prior dual system and in achieving a unitary system in compliance with the mandates of the Court.[21]

The mandatory assignment plan was ordered to be replaced by a magnet school plan with three essential features: (1) "revised attendance zones designed to maximize desegregation through emphasis on a neighborhood school assignment plan"; (2) "magnet programs at eleven predominantly black inner city schools in order to desegregate those schools"; and (3) "a majority-to-minority transfer option to desegregate predominantly white schools."[22] In approving the school district's primarily voluntary plan based on magnets and majority-to-minority transfers, the court stated that "the law does not require that a desegregation plan be mandatory in any way, only that it be effective."[23]

Thus, we see desegregation remedies coming full circle. The first desegregation plans after *Brown* relied on the voluntary transfer of students. These plans did not desegregate school systems, either because blacks were intimidated from transferring to white schools or because, when they attempted to transfer, they were told there was no room for them. As a result, in 1968 the courts began to approve only plans that relied on mandatory reassignment, using such techniques as pairing and clustering and the redrawing of attendance zones.

The court opinions did, however, occasionally point out that voluntary plans per se were not unconstitutional. In *Green* the Supreme Court held: "'Freedom-of-choice' is not a sacred talisman; it is only a means to a constitutionally required end—the abolition of the system of segregation and its effects. If the means prove effective, it is acceptable, but if it fails to undo segregation, other means must be used to achieve this end."[24] In *Swann* the Court held that "an optional majority-to-minority transfer provision has long been recognized as a useful part of every desegregation plan. . . . In order to be effective, such a transfer arrangement must grant the transferring student free transportation and space must be made available in the school to which he desires to move."[25] Thus, voluntary plans and other plans involving race-neutral assignment policies were to be evaluated in terms of their results. Where freedom of choice offers a real promise of achieving a unitary, nonracial system, there should be no objection to allowing it to prove itself in action.

What appears to have changed since 1968 is not the courts' willingness to approve "unworkable" voluntary plans, but their opinion as to whether such plans might work. The growing belief that voluntary plans *can* work is founded on a number of remarkable social changes that have occurred in the intervening years: (1) the overwhelming acceptance by whites of racial integration of the schools; (2) the overwhelming rejection by whites of "forced busing" to achieve this; (3) the public perception of continuing white flight from mandatory reassignment plans; and (4) the creation of magnet school plans that appear to provide an incentive for whites to act in accordance with both their self-interest and their support of integration. The belief on the part of the courts and school district policymakers that magnet plans might work, however, is a relative judgment based on a comparison of voluntary plans with mandatory plans that seemed not to work because they gave whites no incentive to comply.

Departures from Past Research

Is the public choice model the most effective model for school desegregation remedies? This book provides the most recent evidence on this question. The desegregation effectiveness of voluntary plans with magnet schools (the public choice model) is compared with that of mandatory plans with magnet schools (the command and control model) in a sample of 20 school districts, 18 of which were originally studied by Abt Associates (Rossell, 1979; Royster, Baltzell, and Simmons, 1979). This analysis differs from previous research on this subject in three ways. First, it compares the *long-term* impact of voluntary and mandatory plans. Although my own earlier (1979) work and that of Royster and associates (1979) concluded that magnet–mandatory plans produce more desegregation than magnet–

voluntary plans, each of these studies was limited by having only one year of postimplementation data to work with. Often, however, the long-term impact of a policy is very different from the short-term impact (see, for example, Salamon, 1979).

Second, much of the writing in this field has failed to distinguish between the source of the order and the degree of parental choice when defining a mandatory or a voluntary plan. Here "source" refers to whether a plan is board-ordered or court-ordered. The extent of parental choice should determine whether a plan is called "voluntary" or "mandatory," since the most important factor affecting white flight is parental choice, not the source of the order (Rossell, 1983). Thus, "board-ordered" is *not* synonymous with "voluntary," and "court-ordered" is *not* synonymous with "mandatory." In this sample, for example, 56 percent of the voluntary plans are court-ordered whereas 36 percent of the mandatory plans are board-ordered.

Third, even the most recent studies comparing the relative effectiveness of magnet–voluntary plans with magnet–mandatory plans have used dependent variables that are inadequate. This analysis uses a different measure of effectiveness, one that is more closely attuned to the instrumental goal of a desegregation plan as reflected in the desegregation court cases. The measure used here is the exposure of whites and blacks to each other—not merely racial balance, which can be achieved even as white flight reduces the likelihood of meaningful levels of interracial exposure.

In addition to examining the relative effectiveness of voluntary and mandatory desegregation plans, this book also looks at the specific characteristics of magnet programs and their relative attractiveness. Which characteristics are most successful in inducing parents to remove their children from neighborhood schools and enroll them in magnet schools?

Finally, this book assesses what school desegregation plans have accomplished to date and discusses their future. How far have desegregation remedies gone in terms of racial mixing?

Have school districts been required to racially balance all of their schools? How successful have magnet school plans been in big city school districts?

Outline of Chapters

The following chapter discusses the goal of a school desegregation plan. I make a distinction between interracial exposure and racial balance and argue that the goal should be to maximize interracial exposure because the benefits of school desegregation derive from it and not from racial balance. Chapter 3 compares the relative effectiveness of alternative desegregation plans—voluntary versus mandatory—in a 20-school-district subsample from a 119-school-district study. Chapter 4 compares the relative attractiveness of different magnet school programs—a school-level analysis—in the same 20-district sample. Chapter 5 assesses national desegregation trends from the 1960s through 1984 in the whole 119-school-district sample and singles out five big city desegregation plans to compare the relative effectiveness of voluntary and mandatory plans in producing interracial exposure in school districts of this type. Chapter 6 then summarizes the findings, makes policy recommendations, and discusses the model of citizen behavior suggested by these data. I also analyze the alleged superiority of metropolitan desegregation plans and discuss the problems involved in "controlled choice" plans. I compare the three major types of desegregation plans—freedom of choice, mandatory reassignment, and magnet–voluntary—in terms of the three criteria by which policy analysts typically evaluate policy outcomes: equity, efficiency, and effectiveness. The plan I find to be most equitable, efficient, and effective in achieving the goal of interracial exposure is a voluntary plan with incentives.

2

Defining School Desegregation and Its Goal

THE COURTS have proceeded incrementally in defining school desegregation. In 1954 school desegregation was simply the elimination of discrimination. Indeed, 15 years elapsed before there was any change in that legal concept.

By contrast, as early as 1964 the Office for Civil Rights (OCR) in the Department of Health, Education and Welfare (HEW) issued affirmative school desegregation guidelines for complying with the 1964 Civil Rights Act. These guidelines suggested specific yearly changes in the proportion of blacks attending white schools. OCR's measure of remaining segregation was the proportion of black students in schools with enrollments greater than 90 percent black. This is a crude criterion because it is dichotomous—an 89 percent black school is defined as desegregated and a 90 percent black school as segregated. Similarly, a school district with all of its schools at 89 percent black is a desegregated school district, and one with all of its schools at 90 percent black is a segregated school district.

In 1968 in *Green* the Supreme Court finally joined the federal government in placing the emphasis on policy output, racial mixing, rather than on input, a policy of nondiscrimination. In 1971 this was further refined in *Swann* by the finding that racial balance was a starting point. Although *Swann* noted that racial balance was not a constitutional requirement, subsequent decisions strongly emphasized it. If the student enrollment of a school district was 50 percent black and 50 percent white, the schools in that district were required to be 50 percent white and 50 percent black, with marginal deviations allowed.

The most common deviation approved by the courts was a plus or minus 15 percentage point variance for each school from the school district's overall racial proportions.[1] Although giving the appearance of flexibility, this measure, like the OCR guidelines, is crude. A school district could make great strides in reducing racial imbalance, but if it brought imbalanced schools only to within 16 percentage points of the district's overall racial proportions, it would get no credit. A plus or minus 20 percentage point criterion has also been approved in several court decisions in the late 1980s.[2]

The least sensible racial balance criterion in common use is the establishment of an absolute and specific range of racial proportions—such as that all schools must be between 40 and 55 percent black. With this kind of criterion, the school board has to go back to court every few years to get the specific percentages in the range changed as the school system's racial composition changes. For example, if a court order says that all schools have to be between 35 and 65 percent minority when the district's racial composition is 50 percent minority, the school district will have to go back to court to have the permissible percentages changed when its racial composition approaches 65 percent minority. It is physically impossible for a school system that is 66 percent minority to have all schools racially balanced at 65 percent minority. Indeed, for the range 35–65 percent, flexibility is dramatically diminished once the system's minority enrollment reaches 60 percent. Both Milwaukee and Buffalo have this problem with their court orders and as a result must go back to court periodically to change the specific percentages. They would thus be much better off if they had been given a relative range for each school, such as within 15 or 20 percentage points of the school district's racial composition, that would self-adjust to changing demographics.

The courts and the school districts have spent a good deal of time working toward a definition of what constitutes a desegregated school and a desegregated school district and little time explicating the overall goal of school desegregation. As we shall see, however, specifying the goal of a desegregation plan leads one to a definition of what constitutes desegregation at both the school and the district levels.

The primary goal of any school desegregation plan is to eliminate the effects of past discrimination. Because there are an infinite number of such effects, however, the primary goal is more precisely stated as the elimination of the harmful effects of past discrimination. These harmful effects inhere in the stigma of de jure segregation as well as in the unequal distribution of resources that is likely to accompany such segregation. Once these harmful effects have been eliminated, there remain three additional harmful effects that social scientists have identified: (1) the achievement gap between the races; (2) unequal status and conflict between the races; and (3) a lack of minority self-esteem and motivation.

The Effect of Interracial Exposure on Minority Children

Social scientists believe that the harmful effects of de jure segregation are eliminated by interracial exposure. This belief is supported by social science research that shows the educational and social benefits of desegregation to be derived from the percentage of students who are white in the average minority child's school. The most comprehensive and up-to-date research review ever conducted on school desegregation and educational achievement used a statistical technique called meta-analysis to synthesize the research findings of the available studies. Results indicate that although the relationship is not perfectly linear, the greater the percentage white in the average minority child's school, the greater the achievement gains by black children (Mahard and Crain, 1983). Despite disagreement over the size of this effect, I know of no other comprehensive review, or any other research, that has found another variable besides percentage white to be the "cause" of the positive effects of school desegregation. Of course, this does not mean that other factors or educational interventions, such as cooperative learning, could not produce positive effects in a desegregated setting *if* they were implemented.[3] Since they are rarely implemented and it is difficult to obtain information on such interventions in any case, the school desegregation evaluations do not control for these factors.

The research also demonstrates the influence of the student percentage white on black students' subsequent life chances. For example, a recent review conducted by Braddock, Crain, and McPartland (1984) cites 10 major studies that assess the social outcomes for minority adults who had a desegregated education. All but two of these studies had as their causal variable the percentage white in the minority child's school. The higher the percentage white, the greater the social benefits. These studies find that black students from majority-white high schools are more likely to enroll at majority-white four-year colleges, to have white social contacts, to have white friends, to live in integrated neighborhoods, and to have positive relationships with white co-workers. Crain and Strauss (1985) go even further. In their study of the Hartford one-way city–suburban busing program, which found higher educational achievement and career aspirations among the minority students bused into suburban schools, they argue that this effect is a function, not just of the percentage of students who are white in the school, but of the "change of scene." In other words, it is beneficial to minority children's life chances to get them out of minority neighborhoods and into white neighborhoods.

Two studies of the effect of school desegregation on residential integration cited by Braddock, Crain, and McPartland (1984) had change in school district racial balance as their independent variable and change in residential racial balance as their dependent variable. One of these studies (Pearce, 1980) indicates that the school district with the greatest reduction in residential racial imbalance—Riverside—was the school district with no mandatory reassignment of white students, and thus it may also have been the school district with the greatest interracial exposure. Other studies have indicated that what residential integration does occur with school desegregation comes from minority parents moving into the neighborhood of their child's new school, as in Riverside, rather than from whites following their children into minority neighborhoods (Foushee and Hamilton, 1977; Greenwood, 1972; Kentucky Commission on Human Rights, 1975, 1980a, 1980b). None of these studies provides evidence that whites need to be mandatorily reassigned in order to produce positive outcomes for minorities.

These studies do suggest, however, that producing the greatest interracial exposure for minority children—that is, the greatest percentage white in their classrooms—ultimately produces the greatest improvement in their life chances. This appears to be true even if only minorities do the transferring, as in the city–suburban transfer programs.

The Measurement of Interracial Exposure

Although social scientists believe that the harmful effects of segregation can be eliminated by interracial exposure, the literature assessing desegregation plans to date has usually examined the extent of interracial contact by assessing the amount of racial balance. The measure of racial imbalance most commonly used by social scientists is the index of dissimilarity, also called the Taeuber Index or the Duncan and Duncan Index. The formula is as follows:

$$D = \frac{1}{2}\sum \left| \frac{W_i}{W} - \frac{B_i}{B} \right|$$

where W_i is the number of whites (or any other ethnic or racial group) in each school, B_i is the number of blacks (or other group) in each school, and W and B are the numbers of whites and blacks (or other groups) in the school district as a whole. This calculation is then summed for all schools and divided by 2. The index of dissimilarity represents the proportion (or percentage if multiplied by 100) of black students who would have to be reassigned to white schools, if no whites were reassigned, in order to have the same proportion in each school as in the whole school district. The index ranges from 0 (perfect racial balance—that is, no black students need to be reassigned) to 100 (perfect racial imbalance—that is, 100 percent of the black students need to be reassigned, if no whites are reassigned, in order to have perfect racial balance).[4]

Another way of evaluating the contact between the races is to measure interracial exposure directly—specifically, the proportion of students who are white in the average minority child's school.[5] Although the measure can be used for any two groups, for the purpose described here it is used to measure any racial minority's exposure to whites. ("Minorities" are blacks, Hispanics, Asians, and American Indians.) The measure is calculated as follows:

$$S_{mw} = \frac{\sum_k N_{km} P_{kw}}{\sum_k N_{km}}$$

where k stands for each individual school and N_{km} is thus the number (N) of minorities (m) in a particular school (k) and P_{kw} is the proportion (P) white (w) in the same school (k). Hence, the number of minorities in each school is multiplied by the proportion white in the same school. The result is summed for all schools and divided by the number of minorities in the school system to produce a weighted average—the proportion white in the average minority child's school. Since this proportion increases with racial balance reassignments but goes down as the white enrollment decreases, it yields the interracial exposure or *net benefit* resulting from desegregation reassignments.

If the instrumental goal of school desegregation is to bring whites and minorities into contact with each other, then the best measure of its success is interracial exposure—the percentage white in the average black child's school—rather than racial balance. Interracial exposure is a function not only of racial balance, but of the proportions of whites and minorities in the school system. The level of interracial exposure for the average minority child is limited by the proportion white in the school system. Racial balance is an inadequate goal because it ignores how many whites are coming into contact with minorities. This is as true of the precise racial balance measures, such as the index of dissimilarity, as it is of the more imprecise racial balance standards used by the courts, such as the requirement that all schools be within 15 or 20 percentage points of the district's racial proportions. The index of dissimilarity, or any other measure of racial balance, is thus less comprehensive than the index of interracial exposure, because interracial exposure includes racial balance, but racial balance does not include interracial exposure. Racial balance can be achieved with very little interracial exposure, but interracial exposure cannot be achieved without significant racial balance.

This becomes clearer if we consider a hypothetical segregated school system with six schools and the racial composition shown in the first two columns of Table 2.1. Virtually all supporters of school desegregation would prefer a plan that pro-

TABLE 2.1

OUTCOMES OF TWO HYPOTHETICAL DESEGREGATION PLANS

	Original Status		Outcome A		Outcome B	
	Minorities	Whites	Minorities	Whites	Minorities	Whites
	100	0	50	20	50	1
	100	0	50	45	50	1
	100	0	50	40	50	1
	0	100	50	50	50	1
	0	100	50	45	50	1
	0	100	50	45	50	1
District Total	300	300	300	245	300	6
Dist. Percentage	50.0	50.0	55.0	45.0	98.1	1.9

duced outcome A, with considerable racial balance and 245 white students remaining, to a plan that produced outcome B, with perfect racial balance and 6 white students remaining.

Although outcome B has only one white in each school, it has a racial imbalance score of 0 (that is, perfect racial balance),[6] and all schools within 20 percentage points of the school district's proportions (98 percent minority and 2 percent white). If we multiply the number of minorities by the proportion white in each school, however, we find that whites account for only 2 percent of the students in the average minority child's school. Outcome B thus has perfect racial balance, but very little interracial exposure.

Outcome A, by contrast, has an index of dissimilarity of 8.8—that is, it is more racially imbalanced than outcome B. It also has one school (17 percent of the total number of schools) racially imbalanced according to a 15 or 20 percentage point criterion, whereas outcome B had none that were racially imbalanced by that standard. If we multiply the number of minorities by the proportion white in each school, sum across schools, and divide by the number of minorities in the district (300), we find 44.2 percent white in the average minority child's school.

If we have racial balance as our goal, we are forced to choose the intuitively less desirable plan in which there is only one white in each school. If we have interracial exposure as our goal, however, we will choose the intuitively more desirable plan in which the average minority child's school has a 44.2 percent white enrollment. This example also illustrates two basic principles of public policy analysis. Considering only the costs of a public policy (in this case, white enrollment decline) is shortsighted, since even the most desirable of the above plans produced some costs. One would be forced to do nothing if that were the only criterion. By the same token, considering only the benefits of a public policy (in this case, racial balance) would be almost as shortsighted, since one would have to choose the intuitively less desirable plan in which there was very little contact between the races.

Racial balance measures disproportionately reflect benefits because they hold changing demographics constant and hence cannot distinguish between: (1) a desegregation outcome in which 99 percent of the whites have left but the remaining 1 percent are evenly distributed (producing an index of 0 and a situation in which all schools are within 20 percentage points of the district's racial proportions); and (2) an outcome in which none of the whites have left and each school is 50 percent white (producing an index of 0 and all schools within 20 percentage points of the district's racial proportions). Since virtually no one trying to achieve school desegregation would prefer the former to the latter, and social scientists and the courts believe that the goal of a school desegregation plan is the greatest possible interracial exposure, school desegregation ought to be defined and measured as interracial exposure rather than simply the even (or relatively even) distribution of groups.

Moreover, because white flight is a function of the characteristics of a school desegregation plan, using interracial exposure, which reflects white flight, as a dependent variable may enable us to specify plan characteristics that will minimize the costs and maximize the benefits of desegregation. Social science research, for example, suggests that there is greater white flight when whites are reassigned to minority schools, when the busing distance is longer and there are alternatives to the public schools available, when plans are citywide rather than countywide (despite the county plan's involving longer busing distances), when mandatory reassignment plans are phased in over a period of years rather than implemented in one year, when elementary students are reassigned rather than secondary students, when the social class of the white students is higher and that of the minority students lower, when there is greater protest, and when student transfers are voluntary (see Rossell, 1983, 1988; Welch and Light, 1987).

Several courts seem to have recognized that interracial exposure is more useful than racial balance as a guide to designing desegregation plans and to choosing among alternative plans.

These courts have accepted my measure of interracial exposure as a guide to choosing among alternative plans either implicitly, in choosing the plan with the greatest interracial exposure[7] or rejecting the plan with the least interracial exposure,[8] or explicitly, as did the Fifth Circuit Court of Appeals in the Hattiesburg case. As the Appeals Court noted, "It bears emphasis that we do not reject Dr. Rossell's use of 'interracial exposure' as a diagnostic aid. To the contrary, this inquiry can cast light on the potential success of a proposed plan, even its objectives."[9] On the other hand, a federal district court opined in 1989 that

> the index of interracial exposure can be useful in certain contexts. However, because the index is only a measure of the average white enrollment, it does not focus attention on remaining racially identifiable schools and does not assist the Court in ascertaining whether they can be eliminated. . . . A computation of the "index of interracial exposure" cannot be substituted for an inquiry into whether or not vestiges of segregated student assignment patterns continue to exist, as even a high index of interracial exposure can mask the failure to uproot illegally discriminatory assignment patterns.[10]

The last point is, of course, true, and it is why, in this case as in all others, I have compared plans not only in terms of interracial exposure but also in terms of the percentage of students in racially balanced schools (that is, within 20 percentage points of the school district's racial composition). The latter is for the courts and the former is for both the courts and the social scientists who care about creating school desegregation plans that will produce the greatest benefits for black children.

Unfortunately, most academic studies, including a 1987 report for OCR by Welch and Light, continue to use racial balance as a dependent variable because it is easier to use in a comparative analysis—one does not have to control for the pre-desegregation percentage white, as is necessary with interracial exposure.[11] Welch and Light's conclusion that mandatory plans produce more racial balance but also more white flight than voluntary plans tells us little that we do not already know. The most important question not addressed in that and similar reports is what is the net benefit of these two countervailing tendencies—racial balance transfers and white flight? Interracial exposure, unlike racial balance, measures this net benefit. The conclusions of the next chapter are thus based on an analysis that uses interracial exposure as the primary outcome variable.

3

A Comparison of Voluntary and Mandatory Desegregation Plans

━━━━━━━━━━━━━━━━━━━━━━━━━━━━━━━━━━━━

THIS CHAPTER describes the magnet school plans of 20 school districts and compares the desegregation effectiveness of the two types of magnet plans, voluntary and mandatory. The sample was selected from a larger 119-school-district sample in order to update an earlier Abt Associates study of 18 school districts (Royster, Baltzell, and Simmons, 1979), which remains one of the best comparative analyses of magnet school desegregation plans. Royster et al. and I concluded in separate 1979 studies that mandatory desegregation plans with magnet schools were more successful desegregation tools than voluntary plans with magnet schools. These analyses, unfortunately, included only one year of postimplementation data. They could not, therefore, test the proposition that, over the long term, voluntary plans would ultimately produce more interracial exposure than mandatory plans, in part because of lower levels of white flight in the latter (see Rossell, 1979:317). The study presented here tests this proposition.

Sampling Criteria

Originally Abt Associates chose their 18 districts from a sample of districts that were in the OCR annual enrollment survey and were identified by Abt's consultants as having desegregation plans. The school districts with desegregation plans were divided into four categories: those with a student enrollment between 10 and 30 percent minority (black, Hispanic, Asian, and American Indian) and those with an enrollment between 31 and 60 percent minority in the population of magnet–voluntary and magnet–mandatory plans. School districts below 10 percent and above 60 percent minority were excluded from the study, since such districts were not considered to be representative of the districts with desegregation plans. Among the school districts chosen, those with magnet–voluntary and magnet–mandatory plans were identified through a telephone survey. School districts were selected randomly from the sites in each category to produce a sample of 18. For reasons discussed below, I added 2 school districts to this sample to produce a new sample of 20.[1]

The sample of 20 school districts is representative of medium and large school districts with desegregation plans and of school districts with magnet–mandatory and magnet–voluntary plans. Although there are only 9 magnet–voluntary school desegregation plans in this sample, these 9 comprise two-thirds of the school districts that have such plans in the original 119-school-district sample.

Classifying Plans into Magnet–Voluntary and Magnet–Mandatory

The first step in analyzing the comparative attractiveness of the magnet programs in these school districts is to classify them into voluntary and mandatory desegregation plans. A magnet–voluntary plan is one in which desegregation is primarily accomplished through voluntary transfers—that is, by relying on parental choice motivated by incentives. Typically, these plans are characterized by voluntary white transfers to magnet schools placed in minority neighborhoods and voluntary minority transfers to white schools, either because they are magnet schools or under a majority-to-minority transfer program. Many of these plans also include redrawing of contiguous attendance zones to maximize desegregation. The exact implementation of the plan and the amount of desegregation accomplished in each school is largely left to the private choices of consumers. Negative incentives are provided in the form of racial controls on transfers—that is, the denial of a transfer if it does not enhance desegregation at the receiving school (and, in some plans, at the sending school as well).

A magnet–mandatory plan is one in which desegregation is primarily accomplished through mandatory assignment of students to other-race schools. In other words, parents are "forced" to place their children in desegregated schools or to leave the school system. There is a court or board order that specifies in great detail every child's assignment as a function of his or her race and residence. Although parents cannot choose which school their child will be assigned to, they do have the option of entering a "lottery" to get into one of the magnet schools. In such plans, the magnet schools are educational options, not desegregation tools, and their purpose is to reduce conflict and increase parental satisfaction.

In the mandatory desegregation plans, the magnet schools are usually quite successful in achieving racial balance because the alternative is mandatory assignment to a less desirable desegregated school not of one's choice. Boston, for example, initially had long waiting lists for its magnet schools despite considerable white flight from the nonmagnet schools. In the magnet–voluntary situation, on the other hand, some schools will simply fail to attract students because the alternative—one's neighborhood school or another magnet—is more desirable.

Classifying school districts according to these two models is difficult. It is an art, not a science. Table 3.1 shows the outcome of this process. It outlines the current desegregation plans in the 20-district sample, the year of desegregation implementation, the schools and grades included, and the racial composition goals of the plan. It is interesting to note that 55 percent of the school districts in the voluntary category were ordered to desegregate by courts after a finding of intentional segregation. Freedom of choice appears to have been revived in the legal doctrine. Indeed, none of the districts with court-approved vol-

TABLE 3.1

CURRENT DESEGREGATION PLANS FOR 20 DISTRICTS

District	Source of Plan	Deseg. Year	District Desegregation Requirements	
			Schools/Grades Included	Racial Composition Goals
VOLUNTARY				
Buffalo, N.Y.	Court order	1976	All schools	30–65% minority
Cincinnati, Ohio	School board	1970	All schools	No numerical goals
Houston, Tex.	Court order	1975	All schools	No school (nonmagnet) more than 90% white or 90% black and Hispanic
Milwaukee, Wis.	Court order	1976	All schools	25–45% black in each school (25–60% black after 1979)
Montclair, N.J.	Formal pressure from state Board of Education	1977	Elementary, middle schools	25–57% minority in each school
Portland, Oreg.	School board	1970	All schools	No more than 25% minority in middle, high schools; no more than 50% minority in elementary schools
San Bernardino, Calif.	Court order	1978	Elementary, junior high schools	No numerical goals
San Diego, Calif.	Court order	1977	Schools over 50% minority	Reduction of minority population in cited schools
Tacoma, Wash.	School board	1968	All schools	No school more than 40% minority
MANDATORY				
Boston, Mass.	Court order	1974	All schools in 1975 (except those in E. Boston)	Each school in the 8 community sub-districts reflecting overall racial composition of sub-district, ±25% (1975)

TABLE 3.1
(Continued)

| District | Source of Plan | Deseg. Year | District Desegregation Requirements | |
			Schools/Grades Included	Racial Composition Goals
MANDATORY				
Dallas, Tex.	Court order	1971 1976	High schools; grades 4–8 (mandatory); high schools (voluntary)	25–75% minority (grades 4–8)
Dayton, Ohio	Court order	1976	All schools	All schools reflecting district ratio, ±15% pts.
Des Moines, Iowa	HEW adminis- trative action	1977	Cited schools	No more than 50% mi- nority in any school
Louisville, Ky.	Court order	1975	All schools	No more than 12–40% minority (elemen- tary) or 12.5–35.0% minority (secondary)
Montgomery County, Md.	School board	1976	All schools	No more than 50% mi- nority in any school
Racine, Wis.	School board	1975	All schools	No school with a mi- nority population above the district average
St. Paul, Minn.	Formal pres- sure from state Board of Education	1973	All schools	No more than 30–40% minority in any school
Springfield, Mass.	Court order	1974	Elementary schools	No more than 50% mi- nority in any school
Stockton, Calif.	Court order	1975	All schools	All schools reflecting district ratio, ±15% pts.
Tulsa, Okla.	Court order	1971	De jure segregated schools	Court-determined for each school (pairings dismantled, 1985)

Source: Some of the material in this table is adapted from Eugene C. Royster, D. Catherine Baltzell, and Frances C. Simmons (1979), *Study of the Emergency School Aid Act Magnet School Program* (Cambridge, Mass.: Abt Associates).

untary plans even has an explicit mandatory backup in the event the plan fails, although presumably the court-ordered voluntary plans have implicit mandatory backup plans. Although the court decision never mentioned such a possibility, Buffalo, for example, was ordered to reassign some students mandatorily in 1981 after five years of relatively successful voluntary desegregation. The judge was seeking to have 100 percent of the students in racially balanced schools, something few school districts have ever attained.

Despite the lack of a mandatory backup, the voluntary plans are expected to succeed, and all are *comprehensive*—the goal is to desegregate the entire school district by voluntary means. Indeed, Table 3.1 indicates that all but two (San Bernardino and Cincinnati) have explicit and ambitious desegregation goals. The plans are clearly not based purely on freedom of choice, because choices are structured and controls are imposed on the granting of those choices.

Nor is choice the only factor operating in these plans. School districts typically assign students to a neighborhood school on the basis of contiguous zones, but even in a school district without a desegregation plan, living in a certain neighborhood is no guarantee that a child will go to the same school as older siblings or the same school as the children across the street. Schools have limited capacities and lines have to be drawn and often redrawn as populations expand and decline. This is also true of school districts with desegregation plans. As Table 3.2 indicates, none of the voluntary desegregation plans in this sample are entirely voluntary—all use some additional, minimal, mandatory techniques such as selected school closings and contiguous rezoning, particularly at the secondary level. However, these mandatory aspects are common to all school districts in their efforts to accommodate shifting populations.

There is one case, however, where rezoning clearly goes beyond what any school district might do solely to respond to shifting populations. In 1981 Buffalo was ordered to mandatorily reassign 30 percent of its elementary students (15 percent of all students) after five years of successful voluntary desegregation. This phase increased interracial exposure only by a small amount because the judge simultaneously ordered a drastic cutback of the successful voluntary majority-to-minority transfer program, convinced that it was too complicated and placed too great a burden on black students. The trend in interracial exposure in Buffalo during the voluntary period was toward greater interracial exposure than was accomplished by the mandatory plan— that is, if we were to subtract the effect of the mandatory reassignments, we would have more interracial exposure, not less. Despite these mandatory assignments, I still classify the Buffalo plan as voluntary because it began as a voluntary plan and because most of the desegregation that occurred over the time period studied was driven by the choice process. Indeed, the court itself stated in 1983: "The primary method for achieving desegregation in the school system has been through voluntary means."[2]

Not only are the choice plans not pure, but the "command and control" models in this book have choice options as well. Some systems have deliberately avoided additional mandatory reassignments by using magnet schools to desegregate schools that have become resegregated through white flight. Others, such as Boston, placed some magnet programs in schools that could not be desegregated by mandatory means because of extreme white resistance. This was the case in East Boston, where opponents of a "forced busing" plan threatened to blow up the tunnel that connects that neighborhood (and Logan Airport) to Boston, which would have paralyzed the entire city. Although Judge W. Arthur Garrity has always maintained that this was not his reason for excluding East Boston from the plan, most people are skeptical. Whatever the motivation, three magnet schools were placed in East Boston, and desegregation was accomplished solely by voluntary means. Despite the choice options, Boston's plan is still thought of, and rightly so, as the quintessential northern "forced busing" plan.

As this brief discussion suggests, classifying the school dis-

TABLE 3.2

MAGNET SCHOOLS AND OTHER DESEGREGATION TECHNIQUES IN 20 DISTRICTS

District	Role of Magnets in Plan	Racial Composition Goals of Magnets[a]	Additional Techniques Used
VOLUNTARY			
Buffalo, N.Y.	Provide voluntary option for desegregation	50% minority, 50% majority	Majority to minority (M to M) transfer; redrawing attendance zones; grade reorganization (middle schools eliminated); pairing of 20 zone schools (1981)
Cincinnati, Ohio	Desegregate district as a whole	50% majority, 50% minority	M to M transfer; school closings and rezoning
Houston, Tex.	Desegregate district as a whole	Ethnic composition of district	M to M transfer; redrawing of attendance zones
Milwaukee, Wis.	Desegregate district as a whole	Same as district goals (see Table 3.1)	M to M transfer; school closings and rezoning
Montclair, N.J.	Desegregate grades K–5	Same as district goals (see Table 3.1)	Closing of selected schools; elimination of all attendance zones
Portland, Oreg.	Desegregate a particular geographic area	Same as district goals (see Table 3.1)	M to M transfer; grade-level reorganization; consolidation of certain schools
San Bernardino, Calif.	Desegregate district as a whole	No numerical goals (see Table 3.1)	School closings and rezoning; M to M transfer
San Diego, Calif.	Desegregate certain schools	Same as district goals (see Table 3.1)	M to M transfer
Tacoma, Wash.	Desegregate certain schools	Same as district goals (see Table 3.1)	Closing of selected schools; district-wide optional enrollment
MANDATORY			
Boston, Mass.	Provide voluntary option for desegregation and educational options	Racial composition of the district	Redrawing of district boundaries; reassignment by geocodes
Dallas, Tex.	Achieve racial balance in high schools	Capacity of school × ratio of each group in district, ±10% pts.	Redrawing attendance zones; M to M transfer; grade reorganization; pairing and clustering

TABLE 3.2
(Continued)

District	Role of Magnets in Plan	Racial Composition Goals of Magnets[a]	Additional Techniques Used
MANDATORY			
Dayton, Ohio	Provide another option for desegregation	Same as district goals (see Table 3.1)	Redrawing attendance zones; grade reorganization; pairing and clustering
Des Moines, Iowa	Desegregate a particular geographic area	Same as district goals (see Table 3.1)	M to M transfer; redrawing attendance zones; pairing and clustering; closing of selected schools
Louisville, Ky.	Provide another option for desegregation	Same as district goals (see Table 3.1)	Pairing and clustering; closing of selected schools
Montgomery County, Md.	Desegregate a particular geographic area	Same as district goals (see Table 3.1)	Redrawing attendance zones; pairing and clustering
Racine, Wis.	Desegregate a particular geographic area	Same as district goals (see Table 3.1)	Redrawing attendance zones
St. Paul, Minn.	Desegregate a particular geographic area and provide educational options	Same as district goals (see Table 3.1)	Redrawing attendance zones; pairing and clustering; consolidation of schools
Springfield, Mass.	Desegregate a particular geographic area and meet parent demands	Same as district goals (see Table 3.1)	Redrawing attendance zones; grade reorganization; closing of selected schools; pairing and clustering
Stockton, Calif.	Desegregate district as a whole	Same as district goals (see Table 3.1)	Pairing and clustering; closing of selected schools
Tulsa, Okla.	Desegregate the district as a whole and certain schools	50% minority, 50% majority	M to M transfer; redrawing attendance zones; pairing and clustering (dismantled fall 1985)

Source: Some of the material in this table is adapted from Eugene C. Royster, D. Catherine Baltzell, and Frances C. Simmons (1979), *Study of the Emergency School Aid Act Magnet School Program* (Cambridge, Mass.: Abt Associates).

Note:
[a] All goals allow deviation from district's racial or ethnic composition either as a relative standard (i.e., ± 15 or 20 percentage points) or as an absolute standard (i.e., 30–70 percent black).

tricts for analytical purposes in two exclusive categories—mandatory and voluntary—as with every process of categorization involves some distortion. It might be more precise to describe the mandatory–voluntary dimension in terms of a continuum, but I do not believe it would be any easier or any less rife with contradictions. Moreover, describing the policy alternatives as a dichotomy has the advantage of fitting in with the policy debate on the issue.

There will undoubtedly always be disagreement as to how to categorize these plans, not only because of the need to collapse a continuum into two boxes, but also because the plans have changed somewhat over time. Those who study a plan at one time, when it has x characteristics, may classify it differently from those who study it at another time when it has $x + y$ characteristics.

Although this analysis includes the 1979 Abt Associates sample, I disagree with their classification of three school districts. The first of these is Dallas, Texas. Royster, Baltzell, and Simmons (1979) characterize the Dallas plan as voluntary. I believe the Dallas plan is a court-ordered mandatory reassignment plan.[3] The secondary schools were desegregated in 1971 by redrawing attendance zones. The elementary schools, primarily grades 4–8, were desegregated in 1976 by creating six subdistricts and pairing and clustering schools within them. This was accomplished by mandatory reassignment, although magnet schools were added in 1976 to become the primary desegregation tool for the high schools.

I also disagree with their classification of the Racine, Wisconsin, plan as voluntary. The school district administration describes its plan as one that mandatorily assigns students to achieve desegregation in all schools. The 1975 plan reduced racial imbalance by 20 percentage points, and since there are only four magnets, they are clearly limited to serving as educational options.

I also disagree with their categorization of the Montclair, New Jersey, plan as magnet–mandatory. When a school district completely dismantles a mandatory assignment plan and replaces it with a voluntary plan, that district should then be considered to be in the voluntary category. Although the Montclair school district implemented several mandatory plans involving grade reorganization and school pairings between 1971 and 1975, mandatory reassignments were discontinued in 1977. Attendance zones were eliminated and all schools, with the exception of the one high school, are magnet schools with special programs designed to attract students from all over the district. The school district prepares brochures to advertise each school's special theme, and the plan is driven by choice. Clearly, this is a voluntary plan.

Two additional voluntary plans have been added from my 119-school-district sample to replace Racine and Dallas, now reclassified as mandatory. The new districts—Cincinnati, Ohio, and San Bernardino, California—both have nationally recognized voluntary desegregation plans, though neither enjoys a reputation as having an extraordinarily successful one.[4]

Tables 3.1 and 3.2 show, as suggested earlier, that the voluntary plans are not pure choice models—all have some sort of racial controls imposed on the choice process and some contiguous rezoning to maximize desegregation. Indeed, the racial composition goals for the voluntary plans differ little from those for the mandatory plans. The major distinguishing characteristic of the two types of plans can be found in Table 3.2 under the heading "additional techniques used." This column lists the other techniques used to desegregate the school system in addition to magnets. In the voluntary plans the additional techniques are marginal and supplementary; in the mandatory plans the additional techniques are the key to the plan, and the magnets play a marginal and supplementary role. The table shows that, of the districts with voluntary plans, only Buffalo's uses pairing or clustering, and that affects only 20 schools. Of the cities with mandatory plans, by contrast, only tiny Racine does not have either pairing or clustering or (as in Boston) satellite zoning involving busing.

Community Characteristics

The 20 school districts analyzed in this chapter have a wide range of population characteristics, from the huge, predominantly minority Houston district to the tiny, predominantly white Montclair district. The sample, however, consists mostly of medium and large cities (populations of all but Racine and Montclair are over 100,000). Table 3.3 shows the 1970 city or county population (depending on whether the school district is city- or countywide),[5] the percentage white in the city or county population, and the income and educational characteristics of the 20 school districts.

Table 3.4 shows the average community and school district characteristics for the districts in Table 3.3, divided according to whether the districts have mandatory or voluntary plans. The community characteristics include those shown in Table 3.3 plus the white population change in the Standard Metropolitan Statistical Area (SMSA) from 1970 to 1980. The school district characteristics include the percentage of students who are white before desegregation, total enrollment, white enrollment change, interracial exposure, the desegregation year, and racial imbalance. Table 3.4 also shows in the last column the correlation (r) between whether a plan is voluntary and each of these characteristics. Thus, the first characteristic, city population, is correlated (r) .16 with a plan's being voluntary. In other words, districts with a voluntary plan are more likely to be in larger cities. This is a weak correlation, however, and it is not statistically significant. Indeed, none of the correlations are statistically significant.

As Table 3.3 and Table 3.4 indicate, the mandatory desegregation plans were found in cities that before desegregation were smaller in population and percentage of residents who are minority, and higher in income and education, than the cities where voluntary plans were implemented. In other words, in this sample the districts with voluntary plans, because of their social characteristics, are at a disadvantage compared with the

TABLE 3.3
COMMUNITY CHARACTERISTICS FOR 20 SCHOOL DISTRICTS, 1970

District	Population	% White	Population Median Income[a] Total	Black	Median Education[b] Total	Black
VOLUNTARY						
Buffalo, N.Y.	470,528	78%	$6,568	$5,307	10.8	9.9
Cincinnati, Ohio	452,524	71	6,411	4,645	11.1	11.2
Houston, Tex.	1,231,394	61	8,056	5,080	12.1	10.0
Milwaukee, Wis.	717,099	82	8,138	6,168	11.9	10.3
Montclair, N.J.	44,043	72	9,633	6,500	12.7	11.5
Portland, Oreg.	382,619	90	6,705	4,805	12.3	11.3
San Bernardino, Calif.	104,251	84	6,848	5,186	12.1	10.7
San Diego, Calif.	693,931	76	6,225	5,157	12.5	11.7
Tacoma, Wash.	154,581	89	7,293	6,442	12.2	11.6
Average	472,330	78	7,320	5,477	12.0	10.9
MANDATORY						
Boston, Mass.	641,071	79	5,921	5,023	12.0	11.6
Dallas, Tex.	844,403	66	7,984	5,307	12.3	10.2
Dayton, Ohio	243,405	69	7,236	6,831	11.4	10.8
Des Moines, Iowa	200,587	92	7,504	5,358	12.4	11.6
Louisville, Ky.[c]	695,055	86	8,309	4,732	11.6	10.1
Montgomery Co., Md.	522,809	91	14,090	7,460	13.8	12.9
Racine, Wis.	95,162	85	8,982	6,544	11.9	9.6
St. Paul, Minn.	309,980	93	7,695	5,094	12.2	11.2
Springfield, Mass.	163,905	84	7,298	5,646	12.0	10.7
Stockton, Calif.	107,644	58	6,706	3,988	12.1	10.0
Tulsa, Okla.	330,409	85	8,231	3,726	12.4	11.0
Average	377,675	81	8,178	5,428	12.2	10.9
Grand Average	420,270	80	7,792	5,450	12.1	10.9

Notes:
[a] Annual household income.
[b] Highest grade completed.
[c] Jefferson County, Kentucky.

TABLE 3.4
AVERAGES AND CORRELATIONS OF PREDESEGREGATION SCHOOL DISTRICT
AND COMMUNITY CHARACTERISTICS WITH VOLUNTARY AND
MANDATORY PLANS

	Average		Voluntary Plans
	Mandatory	Voluntary	r =
COMMUNITY CHARACTERISTICS			
City population	377,675	472,330	0.16
% White in city, 1970	80.6%	78.1%	−0.14
Income (household), 1970	$8,178	$7,320	−0.25
Minority income (household), 1970	$5,428	$5,477	0.03
Education, 1970 (avg. grade completed)	12.2	12.0	−0.19
Minority education, 1970 (avg. grade completed)	10.9	10.9	0.02
SMSA white population change, 1970–1980	13.3%	3.0%	−0.21
SCHOOL DISTRICT CHARACTERISTICS			
% White T − 2 [a]	73.2%	64.0%	−0.31
Enrollment T − 1	74,088	82,159	0.08
White enrollment change T − 1	−4.5%	−3.7%	0.12
White enrollment change T − 2	−3.0%	−4.7%	−0.34
White enrollment change T − 3	−2.8%	−3.7%	−0.22
White enrollment change T − 4	−2.7%	−4.1%	−0.23
Interracial exposure T − 2	44.3	40.7	−0.09
Year of desegregation plan	1974	1975	−0.03
Racial imbalance T − 2	57.9	52.8	−0.15

Note:
[a] T + 0 is the year of implementation for a desegregation plan; T − 1 is the year before implementation; and so on.

ones with mandatory plans. This suggests that the courts may be more willing to approve a voluntary plan in school districts with a higher percentage of students who are minority where a mandatory reassignment plan seems less likely to succeed or futile. If they do this, judges are projecting their own perceptions of the likelihood of success for a mandatory plan in these types of districts, since only in Houston did a prior mandatory plan actually exist.

An unexpected trend has occurred in the districts with voluntary plans in the decade after desegregation—they experienced a slightly greater increase in median income and educational level than did the school districts with mandatory plans despite being in metropolitan areas that had less growth in the white population than did those of the mandatory plans. By 1980, as a result, there is little difference between the districts with voluntary plans and those with mandatory plans. Did the voluntary plans have some salutary effect on the communities in which they were implemented? Did the mandatory plans have a negative effect on the communities in which they were implemented? These data can only raise such questions; they cannot answer them. But the research suggests that people with the highest income and educational level are most likely to withdraw their children from the public schools (Estabrook, 1980; Giles, Gatlin, and Cataldo, 1976; Lord, 1975; Pride, 1980; Pride and Woodard, 1978, 1985; Ross, 1981; Rossell, 1988). It is thus not unreasonable to hypothesize that mandatory desegregation plans produce enough white flight to have a negative effect on a community's income and educational level, or that choice plans have a salutary effect on a school district and a city's attractiveness to individuals of higher socioeconomic status.

Magnet Programs

The structural characteristics of magnet schools differ according to the type of desegregation plan. There are basically two types of magnet school structures: those where the magnet program is an enclave in a larger regular school (that is, not all the students in the school are in the program); and those where the magnet program encompasses the entire school (that is, all students in the school are enrolled in the magnet program). The former I call a "program within a school" (PWS) and Houston calls a "school within a school" (SWAS). The latter I call a "dedicated magnet."

The general impression among practitioners, although there are certainly no hard data to substantiate this, is that a PWS poses operational problems that a dedicated magnet does not have. These problems concern the interaction between the resident nonmagnet students and the magnet students. How much interaction will be allowed given both black and white preferences for a 50–50 racial balance in the magnet program (see Rossell, 1986a, 1986b)? Are the resident students really in a desegregated school if they only see the opposite race magnet students for part of the day? To what extent are resident students allowed to use the resources of the magnet program? These issues can become such bones of contention between the plaintiffs in a desegregation suit and the school district that most districts try to implement as many dedicated magnets as is possible.

Nevertheless, dedicated magnets—that is, where all students enrolled in the school are in the magnet program—are rarely found in voluntary plans because they have serious implementation problems. With a dedicated magnet the school must be emptied of students and a decision made as to where these students are to be reassigned. Sending them to nearby same-race schools usually does nothing for desegregation and may not even be possible since schools have a fixed capacity. If the goal is to desegregate the school system, these students usually will have to be transported across town to an opposite-race school. If a majority of the dedicated magnets are in minority neighborhoods, most of the students reassigned will thus be minority. But this is usually not politically feasible in a voluntary plan since there is no "equal" assignment of white students to minority schools as in a mandatory plan. Ultimately, for a voluntary plan, the implementation problems of the dedicated magnet outweigh the operational problems of the PWS and thus the PWS magnet is preferred by both the school districts and the courts. In contrast, the dedicated magnet is the preferred model in mandatory reassignment plans because the implementation problems described above are inconsequential in a plan that is already characterized by extensive cross-town reassignments of students of all races.

Some school districts with voluntary plans have been able to make the transition from a PWS model in a particular school to a dedicated magnet as the program becomes more popular and begins to fill the school. This process takes several years, however, because it depends on resident students transferring to other magnets or other regular schools under a majority-to-minority transfer program and thus opening up space for nonresident magnet students to transfer in.

As a result of these implementation problems, Milwaukee is the only school district I know of with a magnet–voluntary plan with more than one or two dedicated magnets (many have none), and it has experienced considerable criticism for the resulting unequal reassignments (Barndt, Janka, and Rose, 1981; Bednarek, 1977; Harris, 1983). In Savannah, the Legal Defense Fund, representing plaintiffs, proposed a "voluntary" plan containing only dedicated magnets, all of them placed in black neighborhoods. Under its plan, when a neighborhood school was converted to a magnet, the black students were to be reassigned to a white school on the other side of the district. No whites were reassigned, however, since none of the magnets was placed in white schools. Both the Justice Department (plaintiff–interveners) and the District Court rejected this plan as burdensome to black students.[6]

The data in Table 3.5 do not distinguish between these two types of programs because only a few school districts provided separate data for students participating in the magnet program. Therefore, all percentages of students participating in magnet schools are based on the 1982 enrollment in schools with magnets. Figures for those school districts that did provide data on program participation (San Diego and Houston) suggest that the district percentage of students actually participating in the magnet programs could be less than half the number of students in that district attending magnet schools. For example, in San

TABLE 3.5

ENROLLMENT IN MAGNET SCHOOLS, BY SCHOOL DISTRICT, 1982

District	Magnet Grade Levels	Magnet Schools No.	% of All Schools	% of Students in Magnets Minority	White	All	Avg. % Minority In Dist.	In Magnets
VOLUNTARY								
Buffalo,	e/m	14						
N.Y.	m/h	3						
	h	2						
	total	19	27.2%	32.9%	31.3%	32.2%	54	54.4%
Cincinnati,	e	26					58	
Ohio	K–12/4–12	4						
	m	7						
	h	2						
	7–12	1						
	total	40	51.3	24.2	24.9	24.5		61.1
Houston,	e/k–8	37					78	
Tex.	m	12						
	h	16						
	total	65	28.0	30.6	37.3	32.1		74.4
Milwaukee,	e	13					58	
Wis.	j	7						
	h	15						
	total	35	26.9	36.7	46.2	40.7		55.1
Montclair,	e	6					48	
N.J.	m	2						
	e & m total	8	100.0	100.0	100.0	100.0		
	total	8	88.9	59.5	65.6	64.5		45.7
Portland,	e	8					27	
Oreg.	K–12	1						
	h	4						
	total	13	13.1	33.4	15.0	19.9		50.2
San Bernar-	e	23					52	
dino, Calif.	m	2						
	e & m total	25	62.5	63.0	54.3	59.0		
	total	25	54.3	47.4	37.7	42.7		56.8
San Diego,	e	24					50	
Calif.	j	5						
	K–12/4–12	3						
	h	8						
	total	40	25.5	32.2	21.0	26.6		60.0

TABLE 3.5
(Continued)

District	Magnet Grade Levels	Magnet Schools		% of Students in Magnets			Avg. % Minority	
		No.	% of All Schools	Minority	White	All	In Dist.	In Magnets
VOLUNTARY								
Tacoma, Wash.	e	5	12.5	22.0	10.0	13.0	26	
	total	5	8.2	12.3	5.4	7.2		44.7
MANDATORY								
Boston, Mass.	e	10					71	
	6–8	3						
	7–12	5						
	9–12	5						
	total	23	19.3	28.9	31.8	29.7		71.4
Dallas, Tex.	e	5					74	
	7–8	4						
	h	6						
	total	15	8.2	10.9	6.2	9.7		82.5
Dayton, Ohio	e	3					59	
	7–9	5						
	10–12	1						
	total	9	21.9	24.7	23.3	24.1		60.2
Des Moines, Iowa	elem total	3	6.9	12.3	4.6	6.0	18	
	total	3	4.9	6.7	2.4	3.1		37.7
Louisville, Ky.	e	4					30	
	K–12	1						
	7–12	1						
	j	1						
	h	1						
	total	8	5.7	4.8	5.6	5.4		27.8
Montgomery Co., Md.	e	12					26	
	j	2						
	h	3						
	total	17	11.4	18.0	5.1	8.4		54.1
Racine, Wis.	e	3					27	
	7–12	1						
	total	4	11.4	7.5	7.5	7.5		23.5
St. Paul, Minn.	e	4					31	
	K–8	1						
	K–12	1						
	total	6	9.2	12.2	9.7	10.5		34.9

TABLE 3.5
(Continued)

District	Magnet Grade Levels	Magnet Schools		% of Students in Magnets			Avg. % Minority	
		No.	% of All Schools	Minority	White	All	In Dist.	In Magnets
MANDATORY								
Springfield, Mass.	e	8					52	
	j	2						
	elem total	10	27.8	42.1	26.6	34.8		
	total	10	25.0	32.0	19.6	26.1		61.7
Stockton, Calif.	e total	3	11.1	8.7	8.3	8.6	68	
	total	3	7.7	5.0	4.9	4.9		66.5
Tulsa, Okla.	e	8					33	
	m	1						
	elem total	9	10.3	25.7	8.3	24.0		
	total	9	9.4	19.9	6.4	10.8		61.2

Note:

[a]The following abbreviations are used: e = elementary school; m = middle school; j = junior high school; h = high school. When there are two sets of summary figures, the first set is the number and percentage of a subset of schools, and the second set is the number and percentage of the total schools in the district. For example, 100 percent of the elementary and middle schools in Montclair have magnets, but only 89 percent of all schools (i.e., including high schools) have magnets.

Diego in 1982 there were 30,834 students enrolled in schools with magnet programs, but only 17,687 were actually participating in those programs.[7] In Houston in 1982 there were 62,343 students enrolled in schools with magnet programs, but only 30,100 students actually participating in them. Since most magnet programs are placed in minority schools, there is less of a disparity between the white enrollment in the school and in the program because almost all of the whites in these schools are there for the program. For example, in San Diego there were 8,000 minority students enrolled in magnet schools but not in magnet programs. In contrast, there were only 4,500 white students enrolled in magnet schools but not in magnet programs.

While these figures may, therefore, exaggerate magnet program enrollment for the voluntary plans, they accurately reflect the average percentage of students who are minority in the schools with magnets. Since the purpose of magnet programs is eventually to desegregate the entire school, not just the program, the percentage minority (or percentage white) for the entire school is the correct statistic to use in comparing plans.

One issue that may be of concern to the reader is the accuracy of the racial statistics. In general, it is rare for children to declare themselves a member of another race in order to be accepted into a magnet program, and it is usually obvious to everyone if a child does so. In San Jose some 300 mixed-race students "changed" their race from white to minority upon the implementation of the desegregation plan. The school district's rule was that a student could only do that once, and that after the implementation year, they were held to the race they had chosen. Nevertheless, although San Jose had the largest number of "race changes" I am aware of, such changes affected only 2 percent of the white population.

The data in Table 3.5 show considerable variation within the two categories of mandatory and voluntary desegregation plans. Among the school districts with voluntary plans, Tacoma—a predominantly white school system with a board-ordered plan affecting only the small number of racially imbalanced black schools in the central city—has the lowest percentages of magnet schools and students participating. Montclair—a tiny, predominantly white school system with a board-ordered plan eliminating all attendance zones—has the highest percentages.

It is also striking that in almost all school districts except San Diego, Tacoma, and Portland, the average percentage minority in magnet schools is within 5 points of the percentage minority in the entire school system. San Diego's average is within 10 percentage points of the district's racial composition. In Tacoma and Portland, the goal of the magnet schools is to achieve a 50–50 racial composition, despite the fact that the percentage minority in these districts is 26 and 27 percent respectively.

A word should be said about Houston, which is often mentioned as a city with an "unsuccessful" voluntary magnet desegregation program. Royster, Baltzell, and Simmons (1979:72) classify Houston's district as one with "low district desegregation/low program effectiveness" because they found that as of 1977–78—the second year of the plan—only 8 percent of students were participating in magnet programs. As data presented here indicate, however, by 1982–83, 28 percent of the schools in Houston were magnet schools, and almost a third of the students in the district were enrolled in them. At least 14 percent of the students were enrolled in the magnet programs themselves, an increase of 6 percentage points since the Royster study. The average percentage minority in these magnet schools, however, was 74.4 percent, and it is from this fact that Houston gets its continuing reputation. Few observers seem to notice that this is within 5 percentage points of the school district's racial composition.

Moreover, contrary to popular belief, the dismantling of the mandatory plan and the adoption of a voluntary plan in Houston in 1975 produced no resegregation whatsoever (see Table 3.16 below). Indeed, the level of racial imbalance dropped by another 13 percentage points over the next decade, and every single year, including the most recent, shows improvement.[8] I doubt that there is any other 82 percent minority school district with as little racial imbalance (57.4 in 1985).

Another surprise is the San Bernardino magnet school plan, which has had a low media profile, generating no national news stories and few articles and case studies. As Table 3.5 indicates, however, San Bernardino has a larger percentage of students in magnet schools than either Milwaukee or Buffalo, the school districts usually touted as possessing the most successful magnet–voluntary desegregation plans. Moreover, although it has a percentage minority (blacks, Hispanics, Asians, and American Indians) that is only 6 percentage points below that of Milwaukee in 1982 and only 2 percentage points below that of Buffalo, the level of interracial exposure of minorities to whites in the

10th year of desegregation in San Bernardino was 9 percentage points higher than in Milwaukee and a half-percentage point higher than in Buffalo. The San Bernardino plan is thus at least as successful as Buffalo's and more successful than Milwaukee's.

In fact, the San Bernardino plan, implemented in 1978 under court order, illustrates several useful lessons. First, the plan began with a number of part-time desegregation programs that most observers, including myself, thought were stalling tactics that would never lead to real desegregation. Second, San Bernardino is one of two school districts in this sample with no specific numerical desegregation goals for its plan, as noted in Table 3.1, despite its being court ordered. Indeed, the state supreme court specifically rejected numerical goals for the plan:

> After the trial court's order was filed, our court upheld the constitutionality of the portion of Proposition 21 that repealed the "racial balance" provisions upon which the trial court had relied. . . . In light of this repeal, California school districts bear no statutory obligation to achieve racially balanced schools. Moreover, as we explain in *Crawford:* "The constitutional mandate articulated in *Jackson* and reaffirmed today is not a constitutional command that each school in a district must reflect the racial composition of the district as a whole. . . . Our decisions, instead, require only that school districts take reasonable and feasible steps to eliminate *segregated* schools, i.e., schools in which the minority student enrollment is so disproportionate as realistically to isolate minority students from other students and thus deprive minority students of an integrated educational experience. . . . It is such segregated schools which traditionally have resulted in the inherently unequal educational opportunities condemned in *Brown*."[9]

Thus, San Bernardino has achieved its present success despite being assured by the state supreme court that it did not have to achieve racial balance in its schools.

On the other hand, Cincinnati, the other school district with no racial balance goals, turned out to be less successful in desegregating its schools than expected, given the rather good national reputation of its comprehensive magnet–voluntary plan.

With regard to racial balance and interracial exposure, it is the least successful magnet–voluntary plan among the districts with the same racial composition in our sample. The Cincinnati school district, however, now has an ambitious numerical desegregation goal and, as a result of a consent decree signed in 1984, has agreed to expand its desegregation program.[10]

Table 3.6 summarizes these data. The voluntary plans clearly rely on magnet schools as their primary desegregation tool— they have almost three times the number and percentage of magnet schools as the mandatory plans. The average number of magnet schools in districts with voluntary plans is 28, representing 35.9 percent of the schools in the district. The average number of magnet schools in districts with mandatory plans is 10, representing 12.2 percent of the schools in the district. The percentage of students in magnet schools in the districts with voluntary plans is 32.3 percent, but only 12.7 percent for the districts with mandatory plans. Finally, the districts with volun-

TABLE 3.6
ENROLLMENT IN MAGNET SCHOOLS UNDER VOLUNTARY AND MANDATORY
PLANS, 1982

| District | % Mi-nority | Magnet Schools | | % of Students in Magnets | | | Avg. % Minority in Magnets |
		No.	% of All	Minority	White	All	
VOLUNTARY							
Sum		250					
Average	50%	28	35.9%	34.4%	31.6%	32.3%	55.8%
(N = 9)							
MANDATORY							
Sum		107					
Average	44	10	12.2	15.5	11.1	12.7	52.9
(N = 11)		—					
Grand sum		357					

tary plans have a slightly higher average percentage minority in their magnet schools because they have a higher percentage minority in their school systems. Interestingly, these data show little difference between white and minority participation in magnet schools at the district level.

We turn now to the systemwide effect of these desegregation plans and their magnet programs to determine which works better—command and control or public choice. The analysis looks at white flight, interracial exposure, and racial imbalance.

White Flight

Of all forms of white response to school desegregation, white flight is probably the most important because it directly affects interracial exposure, the ultimate goal of any desegregation plan. Although the issue of white flight from mandatory desegregation plans has been a hotly debated one since Coleman, Kelly, and Moore's 1975 papers charged that mandatory desegregation plans were counterproductive (see Rossell, 1975–1976, 1978c), surprisingly few studies have specifically compared voluntary and mandatory plans. Most of the research has analyzed aggregate white loss rates in school districts in response to reductions in racial imbalance, but changes in racial imbalance include both mandatory and voluntary transfers. These studies show a significant implementation-year white loss; and the greater the attempted reduction in racial imbalance, the greater the white loss. This is largely a function of the fact that a greater reduction in racial imbalance is highly correlated with more white mandatory reassignments (Rossell, 1978a).

There is disagreement over how long the white flight resulting from desegregation lasts. Virtually all of the research shows, however, that central city school districts above 30 to 35 percent minority with mandatory desegregation plans do not regain in the postimplementation period the white flight incurred in the implementation period (Armor, 1980; Coleman, 1977; Farley,

TABLE 3.7

% WHITE ENROLLMENT CHANGE UNDER VOLUNTARY AND MANDATORY DESEGREGATION PLANS

	Avg. Deseg. Year	% White T−1	N	Years Before and After Major Desegregation Year (T + 0)												
				T − 3	T − 2	T − 1	T + 0	T + 1	T + 2	T + 3	T + 4	T + 5	T + 6	T + 7	T + 8	T + 9
ABOVE 30% MINORITY																
Voluntary	1975	54.9	7	−5.1	−5.9	−5.4	−5.5	−6.2	−6.3	−7.7	−5.3	−3.6	−4.1	−2.5	−3.6	−3.3
Mandatory	1974	56.5	5	−4.4	−4.1	−5.3	−12.7	−9.4	−7.1	−8.2	−7.6	−9.1	−5.1	−8.5	−5.5	−5.1
BELOW 30% MINORITY																
Voluntary	1969	88.6	2	1.5	−1.6	2.0	−1.4	−3.5	−4.1	−4.1	−4.8	−3.2	−4.2	−5.0	−3.8	−4.0
Mandatory	1975	83.9	6	−1.5	−2.2	−3.7	−6.9	−6.2	−5.4	−5.3	−5.6	−4.4	−6.4	−2.9	−4.7	−3.2

Wurdock, and Richards, 1980; Ross, Gratton, and Clarke, 1982; Rossell, 1978a:31; Smylie, 1983). Smylie (1983) and Ross, Gratton, and Clarke (1982) found that even countywide school districts with less than 35 percent minority enrollment, thought to be most resistant to white flight, did not recover, in the post-implementation period, the implementation-year white enrollment loss. The few studies to compare white flight in mandatory and voluntary plans have concluded that the mandatory plans produce more flight in the period surrounding implementation than the voluntary plans and that this loss is not recovered (Smylie, 1983; Welch and Light, 1987).

Table 3.7 compares the average percentage white enrollment change[11] for voluntary and mandatory desegregation plans in

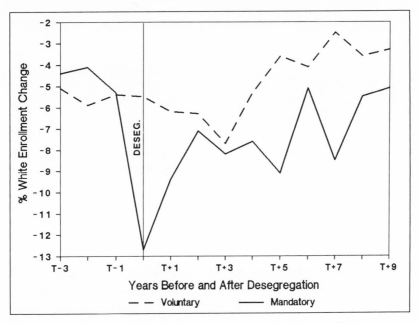

FIGURE 3.1   PERCENTAGE WHITE ENROLLMENT CHANGE IN DISTRICTS ABOVE 30 PERCENT MINORITY

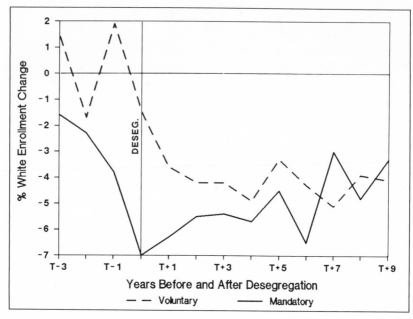

FIGURE 3.2   PERCENTAGE WHITE ENROLLMENT CHANGE IN DISTRICTS
BELOW 30 PERCENT MINORITY

school districts above and below 30 percent minority. The latter
classification is necessary because white flight is also a function of the percentage of pupils who are minority (Armor, 1980;
Coleman, 1977; Farley, Wurdock, and Richards, 1980; Ross,
Gratton, and Clarke, 1982; Rossell, 1978a:31, 1978b; Smylie,
1983). Figures 3.1 and 3.2 illustrate the data in Table 3.7 for
school districts above and below 30 percent minority before
desegregation.

The year of desegregation is indicated by the heading T + 0.
For the voluntary plans this is the year in which the first magnet
programs were established, although most of these school districts had operated majority-to-minority transfer programs for
several years prior to that time. The implementation year for
the mandatory desegregation plans is the year of the major

plan. If there is a court-ordered plan, it is usually the year of that plan, except when a significant plan with mandatory white reassignments precedes a court-ordered plan (as in Stockton, Calif.). Although this rarely happens, in such cases the prior plan would be considered the major plan.

Each year before desegregation is indicated by $T - 1$, $T - 2$, $T - 3$, and each year after implementation of the plan is indicated by $T + 1$, $T + 2 \ldots T + 9$.[12] Because all of the school districts in this sample have magnet schools as a component of their plans, the analysis presented here assesses the effect of voluntary versus mandatory reassignment of white students. These data indicate that, in school districts above 30 percent minority, the mandatory desegregation plans with magnet schools produce greater white enrollment loss than the voluntary plans with magnet schools, not only in the implementation year ($T + 0$), but in subsequent years as well. This is so despite the fact that before desegregation the districts with mandatory plans had less white enrollment decline. The districts below 30 percent minority have, on average, more predesegregation white enrollment loss with mandatory plans than with voluntary plans. The gap between the voluntary and mandatory plans increases dramatically with the implementation of desegregation.[13] The two trend lines cross in the eighth year of desegregation ($T + 7$) and remain essentially the same for the next two years.

Hence, there is a difference between school districts with enrollments above and below 30 percent minority. In the school districts below 30 percent minority, the trend lines for white enrollment loss in the voluntary and mandatory plans cross around the eighth year, although the mandatory plans never recover the much greater white loss they incurred in the early post-implementation years. This finding is contrary to the conclusion reached by Farley, Wurdock, and Richards (1980), Wilson (1985) and me (Rossell, 1978a) that school districts below 30 percent minority did recover their losses, but similar to Ross, Gratton and Clarke's (1982), Smylie's (1983), and Welch and Light's (1987) finding that they did not. In the school districts above 30 percent

minority, however, the voluntary plans have less white enrollment loss than the mandatory plans during the entire postimplementation period.

For districts above 30 percent minority, the total 10-year
white enrollment loss (T − 1 to T + 9) is 37 percent for those
with voluntary plans and 55 percent for those with mandatory
plans. This is a significant difference. The loss for the northern
control group in the 119-school-district sample shown in Table
5.2 (Chapter 5) is 48 percent over the same time period. The
northern control group is not the best comparison group, however, since it has about 20 percentage points less white enrollment than the districts in this analysis with minority enrollment
above 30 percent. From this comparison, the voluntary plans appear to be experiencing less enrollment decline than would be
expected from the declining birth rate, whereas the mandatory
plans appear to be experiencing more.

For districts less than 30 percent minority, by contrast, the
total white enrollment loss (T − 1 to T + 9) shows a much
smaller disparity between mandatory and voluntary plans—34
percent for those with voluntary plans and 41 percent for those
with mandatory plans.

In summary, these data show that in school districts with minority enrollment above 30 percent, the inclusion of magnet
schools in the mandatory plans does not make the two types of
plans comparable in white enrollment decline. For school districts below 30 percent minority, however, the inclusion of magnet schools in a mandatory plan makes the white enrollment
decline under the mandatory plans almost comparable to that
under the voluntary plans. Because these magnet programs are
often placed in the minority schools that would have experienced the most white flight with mandatory assignment, in
districts with a low percentage minority there may be few
minority schools without magnets, and thus white flight is diminished not only at the school level but at the district level
sufficiently to make mandatory plans almost comparable to voluntary plans. In the school districts with a higher percentage

minority and mandatory plans, however, there are so many more minority schools than magnets that the positive effect of the magnets is swamped by the mandatory assignment aspect of the plan.

Interracial Exposure

Although these data are interesting, they are not sufficient for selecting alternative desegregation plans. Considering only the costs of school desegregation plans is not only constitutionally unacceptable, but senseless from a policy analytical perspective. If one were to consider only white flight costs, the desegregation decision would always be to do nothing, since that produces the least white flight (Rossell, 1978a). From both a constitutional and a policy analysis standard, therefore, one must consider both the costs and the benefits of desegregation reassignments.

As discussed in Chapter 2, the measure that most directly reflects both costs and benefits is interracial exposure—the percentage of students who are white in the average minority child's school. Table 3.8 compares interracial exposure under voluntary and mandatory desegregation plans in school districts above and below 30 percent minority. Because interracial exposure is limited by the percentage white before desegregation, districts are divided into those above and below 30 percent minority before desegregation. (Since the predesegregation percentage minority is one of the control variables, this division is abandoned in the multiple regression analysis of interracial exposure that follows.) Because Houston and Montclair dismantled their mandatory reassignment plans (a very limited one in the case of Houston) and replaced them with voluntary plans, their predesegregation data are adjusted slightly to eliminate the effect of the prior mandatory plans. This small adjustment is necessary because the subsequent voluntary plans did not build on the mandatory plans, but replaced them.

Figures 3.3 and 3.4 show interracial exposure in school dis-

TABLE 3.8

INTERRACIAL EXPOSURE (SMW) UNDER VOLUNTARY AND MANDATORY DESEGREGATION PLANS

	Avg. Deseg. Year	% White T − 1	N	Years Before and After Major Desegregation Year (T + 0)												
				T − 3	T − 2	T − 1	T + 0	T + 1	T + 2	T + 3	T + 4	T + 5	T + 6	T + 7	T + 8	T + 9
ABOVE 30% MINORITY																
Voluntary	1975	54.9	7	33.5	33.2	32.8	36.2	37.7	37.6	36.8	36.3	36.5	36.2	35.5	35.0	35.0
Mandatory	1974	56.5	5	29.5	29.6	29.1	38.0	38.3	38.6	37.0	35.5	34.8	33.5	32.0	30.8	29.4
BELOW 30% MINORITY																
Voluntary	1969	88.6	2	60.8	62.5	62.7	68.1	68.1	72.0	73.2	73.3	73.0	73.5	71.9	71.8	70.6
Mandatory	1975	83.9	6	55.5	56.6	57.0	69.1	70.3	70.4	68.8	68.7	67.2	66.7	65.0	64.0	63.6

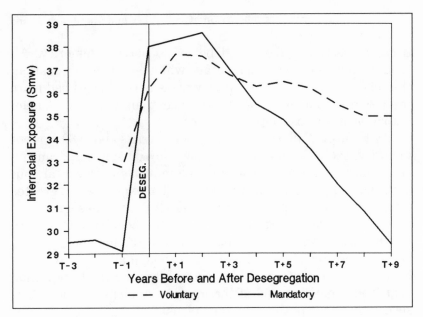

FIGURE 3.3 INTERRACIAL EXPOSURE IN DISTRICTS ABOVE 30 PERCENT MINORITY

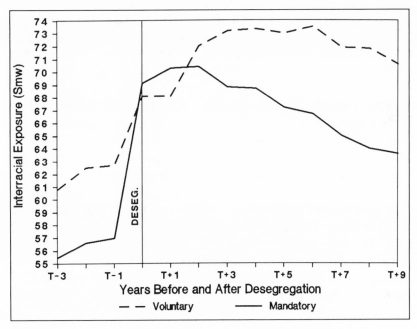

FIGURE 3.4 INTERRACIAL EXPOSURE IN DISTRICTS BELOW 30 PERCENT MINORITY

tricts respectively above and below 30 percent minority. Although they had a lower percentage white before desegregation, the school districts with voluntary plans nevertheless had more predesegregation interracial exposure than those with mandatory plans, across both categories.

As Figure 3.3 illustrates, in school districts above 30 percent minority, the magnet–voluntary plans produce a significant increase in interracial exposure in the implementation year, but both the increase and the absolute level of exposure are greater for the mandatory plans. By the fourth year of desegregation (T + 3), however, the trend lines meet. By the fifth year (T + 4), the districts with voluntary plans surpass the mandatory plans and the gap continues to increase. Although all school districts have decreasing interracial exposure after the implementation year, the negative trend of the mandatory plans is much more severe than that of the voluntary plans.

There is a similar pattern for school districts that are less than 30 percent minority (Figure 3.4). Again, the school districts with voluntary plans had greater predesegregation interracial exposure than those with mandatory plans, but both have a large increase in interracial exposure with the implementation of their plans. The districts with voluntary plans surpass the mandatory plans by the third year of desegregation (T + 2) and continue to show increased interracial exposure until year T + 6, when the trend line begins to decline. As with the school districts above 30 percent minority, the gap between the two types of plans increases over time. Therefore, regardless of whether a school district is above or below 30 percent minority, the mandatory plans do better in the implementation year and for a few years afterward. However, the districts with voluntary plans surpass the mandatory districts within two to four years, and the disparity continues to grow. Ultimately, the voluntary plans produce more interracial exposure.

The 5.6 percentage point gap in interracial exposure between the voluntary and mandatory plans in school districts above 30 percent minority represents roughly 8,500 fewer whites coming into contact with minorities in a school system that began with 80,000 students, 40,000 of them white. The 7.0 percentage point gap in interracial exposure between the voluntary and mandatory plans in school districts below 30 percent minority represents roughly 10,500 fewer white students coming into contact with minorities in a similar school system. Since the average magnet school plan costs $3 to $6 million more a year than the average mandatory reassignment plan, this means that the 8,500 additional whites in the first voluntary plan are valued at $352 to $705 each, and the 10,500 in the second at $285 to $571 each. On the other hand, this "cost" is offset by the larger tax base that accrues from retaining whites and the benefit to black children and society as a whole from greater interracial exposure.

The data in Table 3.8 also show that, in school districts above 30 percent minority, there is only a 2.7 percent decline in interracial exposure in the voluntary plans from the highest point (T + 1) to T + 9. In the districts with mandatory plans, there is an 8.9 decline from the highest point (also T + 1) to T + 9. For the northern control group school districts shown in Table 5.4 below, the decline in interracial exposure over a slightly longer period is 4.5 percentage points. Thus, in districts above 30 percent minority, the voluntary plans have slowed the decline in interracial exposure to half what would be predicted from the declining birth rate, whereas the decline under mandatory plans is about three times higher. In the districts below 30 percent minority, the decline from the highest point to T + 9 is − 2.5 for the voluntary plans and −6.7 for the mandatory plans, again, almost three times higher than the decline with voluntary plans.

In the multiple regression analysis that follows in this chapter, the difference in interracial exposure between the two types of plans is statistically analyzed to determine whether it is significant. The judgment as to whether the difference is important enough to determine the choice of a plan is, however, a matter of one's values and may ultimately depend on the consideration of other factors discussed in more detail below.

TABLE 3.9

RACIAL IMBALANCE (DM) UNDER VOLUNTARY AND MANDATORY DESEGREGATION PLANS

	Avg. Deseg. Year	% White $T-1$	N	$T-3$	$T-2$	$T-1$	$T+0$	$T+1$	$T+2$	$T+3$	$T+4$	$T+5$	$T+6$	$T+7$	$T+8$	$T+9$
ABOVE 30% MINORITY																
Voluntary	1976	54.9	7	55.1	53.7	52.7	46.3	41.3	39.5	37.9	36.6	34.1	33.3	32.9	32.2	31.7
Mandatory	1974	55.2	5	65.4	64.0	62.9	43.1	38.3	34.7	34.5	33.9	32.4	31.1	31.7	32.7	32.2
BELOW 30% MINORITY																
Voluntary	1969	88.3	2	53.0	53.5	52.3	44.7	42.8	36.3	33.4	33.4	33.7	31.6	30.3	29.2	28.9
Mandatory	1975	83.9	6	55.1	52.7	50.4	35.5	33.9	33.0	31.9	30.9	30.5	29.5	29.5	28.4	27.1

Years Before and After Major Desegregation Year ($T+0$)

Racial Imbalance

Not only do voluntary plans produce more interracial exposure, but, as Table 3.9 and Figures 3.5 and 3.6 indicate, they also produce levels of racial imbalance similar to those produced by mandatory plans. Although the districts with mandatory plans consistently surpass the districts with voluntary plans in achieving racial balance, the difference becomes fairly small beginning around the third year of desegregation for school districts below 30 percent minority and around the fourth or fifth year of desegregation for school districts above 30 percent minority. Both plans produce an average level of racial imbalance between 30 and 35 by the fourth to sixth year of desegregation—a level that indicates systemwide desegregation but allows

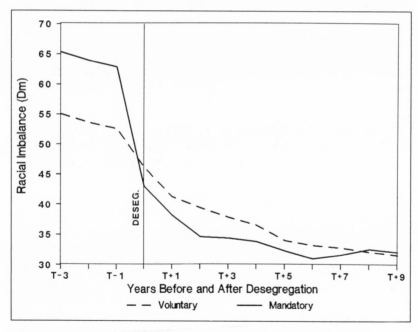

FIGURE 3.5   RACIAL IMBALANCE IN DISTRICTS ABOVE 30 PERCENT MINORITY

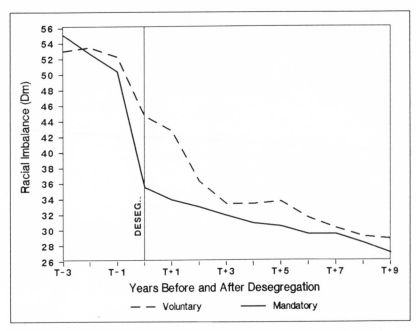

FIGURE 3.6 RACIAL IMBALANCE IN DISTRICTS BELOW 30 PERCENT
MINORITY

for court-approved deviations. In short, even by the traditional
and limited criterion of racial balance, the voluntary plans ultimately produce the same results as the mandatory plans.

This study is not alone in finding voluntary plans doing only
slightly worse than mandatory plans in producing racial balance.
Welch and Light (1987:55) indicate that the average difference
in reduction in racial imbalance between "major–voluntary"
plans and mandatory plans is only 6 percentage points for the
entire desegregation period. Similarly, Smylie (1983) found that
in 1980 all the voluntary plans taken together produced only 14
points less racial balance than all the mandatory plans, although
the mandatory plans had been in effect for almost twice as long.
This is quite a change since the early 1960s in the South, when
the gap between mandatory and voluntary plans was on the
order of 20 to 50 points in favor of the mandatory plans.

Racially Identifiable Schools

The courts rarely use any of the outcome measures discussed above to evaluate school desegregation alternatives because typically they want more control over individual schools than a summary measure allows. The most common standard used by the courts to judge desegregation plans is the extent to which they eliminate racially identifiable schools. If a school district's desegregation plan does not propose to eliminate all racially identifiable schools, the burden of proof is on the district to explain why. As will be shown here and in Chapter 5, however, it is extremely rare for any desegregation plan actually to eliminate all racially identifiable schools and for any court to hold a school district to this standard. But the courts do pay lip service to this notion, and so I compare below the voluntary and mandatory plans in the 20 districts on this measure.

Table 3.10 shows the percentage of students in racially identifiable schools in districts with voluntary and mandatory plans in the 10th year of desegregation. A racially identifiable school is defined here as one whose racial composition is greater than a 20 percentage point deviation from the school district's racial composition. Thus, if a school district is 60 percent minority and 40 percent white, a racially identifiable school is one which is less than 40 percent minority or greater than 80 percent minority. A racially identifiable school could also be less than 20 percent white or greater than 60 percent white. (The same schools are identified as racially identifiable whether whites or minorities are used in the definition.) This criterion is essentially a racial balance criterion and suffers from the problems discussed above, but it is, nevertheless, the most common one used by the courts, although the allowed deviation is often plus or minus 15 percentage points.

The data in Table 3.10 illustrate that the courts do not require that all racially identifiable schools be eliminated—contrary to the assertions of the plaintiffs in these cases—even in school districts which were less than 60 percent minority when they desegregated. The mandatory reassignment plans in school

TABLE 3.10
PERCENTAGE OF STUDENTS IN RACIALLY
IDENTIFIABLE SCHOOLS[a]

Plan	Percentage in T + 9 year
>30% MINORITY	
Mandatory	24.7%
Voluntary	19.4
<30% MINORITY	
Mandatory	13.1
Voluntary	9.2

Note:
[a]These are schools whose racial composition is more than a
20 percentage point deviation (plus or minus) from the
school district's racial composition.

districts below and above 30 percent minority have 13.1 and 24.7
percent of their students in racially identifiable schools. The
school districts below and above 30 percent minority with voluntary plans, by contrast, have only 9.2 and 19.4 percent of their
students in racially identifiable schools. Thus, even by the racial
balance criterion commonly used by the courts, the voluntary
plans do better.

Matched Pairs

Because the districts with successful magnet–voluntary
plans in this sample had already experienced successful predesegregation majority-to-minority programs and began with
more interracial exposure than the districts with magnet–
mandatory plans, it is possible that these districts would have
had more successful desegregation regardless of whether they
used mandatory or voluntary magnets. However, selection bias
seems unlikely in light of research suggesting that districts with
a higher percentage of students who are minority—the districts

with voluntary plans in this sample—have more white flight with mandatory plans than districts with a lower percentage of students who are minority (see, e.g., Armor, 1980; Coleman, Kelly, and Moore, 1975a, 1976b; Farley, Wurdock, and Richards, 1980; Ross, Gratton, and Clarke, 1982; Rossell, 1978a). Moreover, selection bias is unlikely for the school districts above 30 percent minority with voluntary plans, since all but two, Cincinnati and Montclair, desegregated under court order. Of course, it is always possible that judges allow voluntary plans in school districts where they believe school officials are more likely to carry plans out successfully, but this does not seem likely given the lower social status of the school districts with voluntary plans. Most people believe that any type of desegregation plan will be more successful in a higher-class school district than in a lower-class one.

Although we cannot conclusively rule it out, there is evidence to suggest that selection bias is not a confounding factor in this sample. One way to explore this issue is to compare pairs of school districts that have been matched in terms of the extent of predesegregation interracial exposure, percentage of students who are white, the size of the school district, the change in the white population in the metropolitan area (SMSA) from 1970 to 1980, and the extent of racial balance ultimately produced by the plans. Similar levels of racial balance represent similar levels of comprehensiveness. An index of dissimilarity of 30 or above, for example, is associated with a comprehensive, systemwide plan. Controlling for the predesegregation percentage white is necessary because interracial exposure is a function not only of desegregation efforts but of prior racial proportions as well. A school district with a lower percentage white before desegregation is at a disadvantage when compared with a school district with a higher percentage white before desegregation, unless one adjusts for that difference.

Only 6 school districts (three pairs) of the 20-district sample could be matched in this way. Even then, in two of the three pairs the district with the voluntary plan had slightly less inter-

TABLE 3.11

PRE- AND POSTDESEGREGATION CHANGES IN WHITE STUDENT ENROLLMENT, INTERRACIAL EXPOSURE, AND RACIAL IMBALANCE IN BOSTON AND MILWAUKEE SCHOOL DISTRICTS

Years Before and After Desegregation $(T + 0)$	Boston (Mandatory 1974)					Milwaukee (Voluntary 1976)				
	Year	% White	% White Enroll. Change	Smw[a]	Dm[b]	Year	% White	% White Enroll. Change	Smw[a]	Dm[b]
T − 9						1967	73.3%		21.3	81.0
T − 8						1968	73.0	1.4%	23.0	79.0
T − 7	1967	72.7%		33.5	68.9	1969	70.6	−1.7	20.8	79.8
T − 6	1968	68.5	−3.7%	29.6	70.7	1970	70.3	−0.5	22.8	78.5
T − 5	1969	66.0	−2.9	27.1	71.4	1971	67.8	−4.0	21.6	76.8
T − 4	1970	64.1	−1.0	25.7	72.4	1972	65.9	−5.5	21.7	76.1
T − 3	1971	61.5	−4.2	23.8	73.4	1973	64.0	−6.6	23.2	73.6
T − 2	1972	59.6	−3.3	24.9	70.8	1974	61.6	−7.4	23.9	72.0
T − 1	1973	57.2	−6.6	23.8	70.4	1975	60.1	−6.0	24.2	71.1
T + 0	1974	52.3	−16.2	33.1	50.6	1976	56.3	−10.8	35.1	51.3
T + 1	1975	47.0	−16.6	39.7	30.9	1977	52.8	−12.7	39.4	39.4

	Year					Year			
T + 2	1976	44.0	−13.3	36.5	32.8	1978	50.6	−9.5	39.1	36.9
T + 3	1977	41.6	−5.9	35.5	29.7	1979	47.2	−11.1	38.6	33.0
T + 4	1978	39.6	−7.6	33.7	29.2	1980	45.3	−7.4	37.2	32.8
T + 5	1979	37.1	−14.1	31.1	30.9	1981	43.3	−6.0	35.8	33.1
T + 6	1980	35.2	−2.4	29.6	30.8	1982	42.4	−2.9	35.4	32.5
T + 7	1981	32.3	−17.7	27.0	31.4	1983	40.0	−4.8	33.6	32.7
T + 8	1982	29.8	−11.7	25.2	31.6	1984	37.9	−3.1	32.4	31.5
T + 9	1983[c]	27.9	−8.5	22.8	32.6	1985	36.6	−1.4	31.3	31.4
T + 10	1984[c]	27.7	2.8	22.5	33.8					
T + 11	1985[c]	27.4	0.9	22.1	35.9					
10-year difference[d]		−29.3	−70.6	−1.0	−37.8		−23.5	−51.8	7.1	−39.7

Notes:
[a] Smw: Interracial exposure or the percentage of students who are white in the average minority child's school.
[b] Dm: Racial imbalance of whites and minorities.
[c] Smw and percentage white reduced by 0.8 to reflect the difference between the measures with the all-white segregated kindergartens included and the lower index without these kindergartens.
[d] From T − 1 to T + 9.

racial exposure before desegregation than the district with the mandatory plan. Two pairs of school districts were above 30 percent minority before desegregation (Boston–Milwaukee and Buffalo–Dayton), and one pair were below 30 percent minority (St. Paul–Tacoma).

The first pair of cities I will discuss are Boston and Milwaukee. Boston desegregated in 1974 with a mandatory desegregation plan. In 1975 the plan was expanded, and 22 magnet schools were added as educational options. Milwaukee desegregated in 1976 with a magnet–voluntary desegregation plan that included 40 magnet school programs. Both are large school districts (Boston had 93,000 students and Milwaukee 114,000 before desegregation) with similar predesegregation percentages of students who are white, and city–suburban minority-busing programs funded by the state, which during the period of this study were roughly equal in size, although Boston had about a thousand more minority students in its program.

As Table 3.11 shows, Boston's student population was 57.2 percent white in 1973, the year before desegregation, while Milwaukee's was 60.1 percent white the year before desegregation. The level of school interracial exposure (Smw) immediately preceding desegregation was identical in both cities (about 24), but for most of the predesegregation period Milwaukee had much less interracial exposure. In contrast to most districts with voluntary plans, Milwaukee's school interracial exposure surpassed the exposure under Boston's mandatory plan almost immediately to reach a peak of 39.4. By the 10th year of each plan, the consistently greater white flight from the Boston schools (−70.6 percent, as opposed to −51.8 percent for Milwaukee) resulted in a decline in Boston's interracial exposure to 22.8, while Milwaukee had 31.3 percent white enrollment in the average minority child's school. Boston's interracial exposure would show an even larger decrease if we could eliminate the differences between the two districts' minority transfers to the suburbs. Hence, as Figure 3.7 illustrates, Milwaukee's magnet–voluntary desegregation plan consistently produced greater inter-

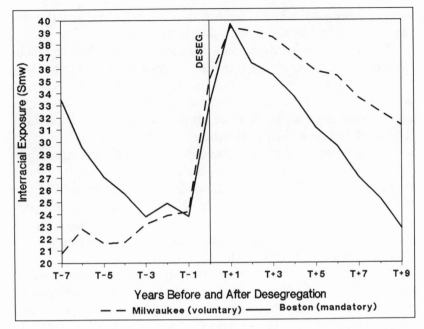

FIGURE 3.7 INTERRACIAL EXPOSURE BEFORE AND AFTER DESEGREGA-
TION IN BOSTON AND MILWAUKEE SCHOOL DISTRICTS

racial exposure throughout the entire postdesegregation period,
although it began with much less exposure. The change in interracial exposure (Smw) before and after desegregation amounted
to a 7.1 percent gain in Milwaukee (voluntary) in comparison
with a 1.0 percent decline in Boston (mandatory) over the same
time period.[14]

Since implementation of desegregation, however, both school
systems have experienced a decline in interracial exposure, although Boston's is much greater. The decline in interracial exposure in Boston from its highest point in the second year of the
plan to the 10th year is a whopping 17.6 percent. The decline in
interracial exposure in Milwaukee, by contrast, is only 7.8 percent, although it is still a decline. Thus, the voluntary plan in
Milwaukee is able to stop only the erosion of interracial ex-

posure caused by white response to desegregation, not the decline caused by the declining white birth rate.

The difference in interracial exposure between the two school
systems is 8.5 percentage points in Milwaukee's favor. Milwaukee had a white enrollment in 1985 of 33,065. This 8.5 percentage point difference in interracial exposure translates into
about 9,600 more white children coming into contact with minorities in Milwaukee than in Boston.

The greater interracial exposure in Milwaukee is not an artifact of changes in the white population of the SMSA.[15] Indeed,
that change is biased against Milwaukee. From 1970 to 1980 the
white population of the Milwaukee SMSA declined by 5.5 percent, whereas that of the Boston SMSA declined by only 2.8 percent. These data thus suggest a real advantage when desegregation plans use incentives rather than force.

Nor is the outcome favoring Milwaukee a function of greater
support for integration in that city. Indeed, the experience of
Milwaukee suggests that judges do not necessarily approve voluntary plans only in those school districts where school officials
are expected to implement such plans successfully. In Milwaukee, as in many other school districts with voluntary plans,
the judge appointed a Special Master to oversee the plan implementation because he did not trust the school board to do it
alone. As for Boston, contrary to popular opinion it was no more
racist than other northern cities in 1974. Bostonians responded
similarly to other northerners when asked about sending their
children to an integrated school that was up to 10 percent black:
12 percent of Bostonians objected and 7 percent of northerners
did so. They were also similar in their opposition to two-way
busing. On the other hand, they were more opposed than other
northerners to an integrated school that could be as much as 50
percent black. On the issues of residential segregation and
"blacks pushing where they are not wanted," however, Boston
residents were strikingly more liberal than other northerners
(Taylor, 1986:46). As Taylor concludes, "The survey data suggest, in fact, that the rejection of the doctrine of social inequal-

ity is more complete in Boston than in other comparable American cities." Thus, there is no reason to suspect that a mandatory plan was ordered in Boston and a voluntary one in Milwaukee because the former was a peculiarly racist city or the latter a particularly enlightened one. Nor is there any reason to believe that the outcome in terms of white flight and interracial exposure in the two cities was a function of the greater racism in Boston.

The history of these plans, however, suggests that minorities may always see themselves as disproportionately "burdened." In both districts plaintiffs, unhappy over what they see as a greater burden on their part, have petitioned the court for plan changes. Black parents in Boston have been requesting since 1982 that the mandatory plan be dismantled and replaced with a voluntary plan because minorities are being mandatorily bused from minority schools in their own neighborhood to minority schools in white neighborhoods (Cooper, 1982). There are few whites left in the schools. When the court failed to grant them relief, a group in Roxbury, the minority community in Boston, asked to secede from the city, citing the "forced busing" of black children across town to attend largely black schools as one of their grievances (*Boston Globe*, 1987). The proposition was defeated in the November 1986 elections.

Similarly, in Milwaukee plaintiffs have complained that minority children, because they choose "other neighborhood" schools at higher rates than white children, are bearing the burden of "busing." As a result, they brought suit against the surrounding suburbs in order to include more whites in the desegregation plan and thus equalize this burden. Hence, the Boston plaintiffs are demanding as relief a voluntary plan—the very situation the Milwaukee plaintiffs are terming burdensome.[16]

Table 3.12 and Figure 3.8 compare two other matched school districts. Both districts were desegregated in 1976 under court order: Dayton, Ohio, with a mandatory plan and Buffalo with a magnet–voluntary plan. Both Dayton and Buffalo began with similar predesegregation percentages of students who are white

TABLE 3.12

PRE- AND POSTDESEGREGATION CHANGES IN WHITE STUDENT ENROLLMENT, INTERRACIAL EXPOSURE, AND RACIAL IMBALANCE IN DAYTON AND BUFFALO SCHOOL DISTRICTS

Years Before and After Desegregation (T + 0)	Dayton (Mandatory)					Buffalo (Voluntary)				
	Year	% White	% White Enroll. Change	Smw[a]	Dm[b]	Year	% White	% White Enroll. Change	Smw[a]	Dm[b]
T − 9	1967	65.8%		9.2	91.0	1967	63.4%		26.1	68.9
T − 8	1968	61.5	−11.7%	12.0	86.3	1968	60.9	−2.1%	26.3	67.2
T − 7	1969	60.4	−3.8	13.5	84.6	1969	59.6	−3.2	27.3	65.5
T − 6	1970	59.0	−5.0	14.8	82.5	1970	58.3	−3.6	27.6	64.6
T − 5	1971	57.0	−6.2	15.4	80.8	1971	57.1	−5.1	28.1	63.1
T − 4	1972	55.0	−8.5	17.5	78.1	1972	54.9	−9.4	27.3	63.0
T − 3	1973	53.3	−9.0	19.3	74.3	1973	53.5	−7.8	26.0	63.5
T − 2	1974	52.1	−6.2	19.8	71.8	1974	52.3	−5.3	26.0	62.7
T − 1	1975	51.1	−5.9	21.3	69.2	1975	49.2	−8.7	26.4	61.0
T + 0	1976	47.7	−17.5	44.6	22.1	1976	50.0	−2.6	29.6	55.3
T + 1	1977	45.7	−6.0	41.9	24.5	1977	49.8	−4.6	36.7	42.5
T + 2	1978	44.8	−8.4	41.6	23.0	1978	48.1	−4.9	38.8	35.4
T + 3	1979	43.5	−6.3	39.8	25.5	1979	46.9	−8.0	39.2	31.6
T + 4	1980	42.7	−5.9	40.0	21.4	1980	46.6	−1.8	40.0	28.4
T + 5	1981	42.0	−3.8	38.7	24.1	1981	46.2	−2.0	42.8	18.7
T + 6	1982	41.3	−4.7	39.3	18.8	1982	45.8	−2.5	43.3	17.5
T + 7	1983	40.5	−5.4	38.3	19.3	1983	45.5	0.6	43.1	16.6
T + 8	1984	39.9	−3.3	37.7	20.2	1984	44.9	−4.3	42.7	15.9
T + 9	1985	39.2	−1.0	37.0	21.0	1985	44.1	−2.4	41.9	16.9
10-year difference[c]		−11.8	−48.0	15.7	−48.2		−5.1	−28.3	15.5	−44.1

Notes:
[a] Smw: Interracial exposure or the percentage of students who are white in the average minority child's school.
[b] Dm: Racial imbalance of whites and minorities.
[c] From T − 1 to T + 9.

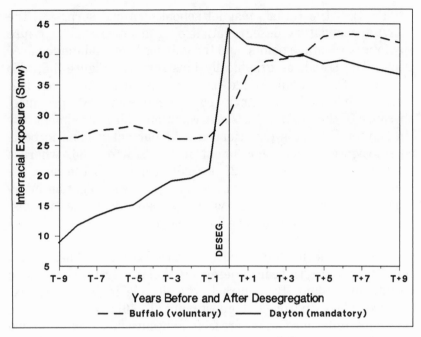

FIGURE 3.8 INTERRACIAL EXPOSURE BEFORE AND AFTER DESEGREGA-
TION IN BUFFALO AND DAYTON SCHOOL DISTRICTS

(51 and 49 percent respectively), and both are medium-sized,
northeastern urban districts. Buffalo's predesegregation student
enrollment was 57,000, while Dayton's was 45,000. Both school
districts had similar predesegregation levels of school racial imbalance, although Buffalo had more school interracial exposure
before desegregation (26.4 versus 21.3 in Dayton), and both had
similar predesegregation changes in white enrollment—a decline of 37 percent in Buffalo to 44 percent in Dayton.

Dayton's mandatory reassignment plan, which later included
nine magnets, produced an implementation-year level of interracial exposure of 44.6, more than 50 percent higher than the
29.6 produced by Buffalo's magnet school plan, which ultimately
included 19 magnets. By 1980, the year the court decided that
desegregation was not moving fast enough in Buffalo, the two
school districts had identical levels of interracial exposure.

By 1981 the Buffalo magnet school plan had surpassed the Dayton mandatory desegregation plan in interracial exposure by four percentage points, and the gap has been maintained over time. The trend, as graphically illustrated in Figure 3.8, also suggests that Buffalo would have surpassed Dayton even if it had not initiated mandatory reassignments in 1981, primarily because of the greater postdesegregation white enrollment loss in Dayton.[17] Dayton experienced a 51 percent decline in post-desegregation white enrollment from 1975 to 1986, whereas Buffalo experienced only a 29 percent decline over the same period. The ultimate change in pre- and postdesegregation inter-racial exposure (Smw) was virtually identical in the two dis-tricts, although Buffalo's absolute level surpassed Dayton's by 5 percentage points.

The decline in interracial exposure from its highest point (T + 6) to the 10th year of desegregation is only 1.4 percentage points in Buffalo. By contrast, the decline in interracial ex-posure in Dayton from its highest point (T + 0) is 7.6 points. The absolute difference in interracial exposure between the two school districts is 4.9 points. Buffalo had a white enrollment in 1985 of 20,162. This difference of 4.9 percent in interracial ex-posure translates into about 4,500 more whites coming into con-tact with minorities in Buffalo than in Dayton.

The greater postdesegregation interracial exposure in Buf-falo is not a function of changing demographics in the two metro-politan areas. Indeed, the data are biased against Buffalo in that regard. Although both Dayton and Buffalo make up about one-fourth of their respective metropolitan areas' population and 3 percent of their land areas, Buffalo has experienced a greater decline in the white population of the metropolitan area than has Dayton. From 1960 to 1970, the white population of the Dayton SMSA grew by 21 percent, but that of the Buffalo SMSA grew by only 1 percent. From 1970 to 1980, the white population of the Dayton SMSA declined by 5 percent, compared with a 10 percent decline in the Buffalo SMSA.

Thus, the evidence suggests that the greater interracial ex-posure in the Buffalo school system is a function of its desegregation plan. In Buffalo mandatory reassignments followed five years of successful voluntary desegregation, and the mandatory reassignments were identified with a highly popular preschool program that has always had a surplus of applicants. Moreover, these mandatory assignments affected only 15 percent of the white student population. In Dayton mandatory reassignment was the primary and initial desegregation tool, affecting close to 30 percent of the white student population and causing white enrollment loss to triple in the year of implementation. Only two of the magnet schools were created in 1976; the rest were added later. By that time, the poor reputation of the desegregation plan had been firmly established.

In Table 3.13 and Figure 3.9, another matched pair of school districts is compared. St. Paul, Minnesota, desegregated in 1973

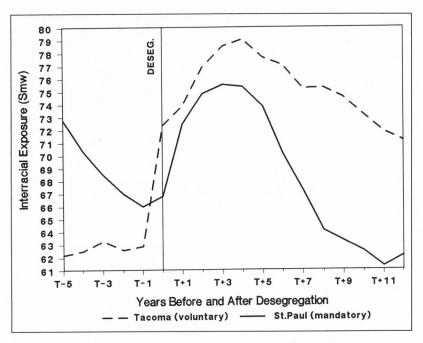

FIGURE 3.9 INTERRACIAL EXPOSURE BEFORE AND AFTER DESEGREGATION IN ST. PAUL AND TACOMA SCHOOL DISTRICTS

TABLE 3.13

PRE- AND POSTDESEGREGATION CHANGES IN WHITE STUDENT ENROLLMENT, INTERRACIAL EXPOSURE, AND RACIAL IMBALANCE IN ST. PAUL AND TACOMA SCHOOL DISTRICTS

Years Before and After Desegregation (T + 0)	St. Paul (Mandatory)					Tacoma (Voluntary)				
	Year	% White	% White Enroll. Change	Smw[a]	Dm[b]	Year	% White	% White Enroll. Change	Smw[a]	Dm[b]
T − 6	1967	90.8%		72.7	51.7	1963	90.2%		62.2	57.4
T − 5	1968	90.7	3.0%	72.9	50.4	1964	89.6	−0.1%	62.5	54.3
T − 4	1969	89.7	−4.9	70.6	51.3	1965	89.0	4.0	63.3	50.3
T − 3	1970	89.2	2.2	68.7	51.3	1966	88.8	−2.0	62.6	53.5
T − 2	1971	88.9	−0.1	67.2	50.9	1967	88.6	5.5	62.9	54.3
T − 1	1972	88.4	−3.7	66.2	49.7	1968	87.2	0.0	72.4	38.2
T + 0	1973	87.6	−5.3	67.0	48.2	1969	86.6	−1.4	73.9	34.5
T + 1	1974	86.5	−12.2	72.6	42.9	1970	85.7	−1.4	76.9	29.1
T + 2	1975	86.3	0.2	75.0	40.8	1971	84.8	−3.6	78.6	27.0
T + 3	1976	83.9	−10.0	75.7	32.9	1972	84.7	−4.6	79.1	26.6
T + 4	1977	82.5	−6.7	75.5	30.1					

	Year				
T + 5	1978	80.4	−8.3	74.0	29.0
T + 6	1979	77.9	−5.7	70.3	30.1
T + 7	1980	74.3	−6.2	67.4	26.9
T + 8	1981	71.0	−6.7	64.3	25.8
T + 9	1982	68.8	−5.4	63.5	24.4
T + 10	1983	68.0	−1.9	62.6	24.2
T + 11	1984	66.8	−1.7	61.5	24.6
T + 12	1985	65.8	1.2	62.3	19.9
T + 13					
T + 14					
T + 15					
T + 16					
T + 17					
13-year difference[c]		−22.6	−51.2	−3.9	−29.8

Year				
1973	83.9	−2.3	77.7	28.9
1974	83.0	−3.2	77.1	28.2
1975	81.3	−3.7	75.3	26.9
1976	81.0	−2.4	75.3	26.7
1977	80.0	−3.0	74.6	25.6
1978	78.6	−6.6	73.2	25.5
1979	77.3	−4.3	71.9	25.6
1980	75.6	−4.4	71.2	23.7
1981	74.3	−2.7	70.2	21.8
1982	73.5	−1.6	69.4	22.2
1983	72.7	−1.1	68.8	21.1
1984	71.6	−1.6	67.8	21.3
1985	71.2	1.0	67.2	21.6
13-year difference[c]	−13.0	−34.3	8.3	−30.6

Notes:
[a] Smw: Interracial exposure or the percentage of students who are white in the average minority child's school.
[b] Dm: Racial imbalance of whites and minorities.
[c] From T − 1 to T + 12.

with a mandatory reassignment plan; Tacoma desegregated in 1968 with a magnet–voluntary plan. Both are medium-sized northern school districts—St. Paul enrolled 48,000 and Tacoma 37,000 students before desegregation. The predesegregation percentage of pupils who are white in St. Paul was 88.4, while in Tacoma it was 88.6. The level of school interracial exposure (Smw) was much higher in St. Paul (mandatory) than in Tacoma (voluntary) for the entire predesegregation period. Although Tacoma began with lower predesegregation and implementation-year levels of interracial exposure than St. Paul, its voluntary plan surpassed St. Paul's mandatory plan by the third year. The gap continues to increase over time, so that by the 13th year of desegregation (T + 12), Tacoma was almost 9 percentage points ahead of St. Paul. The ultimate pre- to postdesegregation change in interracial exposure was 8.3 in Tacoma, but −3.9 in St. Paul.

The decline in interracial exposure in St. Paul from the highest point (T + 3) to the T + 12 year is 13.4 points. The decline in Tacoma from its highest point (T + 4) to the T + 12 year is only 7.9 points. The interracial exposure gap between the two is 8.9 points, favoring Tacoma. In 1985 Tacoma had a white student enrollment of 20,185. The 8.9 point difference translates into about 7,100 more whites coming into contact with minorities in Tacoma than in St. Paul.

The greater interracial exposure in Tacoma is not a function of the changing demographics of the two metropolitan areas. Indeed, as with the previous two comparisons, the demographics are biased against Tacoma, the school district with the voluntary plan. From 1970 to 1980, the St. Paul/Minneapolis SMSA experienced a 14.2 percent increase in white population. The Tacoma SMSA, by contrast, experienced only an 11.9 percent increase in white population. Thus, these matched-pair analyses suggest that even when districts with voluntary plans begin with less predesegregation interracial exposure and a lower predesegregation percentage of students who are white, they may ultimately surpass the mandatory plans in both the change in interracial exposure and the absolute level of interracial exposure.

Net Benefit

Table 3.14 contains a pooled cross-sectional time series analysis in a multiple regression equation of the extent of interracial exposure produced by voluntary or mandatory desegregation, controlling for the change in the white population in the SMSA from 1970 to 1980, the predesegregation percentage of students who are white, interracial exposure and white enrollment change, as well as total enrollment, the year of the plan, the city or county educational level, the time period (from the start of desegregation to the ninth year), and an interaction effect, time period multiplied by a dummy variable, voluntary plan (voluntary = 1, mandatory = 0).

The postimplementation time period is T + 0 to T + 9 and no missing data are filled in as in the interrupted time series shown in Tables 3.7 to 3.9 and Figures 3.1 to 3.6. A pooled cross-sectional analysis increases the N by treating each year as a separate case. Thus, the number of cases would increase from 20 to 200 (20 districts times 10 years) if there were data for all years. Because of missing data, the N is reduced to 186. The average for each one of these variables is thus the average for 186, not 20, school districts.

The two important policy variables for comparing the effectiveness of voluntary and mandatory plans are the dummy variable "voluntary plan" (1 = voluntary, 0 = mandatory), and the interaction effect variable, time period times "voluntary." The dummy variable tests whether voluntary plans produce significantly greater interracial exposure regardless of the time period, and the second variable tests whether voluntary plans produce significantly greater interracial exposure the longer they are in place. The other demographic variables are included in the equation in order to control for confounding variables that might also affect interracial exposure.[18]

This equation shows that voluntary desegregation plans produce significantly more interracial exposure over time than mandatory desegregation plans. The b coefficient for the main effects and the interaction effects are interpreted by solving the

TABLE 3.14

POSTIMPLEMENTATION INTERRACIAL EXPOSURE (SMW) WITH SCHOOL DISTRICT AND PLAN CHARACTERISTICS

Variables	Average	r	b	Beta	SE b
Smw after implementation	48.62				
Voluntary plan	0.44	−0.22	−3.690[b]	−0.10	1.707
Percentage white T − 1	68.61	0.88[a]	1.016[a]	0.82	0.065
Smw T − 2	42.41	0.80[a]	0.248[a]	0.26	0.059
% White enrollment change T − 2	−4.00	0.55[a]	.98[b]	0.12	.43
Enrollment	66,105.49	−0.45[a]	8.05e−7[c]	−0.00	1.75e−5
Year of plan	74.12	−0.04	2.193[a]	0.31	0.297
City/county educational level, 1970	12.08	0.34[b]	−8.308[a]	−0.26	1.404
Time	4.39	−0.09	−0.882[a]	−0.13	0.200
Time × voluntary status	1.90	−0.17	0.903[a]	0.13	0.302
SMSA change—whites, 1970–1980	9.18	−0.20	−0.030	−0.04	0.028
Constant			−84.655		
r²			0.912		
df			184		

Notes:
[a] Significant at the .001 level or better.
[b] Significant at the .05 level or better.
[c] The term e−7 to the right of the b coefficient means the decimal point should be moved seven places to the left; and e−5, five places.

equation for those variables. The equation tells us that a voluntary plan at T + 9, holding all other variables constant, would be expected to have a level of interracial exposure 4.4 percentage points above that of a mandatory plan. For voluntary plans, the equation for Smw in the 10th year (T + 9) is:

$$
\begin{array}{ll}
\text{Smw} \ (T + 9) \ = \ -84.655 \ - \ \underset{[\text{Vol.}]}{3.690(1)} \ + \ \underset{[\% \text{ Wh. T} - 1]}{1.016(68.61)}
\end{array}
$$

$$
+ \ \underset{[\text{Smw T} - 2]}{.248(42.41)} \ + \ \underset{[\% \text{ Wh. Enr. Ch.}]}{.98480(-4.0)} \ + \ \underset{[\text{Enroll.}]}{.000000805(66,105.49)}
$$

$$
+ \ \underset{[\text{Deseg. Yr.}]}{2.193(74.12)} \ - \ \underset{[\text{Educ.}]}{8.308(12.08)} \ - \ \underset{[\text{Time}]}{.882(9)} \ + \ \underset{[\text{Time*Vol.}]}{.903(9)}
$$

$$
- \ \underset{[\text{Smsa Ch.}]}{.03(9.18)}
$$

This produces an index of 49.86 in the 10th year (T + 9). For mandatory plans, the equation for Smw in the 10th year (T + 9) is the same except that the dummy variable "voluntary" is 0 so that it drops out. The interaction effect also drops out, since 0 times anything is 0. This produces an index of 45.42 in the 10th year. The difference between the two is 4.4 percentage points. A quicker way to determine the difference is simply to look at the variable "voluntary" and the interaction effect. The two variables together add up to 4.4 points. Therefore, voluntary plans will produce 4.4 points more interracial exposure (Smw) than mandatory plans.

This equation can be solved for any point in time. For example, at point T + 1 the voluntary plans are estimated to produce 2.8 points *less* interracial exposure than the mandatory plans. The equation will also allow one to plot the decline in interracial exposure over time. Starting with the highest point (T + 1), the voluntary plans produce a level of interracial exposure of 49.65, and the mandatory plans produce a level of interracial exposure of 52.43. By T + 9, the 10th year, the voluntary plans have virtually the same level of interracial exposure as at T + 1—49.86—while interracial exposure under the mandatory plans has dropped to 45.42, a decline of 7 percentage points. Thus, this equation indicates that, on average, the voluntary plans have virtually brought a halt to the normal decline in interracial exposure resulting from the declining white birth rate. The mandatory plans have not.

In addition, interracial exposure is positively related, as would be expected, to the predesegregation percentage of students who are white, predesegregation interracial exposure, the predesegregation percentage change in white enrollment, and the year the desegregation plan was implemented. The most important variable in predicting postdesegregation interracial exposure is the predesegregation percentage of students who are white. Indeed, it is a far more important variable than the type of plan in predicting postdesegregation interracial exposure, and thus it should be statistically controlled in order to detect the effects of plan characteristics.

Postimplementation interracial exposure is negatively related to time and the city or county educational level. This is probably because the higher the educational level of parents, the greater their ability to use private schools or to move from the school district. There is no relationship between interracial exposure and change in the white population in the SMSA from 1970 to 1980 or total district enrollment.

This equation explains almost 91 percent of the variance in postimplementation interracial exposure and is quite robust. The coefficients change little when the data are analyzed without the predesegregation adjustments to Montclair and Houston,[19] when the entire postimplementation time period is analyzed, with its missing data,[20] and when Buffalo's postdesegregation interracial exposure is fixed at the 1980 (pre–mandatory reassignments) level.[21]

The difference of 4.4 between voluntary and mandatory plans increases to 4.9 percentage points when only school districts with more than 30 percent minority enrollment are analyzed. The equation for voluntary plans in school districts greater than 30 percent minority at T + 9 is as follows:

$$\text{Smw (T + 9)} = -137.488 - \underset{[\text{Vol.}]}{3.368(1)} \qquad + \underset{[\%\ \text{Wh. t} - 1]}{.585(55.7)}$$

$$+ \underset{[\text{Smw t} - 2]}{.114(31.8)} \qquad - \underset{[\text{Wh. Enr. Ch}]}{.585(-5.2)} - \underset{[\text{Enroll.}]}{.0001(72092)}$$

$$+ \underset{[\text{Deseg Yr.}]}{2,446(74.8)} \qquad - \underset{[\text{Educ.}]}{3.114(11.9)} \qquad - \underset{[\text{Time}]}{1.25(9)}$$

$$+ \underset{[\text{Time*Vol.}]}{.921(9)} \qquad + \underset{[\text{SMSA Ch.}]}{.010(6.4)}$$

All variables are statistically significant. There is, however, more decline over time in interracial exposure in the school districts above 30 percent minority than in the entire sample. The decline from the highest point (T + 1) to the 10th year (T + 9) is 2.7 points for the voluntary plans and 10 points for the mandatory plans. Thus, school districts with voluntary plans have a 10-year decline in interracial exposure that is less than the average decline of 4.5 points over a slightly longer time period for the control group of northern school districts shown in Tables 5.1 through 5.8 in Chapter 5. The mandatory plans, by contrast, have substantially more decline in interracial exposure than the control group shown in Chapter 5, almost four times more decline than the voluntary plans.

The 4.9 percentage point gap in interracial exposure between the voluntary and mandatory plans in school districts above 30 percent minority represents about 7,600 fewer whites coming into contact with minorities in a school system with a mandatory plan that began with 40,000 white students. The 4.4 percentage point gap in interracial exposure between all the voluntary and mandatory plans represents about 6,800 fewer white students in contact with minorities.

This analysis and the matched-pair analysis suggest that there is little danger of a selection bias. Thus, we can be fairly confident that the voluntary plans really do produce more interracial exposure than the mandatory plans. The voluntary plans do not, however, halt the normal decline in interracial exposure that results from the declining birth rate.

Dismantling Mandatory Plans

It has been almost 20 years since the wave of mandatory reassignment plans swept the South after *Alexander* and desegregated virtually the entire region. Many of these school districts are now returning to court to attain unitary status; others are seeking only to change their plan from a "forced busing" to a freedom-of-choice model. The outcome of these decisions to move from mandatory reassignment plans to choice plans or neighborhood school systems will have a major impact on future education policy.

There are 7 school districts in the 119-school-district sample that dismantled mandatory desegregation plans and replaced them with voluntary plans during the period of this study. They are: Montclair, New Jersey; Houston, Texas; Rochester, New York; Cambridge, Massachusetts; Los Angeles, California; Tulsa, Oklahoma; and Oklahoma City, Oklahoma. I have complete data for Montclair, Houston, Los Angeles, and Cambridge, and almost complete data for Oklahoma City.

In the Montclair magnet–voluntary desegregation plan, every elementary school is a magnet school, and all attendance zones are eliminated. As Table 3.15 demonstrates, this plan continued the trend of decreasing racial imbalance begun with the mandatory desegregation plan implemented in 1969 and 1971. Moreover, contrary to the trend for all school districts, and particularly those above 50 percent minority, the Montclair school district has had no decline in interracial exposure since 1982. In short, the choice plan not only maintained the desegregation achieved by the prior mandatory plans, but actually increased desegregation.

The Houston school district was 60 percent minority when its mandatory plan was dismantled in 1975 in favor of a magnet–voluntary plan. The mandatory plan was limited, but it was about average by the standards of predominantly minority school districts, reassigning less than 6 percent of the white students and increasing interracial exposure by 2.4 percentage

TABLE 3.15

MONTCLAIR: ENROLLMENT AND SEGREGATION INDICES
BEFORE AND AFTER DISMANTLING OF MANDATORY PLAN

Year	White Enrollment	% White Enrollment Change	Interracial Exposure Actual Smw	Interracial Exposure Predicted Smw	Racial Imbalance Actual Dm	Racial Imbalance Predicted Dm
1967	4,977		49.6		33.7	
1968	5,039	1.2%	48.9		32.6	
1969	5,161	2.4	55.3		28.8	
1970	4,771	−7.6	49.2		30.9	
1971 MANDATORY DESEGREGATION						
1971	4,753	−0.4	53.4		24.4	
1972	4,341	−8.7	57.5		12.9	
1973	4,148	−4.4	56.6		13.1	
1974	4,003	−3.5	55.8		13.1	
1975	3,710	−7.3	54.4		14.5	
1976	3,641	−1.9	55.3		12.3	
1977 MAGNET–VOLUNTARY						
1977	3,579	−1.7	55.1	54.0	8.0	13.2
1978	3,465	−3.2	54.8	53.3	6.1	13.3
1979	3,331	−3.9	54.4	52.7	6.7	13.3
1980	3,190	−4.2	53.2	52.1	5.4	13.3
1981	3,090	−3.1	50.8	51.4	8.2	13.3
1982	3,073	−0.6	51.4	50.8	5.5	13.3
1983	2,869	−6.6	51.0	50.1	4.8	13.4
1984	2,800	−2.4	51.4	49.5	3.4	13.4
1985	2,535	−9.5	51.7	48.9	3.9	13.4
Change under mandatory plan (6 years) 1970–1976	−1,130	−23.68	6.18		−18.56	
Change under voluntary plan (6 years) 1976–1982	−568	−15.60	−3.9		−6.8	
Change since voluntary plan 1976–1985	−1,106	−30.38	−3.63		−8.46	

points, as shown in Table 3.16. Although it produced about half the increase in interracial exposure of the 1980 St. Louis mandatory reassignment plan, it nevertheless achieved twice as much as the 1978 Los Angeles mandatory plan. The magnet–voluntary plan, by contrast, has managed to decrease racial imbalance every year from 1975 through 1985, for a total decrease of 13 percentage points. The decline in interracial exposure since the voluntary plan was implemented—4 percentage points—is about what would be predicted for a school district whose student percentage minority increased by 22 percentage points over that time period (from 60 percent to 82 percent).

As Table 3.17 shows, after dismantling the mandatory desegregation plan that had been in effect for three years, Los Angeles was able to produce greater interracial exposure with a return to sole reliance on magnets and the majority-to-minority transfer program than would have been predicted if the mandatory plan had continued. Despite the fact that the mandatory plan included only grades 4 to 8, Los Angeles experienced extraordinary white flight in 1978. As a result, the mandatory desegregation plan increased interracial exposure by less than a half a percentage point and reduced racial imbalance by only 5 percentage points. When the program was expanded in 1980 to encompass all grades, interracial exposure *declined* by 1 percentage point. With a return to voluntary desegregation in 1981, the decline in interracial exposure was slowed as whites returned to the public schools. By 1982 the white enrollment loss rate had been reduced to 2 percent, one of the lowest in this sample.[22] This trend continued at least through 1985.

Table 3.18 shows the trends in interracial exposure and racial balance in Cambridge from 1968 through 1985. These data indicate that the dismantling of the mandatory reassignment plan implemented in 1979, and its replacement in 1981 with a "controlled choice" plan (similar to Montclair's but with no magnets) in which all attendance zones are eliminated, did not resegregate the school system. In fact, racial imbalance has continued to decline every year since the controlled choice plan was imple-

TABLE 3.16

HOUSTON: ENROLLMENT AND SEGREGATION INDICES
BEFORE AND AFTER DISMANTLING OF MANDATORY PLAN

Year	White Enrollment	% White Enrollment Change	Interracial Exposure		Racial Imbalance	
			Actual Smw	Predicted Smw	Actual Dm	Predicted Dm
1967	131,803		84.6		90.9	
1968	131,099	−0.5%	15.4		80.4	
1969	124,451	−5.1	16.0		79.1	
1970 MANDATORY DESEGREGATION						
1970	119,181	−4.2	18.4		74.9	
1971	107,587	−9.7	18.2		73.7	
1972	98,282	−8.6	17.6		72.7	
1973	87,776	−10.7	17.3		71.3	
1974	81,459	−7.2	17.0		70.5	
1975 MAGNET−VOLUNTARY						
1975	75,085	−7.8	16.8	16.6	69.6	69.3
1976	71,430	−4.9	16.8	16.2	68.2	68.2
1977	66,439	−7.0	16.6	15.8	67.3	67.1
1978	59,407	−10.6	16.1	15.4	66.0	66.0
1979	53,086	−10.6	15.9	15.0	64.2	64.9
1980	48,811	−8.1	15.7	14.6	62.1	63.8
1981	45,048	−7.7	15.1	14.2	60.5	62.7
1982	42,136	−6.5	14.7	13.8	59.3	61.6
1983	38,481	−8.7	14.1	13.4	58.3	60.5
1984	35,604	−7.5	13.6	13.0	57.5	59.4
1985	34,111	−4.2	12.8	12.7	57.4	58.3
Change under mandatory plan (5 years) 1969–1974	−42,992	−34.5	1.1		−8.7	
Change under voluntary plan (5 years) 1974–1979	−28,373	−34.8	−1.1		−6.2	
Change since voluntary plan 1974–1985	−47,348	−58.1	−4.2		−13.1	

TABLE 3.17

LOS ANGELES: ENROLLMENT AND SEGREGATION INDICES
BEFORE AND AFTER DISMANTLING OF MANDATORY PLAN

Year	White Enrollment	% White Enrollment Change	Interracial Exposure Actual Smw	Interracial Exposure Predicted Smw	Racial Imbalance Actual Dm	Racial Imbalance Predicted Dm
1966	351,817		20.8		73.9	
1967	350,177	−0.5%	20.6		73.5	
1968	347,967	−0.6	20.5		72.9	
1969	335,511	−3.6	20.5		72.1	
1970	318,431	−5.1	20.5		71.1	
1971	300,079	−5.8	20.2		70.2	
1972	283,199	−5.6	20.1		69.3	
1973	269,768	−4.7	19.7		69.0	
1974	250,914	−7.0	19.8		67.3	
1975	240,787	−4.0	19.6		66.7	
1976	219,359	−8.9	18.9		65.9	
1977	194,808	−11.2	18.9		62.9	

1978 MANDATORY DESEGREGATION

Year	White Enrollment	% White Enrollment Change	Interracial Exposure Actual Smw	Interracial Exposure Predicted Smw	Racial Imbalance Actual Dm	Racial Imbalance Predicted Dm
1978	163,912	−15.9	19.2		58.7	
1979	146,535	−10.6	17.9		58.1	
1980	127,281	−13.1	16.9		57.3	

1981 MAGNET–VOLUNTARY

Year	White Enrollment	% White Enrollment Change	Interracial Exposure Actual Smw	Interracial Exposure Predicted Smw	Racial Imbalance Actual Dm	Racial Imbalance Predicted Dm
1981	120,729	−5.1	15.3	15.7	60.7	56.8
1982	118,120	−2.2	15.0	14.6	59.9	56.1
1983	113,964	−3.5	14.3	13.4	60.7	55.4
1984	110,313	−3.2	13.8	12.3	60.5	54.7
1985	107,216	−2.8	13.1	11.1	61.3	54.0

	White Enrollment	% White Enrollment Change	Actual Smw	Predicted Smw	Actual Dm	Predicted Dm
Change under mandatory plan (3 years) 1977–1980	−67,527	−34.7	−2.0		−5.6	
Change under voluntary plan (3 years) 1980–1983	−13,317	−10.5	−2.6		3.4	
Change since voluntary plan 1980–1985	−20,065	−15.8	−3.8		4.0	

TABLE 3.18

CAMBRIDGE: ELEMENTARY[a] ENROLLMENT AND SEGREGATION INDICES
BEFORE AND AFTER DISMANTLING OF MANDATORY PLAN

Year	White Enrollment	% White Enrollment Change	Interracial Exposure (Actual)[b]	Racial Imbalance (Actual)[b]
1968	6,705		71.3	36.6
1969	6,692	−0.2	72.5	36.8
1970	6,438	−3.8	71.4	37.1
1971	6,253	−2.9	69.2	39.9
1972	6,076	−2.8	68.7	37.3
1973	6,050	−0.4	68.2	33.9
1974	5,356	−11.5	65.9	31.3
1975	5,184	−3.2	60.5	37.9
1976	4,929	−4.9	58.7	38.8
1977	4,674	−5.2	57.1	39.7
1978	4,325	−7.5	55.6	38.6
1979	4,138	−4.3	55.2	35.1
1980 MANDATORY DESEGREGATION				
1980	3,806	−8.0	60.1	26.0
1981	3,449	−9.4	59.1	17.8
1982 VOLUNTARY DESEGREGATION				
1982	3,251	−5.7	57.5	15.8
1983	3,013	−7.3	56.1	14.7
1984	2,839	−5.8	54.1	10.9
1985	2,805	−1.2	54.1	9.9
Change under mandatory plan (2 years) 1979–1981	−689	−16.7	3.9	−17.3
Change under voluntary plan (2 years) 1981–1983	−436	−12.6	−3.0	−3.1
Change since voluntary plan 1981–1985	−644	−18.7	−5.0	−7.9

Notes:

[a] Cambridge has only one high school.

[b] With only two years of mandatory desegregation, a trend could not be established by which to predict interracial exposure and racial imbalance if the plan had continued.

mented, and racial balance is now nearly perfect. Although interracial exposure has also declined every year due to a declining white enrollment, this trend had stabilized by 1985.

Cambridge and Montclair are the only school districts in the 119-district-sample to eliminate their school attendance zones. They are also both tiny school districts of less than 10 square miles. The logistics of adopting such plans in large school districts appear to be overwhelming, as discussed in Chapter 6. Cambridge has no magnets and relies simply on people's knowledge of the schools and publicity from the Parent Information Centers. It helps that it is tiny—virtually every school is within walking distance from home for most of the population. It is also one of the more residentially integrated cities in the United States; if all parents simply chose the school nearest to their home, the school district would still be quite integrated.

Table 3.19 shows the trends in interracial exposure in Oklahoma City from 1968 through 1985. Oklahoma City dismantled its mandatory reassignment plan in 1985 and replaced it with a neighborhood school plan and majority-to-minority transfer program. Unlike Montclair, Houston, and Los Angeles, however, Oklahoma City has no magnet programs in minority schools, and unlike Cambridge, it is large and quite residentially segregated. The Oklahoma neighborhood school plan increased racial imbalance by 15 percentage points and reduced from 56.4 to 45.1 the percentage white in the average black child's school from 1984 to 1986.

These data suggest that dismantling a mandatory plan and replacing it with a voluntary plan will resegregate a large school system beyond what would have occurred under the mandatory plan *only* if the plan does not include magnet programs in minority schools and if there are no racial controls on school transfers. In other words, public choice plans will usually produce more interracial exposure than command and control plans, but only if the proper incentives are adopted. These include programs in minority schools to encourage socially appropriate behavior on

TABLE 3.19

OKLAHOMA CITY: ENROLLMENT AND SEGREGATION INDICES
BEFORE AND AFTER DISMANTLING OF MANDATORY PLAN

Year	White Enrollment	% White Enrollment Change	Interracial Exposure		Racial Imbalance	
			Actual S_{mw}	Predicted S_{mw}	Actual D_m	Predicted D_m
1967	59,417					
1968	58,472	−1.6	12.2		88.6	
1969	53,470	−8.6	26.0		71.5	
1970	50,495	−5.6	28.5		68.5	
1971	49,571	−1.8	30.3		66.7	
1972 MANDATORY DESEGREGATION						
1972	42,224	−14.8	63.7		26.8	
1973	37,461	−11.3	64.2		24.4	
1974	34,568	−7.7	62.8		22.3	
1975[b]	31,944	−7.6	60.2		22.5	
1976	29,319	−8.2	57.5		22.6	
1977[b]	27,997	−4.5	56.3		22.4	
1978	26,674	−4.7	55.0		22.1	
1979	24,964	−6.4	53.2		22.1	
1980	22,713	−9.0	51.4		22.1	
1981[b]	22,449	−1.2	50.3		22.6	
1982	22,185	−1.2	49.2		23.0	
1983[b]	21,111	−4.8	52.8		23.7	
1984	20,037	−5.1	56.4[a]		24.4[a]	
1985 VOLUNTARY DESEGREGATION						
1985	19,557	−2.4	46.2[a]	55.2	38.2[a]	24.4
1986	18,975	−3.0	45.1[a]	54.2	39.4[a]	24.4
Change under mandatory plan (2 years) 1971–1973		−24.0	33.9		−42.3	
Change under voluntary plan (2 years) 1984–1986		−5.3	−11.3		15.0	

Notes:
[a] Blacks and nonblacks.
[b] Data in these years extrapolated from adjoining years.

the part of whites and negative incentives in the form of racial controls on transfers to further structure the process toward its goal—a desegregated school system.

Conclusions

The analysis presented here suggests that the public choice model is relevant for school desegregation. Many parents behave, in general, like rational utility maximizers. Previous research suggests that when confronted with mandatory reassignment, parents weigh the costs and benefits of alternative courses of action and choose the alternative with the least cost (Rossell, 1983, 1988), which often means withdrawing their children from the school system. When asked to choose between their neighborhood school and a superior magnet school, sufficient numbers will choose the latter, so that plans based primarily on choice will produce more interracial exposure than those based primarily on mandatory reassignment. But part of the reason the magnet–voluntary plans ultimately produce more interracial exposure is that, even with magnet schools, the mandatory plans produce more white flight than the voluntary plans.

The mandatory plans *do* produce more interracial exposure in the implementation year than the voluntary plans—the primary reason I (1979) and Royster, Baltzell, and Simmons (1979), with one year of postimplementation data, concluded that mandatory plans produce greater interracial exposure. But even when magnet schools are included as educational options, mandatory desegregation plans begin to resegregate shortly after the implementation year at a more rapid rate than the voluntary plans. Around the third or fourth year of desegregation, the two trend lines cross, and the magnet–voluntary plans produce greater interracial exposure than the mandatory plans, all other things being equal. This appears to be true regardless of whether a school district's enrollment is more or less than 30 percent minority and regardless of the extent of predesegregation interracial exposure. It must be stressed, however, that none of the mandatory plans in our sample could by any stretch of the imagination be called "failures." Every school district with a mandatory desegregation plan has more interracial exposure in the 10th year of desegregation than it would have had if no plan at all had been implemented.

Whether one considers the 4.4 percentage point gap between the two types of plans to be important and worth the added expense depends on how one values a situation in which roughly 6,800 more whites come into contact with minorities in the hypothetical school system of 40,000 whites. This in turn will depend upon the value to the school district of having higher-tax-paying whites in the school system, as well as the other social benefits such people add to public education. On the other hand, voluntary plans do not reverse the decline in interracial exposure resulting from the decline in the white birth rate. They merely eliminate the decline in interracial exposure due to white flight from desegregation and slow down the decline in interracial exposure due to the declining white birth rate. Mandatory plans do not appear to do either. Moreover, since voluntary plans are preferred by parents (Rossell, 1986a, 1986b, 1987), all that such plans would have to produce to be superior to mandatory plans is the same interracial exposure.

Although the finding that primarily voluntary plans produce more interracial exposure over time than mandatory plans contradicts several decades of school desegregation research, it must be emphasized that the voluntary plans analyzed in this report are qualitatively different from the old southern freedom-of-choice plans or northern one-way majority-to-minority programs. They are different in that incentives are provided to motivate whites to act in a socially desirable manner—that is, to transfer to minority schools. They are also different in that the choice plans analyzed here are not complete "marketplace solutions." Negative incentives are imposed in the form of racial controls on transfers, and, although racial balance goals were perhaps not necessary for successful outcomes, most of the school districts had them. Some used minimal redrawing of attendance zones and included a small number of mandatory transfers.

The whites in this study are also different from the whites of the 1960s, when freedom-of-choice plans consistently failed. As attitudes toward desegregation have improved over time, we would expect voluntary plans to be more successful. Magnet schools thus provide white parents with an incentive to act in a manner consistent with their stated support for integration.

This analysis also shows that mandatory plans can be dismantled with no harm *if* they are replaced with comprehensive voluntary plans with both positive and negative incentives. Returning to neighborhood schools and relying solely on majority-to-minority programs will probably produce some resegregation beyond the "normal" decline in interracial exposure in large school districts (e.g., Oklahoma City). Pure freedom of choice undoubtedly has some important philosophical advantages over the incentives approach, but it will, in most cases, produce less interracial exposure.

4

What Is Attractive About Magnet Schools?

AN IMPORTANT assumption of the public choice model of school desegregation policy is that citizens are capable of making programmatic choices among schools. If money is poured into magnet schools that are also given special themes or curricula, parents will compare the resources of that school with those of their neighborhood school and other schools. On that assumption, school districts with magnet schools prepare elaborate, detailed booklets, leaflets, and newsletters with enticing descriptions of their magnet programs.

Milwaukee, for example, mails a 12-page newsletter to parents. The Montessori program in two schools, Greenfield and MacDowell, accepts children between the ages of three and six. It is described in the following terms:

> The Montessori approach to education is based on the work of Maria Montessori, an Italian physician, and was introduced in the United States in the early 1900s. Everything in the Montessori classroom is designed for learning. Children use a wide variety of materials which help them learn through their senses about practical life, mathematics, language, and cultural subjects. They choose activities which interest them and develop skills and acquire knowledge as they work. These experiences in a multi-age classroom develop children's intelligence and the ability to learn from each other. Children enjoy mastery and feel a real sense of accomplishment in this approach. At the advanced level, students use their past experiences in the Montessori environment to move into new levels of functioning and creative thinking. The role of each spe-

111

cially trained teacher in the Montessori classroom is to observe and direct the activity of each child. Through class observation and educational sessions, parents are encouraged to use Montessori approaches at home. (Milwaukee Public Schools, 1985:6)

Montclair mails nine four-page brochures, one for each school, to parents. The science and technology magnet is portrayed in the following terms:

> Watchung is a K–5 elementary school that specializes in science and technology. . . . Microcomputers are a part of the regular curriculum which utilizes LOGO as the programming language. Word processing is taught as a tool for editing student writing. Twice weekly, students receive formal instruction in the school's computer lab. . . . The science curriculum reflects the magnet's specialized commitment to science and technology and is used regularly in reading and writing assignments. Units in astronomy, ecology, electricity, basic electronics and marine biology are special parts of the curriculum, and fifth grade students participate in an environmental education program at Stokes State Park. . . . Mini-courses, taught by parent volunteers, as well as the staff, include ceramics, photography, cooking, microcomputers, astronomy, and filmmaking. (Montclair Public Schools, 1985)

San Diego mails to parents an 11-page elementary magnet brochure and a 7-page junior and senior high magnet brochure that describe approximately three magnet themes per page. The school district characterizes the creative and performing arts magnet at O'Farrell as follows:

- Features specialized professional instruction in dance, drama, music, (vocal/instrumental/electronic), visual art, t.v. production, and technical theatre.
- Offers Gifted and Advanced Placement Programs, emphasizing a strong program of basic skills instruction.
- Produces an extensive calendar of art events including plays, musicals, and departmental concerts.
- Provides extended day for students. (San Diego City Schools, 1988–89:5)

The Buffalo school system mails a 23-page brochure to parents. In most cases the description of the magnet program plus photographs takes up a full page. The School 59 Science Magnet (also called the "Zoo School") is described as:

> structured to foster a responsible educational experience which values all life, freedom of choice, and individuality—and which stresses questioning, hypothesizing, evaluating, communicating, and cooperating. . . . To implement the philosophy fully, the student population will move through three phases of a developmental program, housed at a main building and two satellites. The main building will be designed to accommodate multiple activities . . . for Grades Pre-K through 4. The Buffalo Museum of Natural Science serves as the satellite location for the basic instructional program of students in Grades 5 and 6. The Buffalo Zoological Gardens serves as the satellite location for the basic instructional program of students in Grades 7 and 8. (Buffalo Public Schools, 1987–88:17)

Even the school districts with mandatory desegregation plans create elaborate brochures to sell the magnet programs. Boston, for example, prepares a 44-page brochure describing not only the magnet school programs, but the curriculum in each of the regular schools as well. The magnet school programs cover 11 pages, with up to three programs per page. Copley Square International High magnet is:

> one of two public high schools in the United States that features a full curriculum of international studies. The studies include foreign language, government, politics, science, business, art, theatre and computers. Students are required to complete at least four years of at least one foreign language (i.e., French, Spanish, Mandarin Chinese or Japanese). Eleventh and twelfth grade students must enroll in one of five "strands" (a major area of concentration) in either Diplomacy, Culture and Art, Foreign Language, Business or Technology. Attendance and academic achievement is stressed. Students will have an opportunity for advanced computer instruction and career exploration through internships, and university placements for grades 11–12. A selected number of students will be able to

participate in student exchange and travel study programs outside and inside the United States. (Boston Public Schools, 1987–88:42)

These excerpts from the magnet school brochures are typical of the genre. They illustrate the way in which the magnet programs are "sold" to parents and suggest that school system administrators believe parents are capable of choosing among schools if given adequate information, including information in the form of photographs of black and white children in the classroom. Indeed, nothing illustrates more vividly than these photographs that school officials believe that white parents are able to look beyond issues of race in assessing educational quality. But these brochures do not tell us whether any magnet is more attractive than another and whether black and white parents differ in their educational preferences. This chapter examines previous research on these issues. This chapter also presents an analysis of the relative success of the magnet schools in the 20 districts examined in Chapter 3.

The Literature

The literature on magnet schools is characterized by case studies of the curriculum and interracial contact in one or two schools. There are few systematic, comparative analyses of which school characteristics are most attractive to parents and students, or their overall desegregation effectiveness. There are even fewer systematic analyses of the educational effectiveness of the different magnet curricula, although curriculum is presumably one of the factors that motivates parents to enroll their children. In addition, since most of the writing in this field consists of case studies, the authors have typically failed to consider the environmental context—that is, whether a magnet operates within a mandatory plan or a voluntary plan. Because it is less difficult to attract students to a magnet school in the mandatory situation than in the voluntary, the characteristics that appear to be important in attracting students may also differ in these two situations.

LOCATION AND PERCENTAGE OF STUDENTS
WHO ARE MINORITY

It is by now a truism that schools located in black neighborhoods, regardless of whether assignment is mandatory or voluntary, have difficulty in attracting whites (see Rossell, 1985b). As
discussed in the previous chapter, on average 50 percent of the
whites assigned to schools formerly above 90 percent black will
not show up. It should not be surprising, then, that when attendance at a formerly black school is voluntary, the research suggests that it is also difficult to get whites to enroll (Fleming et
al., 1982:117; Larson, 1980:5; Royster, Baltzell, and Simmons,
1979; Weaver, 1979).[1] Parent surveys conducted in Yonkers and
Savannah in 1986 indicate that the percentage of white parents
who will definitely send their children to magnet programs decreases from 20 percent (Yonkers) and 29 percent (Savannah)
when the school is two-thirds white and located in a predominantly white neighborhood in the suburbs to 15 and 10 percent
respectively when the school is two-thirds black and located in a
black neighborhood (Rossell, 1986b, 1986c). There is also evidence that the rate of return to a magnet school in subsequent
years is a function of the percentage of students who are minority attending the desegregated magnet school (Larson, 1980:5;
Rossell and Ross, 1979). It appears, then, that initial success in
attracting whites is a function not just of past racial composition, but also of the new, projected racial composition. What we
do not know from this research is whether this is a function of
racial prejudice, class prejudice, or concern about the lower educational quality often associated with schools that contain a large
percentage of black and/or lower-class students.

CURRICULUM

A good deal of research demonstrates that social class is related to values and attitudes toward education and desegregation. Class differences in racial attitudes have been documented
and publicized in three decades of survey research. In general,

the higher the social class, the greater the racial tolerance and support for integration. Less well publicized, but of importance for magnet schools, are the strong class differences in educational values and preferences that might interact with the more well known racial attitudes.

Kohn (1976), for example, found that although parents of all social classes appear to share the same values with regard to child rearing, their priorities differ. Working-class parents stress conformity to external standards and external control, as well as obedience to authority, more than middle-class parents do. Middle-class parents place more emphasis on self-direction and inner control than working-class parents.

Similarly, Sieber and Wilder's (1973) analysis of parental preferences for teaching styles demonstrated that working-class parents prefer more traditional, less child-centered practices. There are other differences as well. When asked to evaluate the relative importance of six basic high school goals (teach job skills, teach academic skills, develop respect for authority, provide a setting for making friends, keep children out of trouble, and make them aware of their cultural identity), all classes rated job skills highest and cultural identity lowest. However, those with less education placed substantially greater emphasis on respecting authority and keeping children out of trouble, whereas those with more education showed greater concern for academic skills and making friends.

Thus, the research on class differences in racial attitudes and educational preferences suggests two things. First, whites who volunteer for magnet schools in black neighborhoods will tend to be of higher social class than those who do not volunteer, and, second, they will prefer more child-centered, nontraditional instructional styles than the general white public school population.

The Yonkers and Savannah surveys (Rossell, 1986b, 1986c) substantiate this in part. There was greater willingness among parents of higher social class to enroll their children in a magnet school regardless of the racial composition of the school and neighborhood. In Yonkers and Savannah, 25 and 32 percent respectively of white parents with more than a high school education were willing to enroll their children in a magnet program in a 50 percent black school in a minority neighborhood. In contrast only 11 percent and 24 percent of white parents with less than a high school education were willing to do so.

On the other hand, the Yonkers and Savannah surveys do not show the expected relationship between education or income and support for child-centered, nontraditional programs like Montessori. In fact, less educated whites were significantly more likely to be interested in Montessori programs than more educated whites. The only programs in which there was greater interest on the part of whites with more education were the accelerated (i.e., "gifted and talented") and foreign language magnets in both Yonkers and Savannah, the math/science magnet in Savannah, and the extended day magnet in Yonkers. The remedial education magnet was of more interest to less educated whites, as would be expected, but, contrary to expectations, the fundamental magnet was *not* more attractive to them.

Royster, Baltzell, and Simmons (1979:91) found that at the elementary school level, the magnet schools in minority neighborhoods that had the most success in attracting whites were those that had nontraditional programs that stressed the need for children to follow their own interests and to proceed through the learning process at their own pace. Their analysis did not, however, differentiate among whites by class. At the senior high school level, the academic programs were more attractive to white students than to minorities. Indeed, they often had problems meeting minority enrollment goals (Royster, Baltzell, and Simmons, 1979:91), but this may also have been a function of the selection criteria.

Examples of successful magnets found in the literature substantiate the conclusions of the Abt study. Case studies suggest that gifted and talented magnets that select on the basis of academic ability are always popular with middle-class whites (Fleming et al., 1982; Flood, 1978:8, 10; Levine and Eubanks, 1980;

Los Angeles Monitoring Committee, 1979:8; Rosenbaum and Presser, 1978; Weaver, 1979:16). The minority neighborhood magnet that Stancill (1981) claims is the most popular elementary school magnet in Houston is a Montessori preschool program that accepts children at age three. Similarly, the early childhood centers in Buffalo are highly popular and have long waiting lists, despite originally being mandatory assignment schools (Rossell, 1987).

There is some evidence that the selectivity, or perceived selectivity, of magnet programs is more important to many parents than the specific theme. A 1977 survey of parents whose children were in magnet schools in Boston and Springfield (both with court-ordered mandatory desegregation plans) found that 87 percent did not know the magnet theme of their child's school. Their attraction to the magnet school was based on a perception of magnets in general as "good schools" (Citywide Educational Coalition, 1978). A survey of parents in Montgomery County, Maryland, elementary magnet schools (a board-ordered mandatory plan) found that although 64 percent knew that their child's school was a magnet, only 36 percent (48 percent of the whites and 24 percent of the minorities) could name a magnet program feature (Larson, 1981:43). Nevertheless, ignoring curriculum would be foolhardy because it is important to many individuals and might be generally important in creating a school's image, even if many parents cannot remember its content.

Indeed, survey research conducted in Savannah and Yonkers prior to implementation of a plan suggests that parents are able to distinguish among magnet themes (Rossell, 1986a, 1986b). The Yonkers and Savannah surveys not only found considerable variation in support for different themes, but consistency between the two districts and between black and white parents in support for magnet themes. The support ranged from above 50 percent in both districts for computer science, accelerated, or math/science magnet programs to 29 percent in Yonkers and 14 percent in Savannah supporting extended day magnet programs.[2] Contrary to popular belief, the Montessori magnets were among the less popular ones, with 38 percent support among Yonkers white parents and 30 percent support among Savannah white parents. This may have been due, however, to lack of understanding of what a Montessori education is.

PUPIL–TEACHER RATIOS

One measure of educational quality that most parents are aware of is the pupil–teacher ratio. Rarely do parents remain in their child's classroom in order to evaluate the instruction he or she is receiving, but parents do seem to be interested in the size of their child's class. Indeed, the Houston school district found that a lower pupil–teacher ratio was cited as one of the most attractive features of magnet schools by both magnet and nonmagnet parents (Stanley, 1982:9, 12). Similarly, parents of children in a formerly black magnet school in St. Paul indicated that the most important selection factor for them was the low pupil–teacher ratio (Levine and Eubanks, 1980:57).

PHYSICAL APPEARANCE

In the absence of information about the quality of instruction, parents may also rely on such surrogates as the physical appearance of a school. Levine and Eubanks (1980:57) found that one of the characteristics shared by the three successful minority neighborhood magnets they studied is that they all had attractive buildings, even though old and remodeled. Similarly, a survey of parents in Houston found that 48 percent of the magnet school parents and 40 percent of the nonmagnet parents agreed that the physical appearance of the school would influence their decision to enroll their child (Stanley, 1982:8, 12). Royster, Baltzell, and Simmons (1979:33) argue, however, that although newer physical plants with newer equipment and more extensive facilities are an added inducement for parents to enroll their children, the physical plant per se is not a critical element. Comerford (1980:52–53) makes a similar argument, although he adds that the lower the social class of a parent, the greater the importance of an attractive school building.

DISTANCE

One of the fascinating aspects of the research on the effect of desegregation remedies on white flight and the research on the causes of magnet school attractiveness is the similarity in the relationships. In a sense, one can think of white flight from a mandatory plan and volunteering for a magnet as opposite sides of the same coin. The factors that cause a great deal of white flight will also discourage whites from volunteering for magnet schools. Thus, just as greater busing distance increases white flight, greater distances also lower the percentage volunteering for a magnet in a voluntary plan. In a mandatory desegregation plan, on the other hand, the distance to a magnet school is less of a problem because it is not competing with neighborhood schools, but with other schools to which students are bused. The magnet schools in Boston, for example, had much longer travel times than the other desegregated schools, but achieved a higher percentage of their projected enrollment (Massachusetts Research Center, 1976:54). Thus, busing distance is only a problem for magnet schools when there is no mandatory desegregation stimulating magnet school enrollment. In Houston, where there are no mandatory reassignments, the most frequently cited major weakness of the magnet school program is the busing distance (Stanley, 1982:12).

EDUCATIONAL BENEFITS

The public choice model of desegregation assumes that parents will act in their own self-interest; that is, they will leave their neighborhood school if another school offers their child a superior education. However, there are few empirical assessments of the actual quality of education (or lack thereof) in magnet schools. Numerous studies document higher achievement among magnet school students (Alkin, 1983:7-8; Blank et al., 1983:41; Bortin, 1982:256, 266-73, 280-83; Charpentier, 1984; Comerford, 1980:51; Fleming et al., 1982:126a, 134a; Gaines, 1987; Larson, 1981:55; Larson and Allen, 1988; Mayesky, 1980; Smith 1978:212; Weber, McBee, and Lyles, 1983:10), but only a few of these studies have a comparison group of students who are not in the magnet and a statistical control for premagnet achievement. These are both essential features for determining causality. There are also two case studies of Buffalo (Rossell, 1987) and Cambridge (Rossell and Glenn, 1988) that show large increases in achievement some years after the implementation of choice plans, even while the average median income and percentage white were declining. But, again, it is difficult to determine causality without a "control group" and control for pretreatment difference. The few studies that do have these features show significant achievement gains in a fundamental magnet (Weber, McBee, and Lyles, 1983), an extended day magnet (Charpentier, 1984), and math/science magnets (Gaines, 1987; Larson and Allen, 1988). Blank (1989) reports on three additional studies conducted by the Austin, Dallas, and San Diego school districts that included statistical controls for student background characteristics. The findings of these studies show magnet schools have a positive effect on student achievement. In particular, the Austin study found significantly higher scores for students in a high school science magnet compared to similar nonmagnet students in science and math in grades 9, 10, and 11. The San Diego evaluation found no difference between a high school "writing" magnet and nonmagnet school scores on a measure of critical thinking, but significant gains on the writing measure for magnet students. Although it is not clear what the causal mechanism is—smaller classes, increased time on task in the extended day, better programs, more parent involvement—the limited evidence does suggest that magnet schools have a positive effect on achievement. Thus, parents may indeed be acting in their self-interest when they choose a magnet school for their child.

Magnet Success in 20 School Districts

We now turn to the analysis of the success of individual magnet programs in the 20-school-district sample analyzed in Chapter 3. Table 4.1 lists the different types of magnet school

TABLE 4.1

MAGNET SCHOOL PROGRAMS BY TYPE: TOTALS FOR ALL DISTRICTS

Magnet Programs	Total N	%	Magnet Programs	Total N	%
ELEMENTARY/MIDDLE SCHOOL			HIGH SCHOOL		
Basic skills/Individualized	32	12%	Science/aviation/		
Foreign languages	31	11	engineering/computers	14	19%
Science/math/computers	31	11	Vocational/career		
Gifted and talented	27	10	preparation	10	14
Visual/performing/			Business/marketing	8	11
creative arts	26	10	Creative and performing		
Fundamental/traditional	22	8	arts	7	10
College preparatory	20	7	College prep	5	7
Early childhood/			Medical careers	5	7
Montessori	18	7	International/multicultural	4	6
Multicultural/international	13	5	Communications/		
Extended day	11	4	mass media	4	6
Physical education	7	3	Law and criminal justice	3	4
Life skills/careers	7	3	Foreign languages	2	3
Reading/writing/			Teaching careers	2	3
humanities	6	2	Fundamental	2	3
Open school	6	2	Transportation	1	1
University laboratory	5	2	Individualized, open ed	2	3
Ecology/environment	3	1	University laboratory	1	1
Other	3	1	Community/government/		
Special needs	2	1	life skills	1	1
Total	270	100	Hotel and restaurant		
			careers	1	1
			Total	72	100
Total number of magnet schools [a]	355	100			

Note:
[a] Total in each category does not add up to total number of magnets in the 20-district sample (279 elementary/middle; 76 high school), because data are missing on some magnet programs.

programs. In the total sample there are 355 magnet schools, of which 226 are elementary schools, 53 are middle schools, and 76 are high schools. Middle schools are classified with the elementary schools because the programs at this level are more like those at the elementary level than they are like those at the high school level. In addition, there are several K–8 magnet schools. For instance, Buffalo has no middle schools at all; schools are either K–8, preschool–8, or high school.

Elementary and middle school programs tend to be more curriculum-oriented and high school programs tend to be more career-oriented or vocational, but there is some overlap. Both groups include college preparatory programs, foreign languages, creative and performing arts, and math/science/computer programs, although it is really only the last two that seem to be equally popular at all grade levels.

Most of the magnet programs are in elementary schools for two related reasons. First and most important, the majority of the schools in any district are elementary schools. Second, because elementary schools have smaller attendance zones, they are less likely to be desegregated by the redrawing of contiguous zones. Thus, in a voluntary plan elementary schools are more likely to be in need of a magnet program to attract students of the opposite race. In a mandatory plan, the elementary schools and middle schools typically will have suffered more white flight and thus will be more in need of a magnet program to desegregate them than the high schools (see Rossell, 1978a).

Table 4.2 shows the location of magnet schools for the entire sample and for voluntary and mandatory plans. Since I have no data on the racial composition of the neighborhood in which these schools are located, location is operationalized as the pre-desegregation percentage of students who are minority in the school.

"White locations" are schools that were less than 25 percent minority before desegregation; "integrated locations" are schools that were between 25 and 49 percent minority before desegregation; and "minority locations" are schools that were at or above 50 percent minority before desegregation. These data show that for the entire sample, 33 percent of the magnet programs are in white locations, 21 percent are in integrated locations, and 46 percent are in minority locations. There is no significant difference between the two types of plans in this pattern.

It is surprising that, among districts with voluntary plans,

TABLE 4.2

MAGNET LOCATIONS BY RACIAL COMPOSITION OF LOCATION

| | Percentage | | | |
Location	Mandatory	Voluntary	Total	N
White locations[a]	37%	31%	33%	111
Integrated locations[b]	18	22	21	69
Minority locations[c]	44	47	46	154
	100[d]	100	100	334[e]

Notes:
[a] School < 25 percent minority before desegregation.
[b] School 25 to 49 percent minority before desegregation.
[c] School ≥ 50 percent minority before desegregation.
[d] Percentages do not add to 100 due to rounding error.
[e] Total is less than 355 because of new schools with no prior racial composition (i.e., missing data).

almost a third of the magnet programs are found in white locations. Since school districts have limited resources, one would think that they would put their money into the most difficult-to-desegregate schools—those located in minority neighborhoods. Either administrators do not understand this, or they have other goals that they wish to accomplish with these magnets. My discussions with school district personnel over the last decade suggest the former. There is a general disbelief in the willingness of minority students to transfer to white schools under majority-to-minority programs because of their reputation from the days when no transportation was provided and when there was no "selling" of the programs or "targeting" of schools. The majority-to-minority programs are viewed as pure freedom-of-choice programs, and "everyone knows" that that model did not work. Utilizing a majority-to-minority program as a supplement to a magnet school plan is a relatively new idea that many school administrators have not previously considered.

School district personnel do, however, seem to consider the location of particular kinds of magnets. Table 4.3 shows the correlation between predesegregation percentage minority—that

TABLE 4.3
CORRELATION BETWEEN PREDESEGREGATION PERCENTAGE OF PUPILS WHO
ARE MINORITY AND CURRICULUM[a]

Curriculum	*Predesegregation % Minority*	
	r	
	Voluntary	*Mandatory*
Careers	0.28[b]	0.12
Math/science	0.14[b]	−0.08
Creative and performing arts	0.03	−0.02
Early childhood/Montessori	0.03	−0.08
Multicultural/international	0.01	−0.09
Physical education	0.00	—[c]
College preparatory	−0.04	0.30[b]
Gifted and talented	−0.04	0.22[b]
Fundamental	−0.04	−0.03
Other	−0.06	−0.13
Basic skills/individualized	−0.07	−0.13
Extended day	−0.12[b]	—[c]
Foreign languages	−0.16[b]	−0.08

Notes:
[a]A positive figure (no sign) means that the magnet theme is found in a minority location; a negative sign means that it is found in a white location.
[b]Significant at .05 or better level.
[c]No data.

is, racial composition of location—and the type of magnet school program. These data tell us whether school district personnel have a conception of selling a certain kind of magnet to a certain constituency. The "constituency" for a magnet in a minority location—that is, the group that has to be recruited—is the white population; the "constituency" for a magnet in a white location is the minority population.

The location of themes is different in the two types of plans. In voluntary plans, careers and math/science magnets tend to be placed in minority neighborhoods, the latter perhaps because of a perception that math/science magnets are attractive to whites. What is not clear is why the foreign language and extended day magnets are put in white neighborhoods, since one would think

that the greatest constituency for these would be whites. A
strong possibility is that school district personnel also use magnets to satisfy white demands for certain programs in their
schools rather than as desegregation tools.

The mandatory plans show a different pattern. The magnet
programs that are most likely to be placed in minority neighborhoods are college preparatory and gifted and talented. Since
surveys (Rossell, 1986b, 1986c) and case studies (Fleming et al.,
1982; Levine and Eubanks, 1980; Rosenbaum and Presser, 1978)
show that these are quite popular with whites, the school district personnel in the mandatory plans appear to be as interested as those in voluntary plans, if not more so, in "selling" the
magnet schools placed in minority neighborhoods. What is surprising is that the voluntary plans do not also place most of their
gifted and talented programs in minority neighborhoods.

INDICATORS OF SUCCESS

Table 4.4 analyzes voluntary and mandatory plans in terms
of a number of possible indicators of magnet success: the percentage of students who are minority in schools in white locations, the percentage of students who are white in schools in minority locations, deviation from a 50–50 racial balance, and the
percentage of predesegregation enrollment maintained. The
percentage of predesegregation enrollment is an imperfect measure of the extent to which the school utilizes its full capacity as
opposed to having a small but racially balanced magnet school
program. Deviation from "racial balance" was chosen as a criterion because a goal of magnet programs is to have schools that
are in some sense "balanced," and we would want to know the
extent to which they achieve this. Deviation from a 50–50 racial
balance was chosen for several reasons. First, most of the magnets have a goal whose permissible range of 15 to 20 percentage
points includes 50 percent white and 50 percent minority. Second, and most important, the allowable deviation for most of
these magnet schools is so broad that almost all fall within it.
Thus, if deviation from the *allowable* range for each district

were an outcome measure, there would be almost no variance—virtually all of the magnets have zero deviation from their allowable range. Finally, most people consider a racial composition of 50 percent minority and 50 percent white to be the ideal, as indicated by the fact that so many desegregation plans have this as the goal for their magnet schools and/or regular desegregated schools. Indeed, as discussed in Chapter 5, school districts above 65 percent minority routinely implement court-approved plans that limit the racial composition of the schools to 50 percent white and 50 percent minority rather than the levels of the school district's racial composition.

The results seen in Table 4.4 are surprising. Although the mandatory plans have the presumed threat of mandatory reassignment as a stimulus to "volunteering," there is virtually no difference between districts with voluntary plans and mandatory plans in the percentage minority in schools in white locations, the percentage white in schools in minority locations, deviation from racial balance, and the percentage of predesegregation enrollment achieved in magnet schools. Both types of plans have magnet schools with close to 50 percent minority enrollment in white locations, close to 35 percent white enrollment in minority locations, and an average deviation from racial balance that is a little less than 20 percentage points; both types of plans have managed to fill their schools to their predesegregation levels.

Table 4.5 shows the average percentages of students who are white and minority in magnet schools in minority locations, inte-

TABLE 4.4
MAGNET SUCCESS IN VOLUNTARY AND MANDATORY PLANS, 1982

Success Indicators	*Voluntary*	*Mandatory*
% Minority in white locations	52.0	51.6
% White in minority locations	36.6	32.1
Deviation from 50% white		
(in % points)	17.2	19.4
% of predesegregation enrollment	101.0	103.0

TABLE 4.5
RACIAL COMPOSITION OF MAGNET SCHOOLS BY LOCATION, 1982

Location	% White		% Minority	
	Voluntary	Mandatory[a]	Voluntary	Mandatory
Minority location	27.7	31.3	72.2	68.6
Integrated location	39.9	43.3	60.1	56.7
White location	53.7	51.1	46.3	48.9

Note:
[a] Figures for percentage white and percentage minority for the same type of plan and location should add to 100. If they do not, it is due to rounding error.

grated locations, and white locations under voluntary and mandatory plans. In a residentially segregated world, location is basically synonymous with busing distance for both white and minority students. These data show that the longer the busing distance, the lower the percentage of the opposite race enrolled in the magnet school. For whites, these data may also reflect prejudice against blacks, as well as fears about the quality of education in formerly minority schools.

Table 4.6 shows the average percentage of students who are white by grade level, location, and curriculum for magnet schools in minority locations. High schools are a problem in voluntary plans. Because of their size, it is rare for the entire school to become a magnet (i.e., a dedicated magnet). Therefore, the most common type of magnet structure for a high school is a program within a school (PWS) consisting of several hundred white and minority students. Because the average high school typically has over a thousand students, a PWS will not produce racial balance in a school with a large resident minority population.

Table 4.6 also shows the percentage of students who are white in different kinds of programs. The success of basic skills/individualized programs may be in part a corroboration of the research that suggests that parents care about the pupil–teacher ratio of their children's school. If parents want a smaller pupil–

TABLE 4.6
AVERAGE PERCENTAGE WHITE BY MAGNET SCHOOL CHARACTERISTICS
IN MINORITY LOCATIONS

| | % White 1982 | |
Characteristic	Voluntary	Mandatory
GRADE LEVEL		
Elementary	27.4	31.7
Middle	30.3	30.9
High	19.8	29.1
PREDESEGREGATION RACIAL COMPOSITION		
Minority location	27.7	31.3
Integrated location	—[a]	—[a]
White location	—[a]	—[a]
CURRICULUM		
Basic skills/individualized	43.1	42.1
Physical education	41.4	—[a]
Gifted and talented	34.8	37.2
Early childhood/Montessori	34.2	—[a]
College preparatory	30.4	26.1
Multicultural/international	29.4	38.5
Creative and performing arts	28.1	34.1
Other	27.3	—[a]
Fundamental	26.0	51.8
Math/science	24.3	30.3
Foreign language	21.5	14.1
Extended day	18.6	32.4
Careers	15.3	23.0

Note:
[a] No data.

teacher ratio because they want more individualized attention for their children, then basic skills and individualized instruction programs will be popular, as suggested here and by Royster, Baltzell, and Simmons (1979). If white parents worry about the quality of education in minority schools, then gifted and talented magnet programs will be popular, as suggested here. What is surprising is the attractiveness of the physical education magnets, but perhaps a self-selection factor is operating here. There apparently are white parents who care about athletic training for their children and for this magnet theme the issue of the quality of education in minority schools is not pressing.

Under the mandatory plans, we see that the high schools are doing about the same as elementary and middle school magnets because there are more dedicated high school magnets in mandatory plans. The most popular magnet under the mandatory plans is the fundamental magnet, followed by the basic skills/individualized magnets. Some research suggests that fundamental magnets appeal to the working-class white parents who are least likely to be able to leave the school system. (Indeed, the gossip in Boston is that the only middle-class whites left in the school system are enrolled in Boston Latin.) The basic skills/individualized magnets, on the other hand, should appeal to parents of all classes, working-class as well as middle-class, since the research suggests that all parents care about the pupil–teacher ratio in their children's schools.

The correlation between the percentage white for each magnet theme in the two types of plans is .50. This means that in both plans the magnet themes are somewhat similarly successful in attracting whites.

Table 4.7 shows the average percentage minority by magnet school characteristics in schools in nonminority locations—that is, locations less than 50 percent minority. Again, under the voluntary plans the high schools, which tend to have PWS magnets, have the smallest percentage of the opposite race. This is not true of the mandatory plans, where high schools have the highest percentage of pupils who are minority in white schools. It is not clear if this is a result of white flight or of the greater willingness of minority high school students, who would in any case be bused long distances, to volunteer for magnet high schools.

The most popular magnets in white locations under the voluntary plans are, contrary to Royster, Baltzell, and Simmons

TABLE 4.7

AVERAGE PERCENTAGE MINORITY BY MAGNET SCHOOL CHARACTERISTICS
IN NONMINORITY LOCATIONS

| | % Minority 1982 | |
Characteristic	Voluntary	Mandatory
GRADE LEVEL		
Elementary	52.8	48.8
Middle	58.1	59.2
High	47.3	73.8
PREDESEGREGATION RACIAL COMPOSITION		
Minority location	—[a]	—[a]
Integrated location	60.1	56.7
White location	46.3	48.9
CURRICULUM		
Gifted and talented	66.6	19.3
Extended day	56.9	—[a]
College preparatory	55.3	43.1
Math/science	54.9	51.5
Fundamental	54.9	37.3
Early childhood/Montessori	53.7	25.7
Physical education	53.0	—[a]
Multicultural/international	49.4	66.6
Foreign language	49.1	49.0
Careers	48.3	69.9[b]
Basic skills/individualized	48.1	39.6
Other	47.8	55.4
Creative and performing arts	42.1	51.7

Notes:
[a] No data.
[b] Significant at .05 or better level.

(1979), the gifted and talented magnets. These are followed by the extended day magnets and the college preparatory magnets. Least successful in enrolling minorities are the creative and performing arts magnets. Under the mandatory plans, the most successful magnets in enrolling minorities are the careers and multicultural/international magnets. The least successful are the gifted and talented magnets, contrary to the situation under voluntary plans. These data suggest that under the mandatory plans the gifted and talented magnets serve as a means of retaining middle-class whites in the school system by offering them a selective, elite education. Gifted and talented magnets appear to be much less selective in the voluntary plans, however, where they are merely another desegregation tool rather than a means of reducing white flight. The early childhood/Montessori magnets are also differentially successful in the two types of plans. They are more successful in enrolling minorities under the voluntary plans than under the mandatory plans. It is difficult to say why this is the case.

The correlation between the percentage minority for each magnet theme in the two types of plans is $-.67$; that is, there is a negative relationship. Most of this is caused by the diametrically different percentages of minorities in the gifted and talented and early childhood/Montessori magnets under the two types of plans.

Table 4.8 shows the average absolute deviation from racial balance by grade, location, and curriculum for voluntary and mandatory plans. Under both voluntary and mandatory desegregation plans, the greatest deviation from racial balance is found in high schools. Location is also important. The smallest deviation from balance under voluntary plans is found in the white locations—it is easier to get minorities to go to white neighborhoods than the reverse.

There is greater deviation from racial balance under voluntary plans, with the physical education magnets having the least (10.3) and the careers magnets having the most (23.0). The gifted and talented magnets, because of their selection criteria, have a relatively large deviation from racial balance, as do the careers magnets because of the difficulty they have in attracting whites to minority locations.

Table 4.9 shows the relative strength of all of the school district variables, the school characteristics, and the magnet programs, when compared with each other and simultaneously con-

TABLE 4.8
AVERAGE DEVIATION FROM RACIAL BALANCE

Characteristic	Absolute Deviation from Racial Balance	
	Voluntary	*Mandatory*
GRADE LEVEL		
Elementary	17.0	18.7
Middle	18.2	17.2
High	22.0	24.9
PREDESEGREGATION RACIAL COMPOSITION		
Minority location	23.0	23.4
Integrated location	14.4	11.9
White location	9.4	17.7
CURRICULUM		
Physical education	10.3	—[a]
Multicultural/international	10.8	19.3
Basic skills/individualized	13.2	19.9
Foreign language	13.7	16.3
Early childhood/Montessori	16.0	24.3
Other	17.1	13.7
College preparatory	17.6	17.1
Extended day	18.5	—[a]
Creative and performing arts	18.8	20.4
Fundamental	18.9	19.0
Math/science	19.7	16.4
Gifted and talented	20.2	20.0
Careers	23.0	24.5

Note:
[a] No data.

trolled, in predicting a magnet school's percentage of students who are white in 1982. This multiple regression equation indicates that the higher the percentage of students who are minority in the school district, the lower the percentage white in a magnet school. Obviously, the percentage white in the district is something of a constraining factor for the percentage white in any one magnet school that is competing with a number of other

TABLE 4.9

PREDICTORS OF MAGNET SCHOOL STUDENT PERCENTAGE WHITE PUPILS, 1982

Variables	Avg.	r	b	Beta	SE b
% white, 1982	39.34				
SCHOOL DISTRICT CHARACTERISTICS					
% minority in district, 1982	55.54	−0.475	−0.606	−0.498[a]	0.058
City/county educational level (by grade)	12.00	−0.034	−4.740	−0.200[a]	1.029
Year of major plan	74.52	0.070	1.148	0.148[a]	0.335
Voluntary plan	0.70	−0.046	1.440	0.033	1.883
Total district enrollment, 1982[b]	54,539.97	−0.144	−9.10e−7	−0.001	2.75e−5
SCHOOL CHARACTERISTICS					
% minority in year before desegregation	50.40	−0.523	−0.290	−0.514[a]	0.023
High school	0.21	−0.034	8.334	0.169[a]	3.217
Total enrollment, 1982	718.84	−0.064	0.003	0.083	0.002
New school	0.05	−0.032	6.212	0.066	3.785
Elementary school	0.64	0.087	0.734	0.018	2.520
MAGNET PROGRAMS					
Basic skills/individualized	0.12	0.153	11.465	0.182[a]	3.805
Careers × high schools	0.10	−0.179	−9.303	−0.136	11.323
Creative and performing arts	0.11	−0.014	8.007	0.123	3.850
Gifted and talented	0.09	−0.049	7.188	0.100	3.964
Physical education	0.02	0.030	10.155	0.076	5.886
Fundamental	0.07	0.076	4.803	0.062	4.157
Careers × elementary schools	0.01	−0.002	9.828	0.058	12.656
Early childhood/Montessori	0.05	−0.005	4.586	0.050	4.727
College preparatory	0.07	−0.004	3.857	0.049	4.423
Foreign language	0.10	0.030	3.175	0.046	3.932
Math/sciences	0.11	−0.035	−2.333	−0.036	3.807
Careers/life skills (all schools)	0.12	−0.168	−2.063	−0.033	11.162
Multicultural/international	0.05	0.050	−0.984	−0.011	4.700
Extended day	0.03	−0.048	−0.213	−0.002	5.274
Constant			50.171		
r²			0.569		
df			300		

Notes:
[a]Significant at .05 or better, level.
[b]The term e−7 or e−5 to the right of the b coefficient means to add 7 or 5 decimal places respectively to the left of the decimal place shown.

programs. This is particularly true when school districts and courts try to maintain racial balance in all or almost all of the schools. The higher the median educational level in the school district, the lower the percentage white in the magnet schools. In other words, magnet schools do better in school districts where the social class of the community is lower and the competition with private schools is not as great.

The more recent the year of implementation of a magnet program, the higher the percentage white in a magnet. If all desegregation plans cause some white flight,[3] the later this occurs, the less reduction in percentage white by 1982. In part this may be a function of changing attitudes in American society. Whites have become more supportive of desegregation, and so plans implemented in recent years may produce less white flight. This relationship may also be a function of a tapering off of the dramatic declines in white birth rates in the 1970s.

The school district's total enrollment is a surrogate for busing distance, but in this combined equation there is no relationship between busing distance and a magnet school's percentage white. Whether or not a plan is voluntary also makes no difference in a magnet school's percentage white.

Only two school characteristics are statistically significant predictors of percentage white. First, the higher the predesegregation percentage minority in a magnet school, the lower the percentage white. Second, high school magnets that are not career or vocational specialty magnets have a higher percentage white.[4] Only the basic skills/individualized curriculum magnet program is significantly better than the others. The variable "new school" may be a surrogate for physical appearance as well as the quality of the facilities. It is undoubtedly a poor surrogate—only a small percentage of the magnet schools in this sample are new—and so the lack of a relationship with percentage white should be treated cautiously.

Table 4.10 shows the school district, school, and magnet program characteristics that predict deviation from (50–50) racial balance.[5] In this equation, a positive figure (without a sign)

TABLE 4.10

PREDICTORS OF MAGNET SCHOOL DEVIATION FROM RACIAL BALANCE, 1982[a]

Variables	Avg.	r	b	Beta	SE b
Deviation from racial balance, 1982	17.85				
SCHOOL DISTRICT CHARACTERISTICS					
% minority in district, 1982	55.54	0.308	0.265	0.309[b]	0.050
City/county educational level (by grade)	12.00	0.061	2.865	0.171[b]	0.893
Year of major plan	74.52	−0.134	−1.071	−0.196[b]	0.291
Voluntary plan	0.70	−0.068	−3.381	−0.109[b]	1.635
Total district enrollment, 1982[c]	54,539.97	0.166	2.62e−5	0.057	2.39e−5
SCHOOL CHARACTERISTICS					
% minority in year before desegregation	50.40	0.396	0.159	0.400[b]	0.020
High school	0.21	0.111	−1.376	−0.040	2.793
Total enrollment, 1982[c]	718.84	0.102	−4.42e−4	−0.016	0.002
New school	0.05	0.034	−3.811	−0.057	3.285
Elementary school	0.64	−0.096	1.263	0.043	2.187
MAGNET PROGRAMS					
Basic skills/individualized	0.12	−0.074	−3.032	−0.068	3.303
Careers × high schools	0.10	0.190	13.079	0.271	9.829
Creative and performing arts	0.11	0.038	−2.553	−0.056	3.342
Gifted and talented	0.09	0.052	−1.677	−0.033	3.441
Physical education	0.02	−0.082	−7.952	−0.084	5.110
Fundamental	0.07	0.023	2.231	0.041	3.609
Careers × elementary schools	0.01	−0.045	−5.229	−0.044	10.987
Early childhood/Montessori	0.05	−0.022	−3.576	−0.056	4.103
College preparatory	0.07	−0.005	−0.964	−0.017	3.840
Foreign language	0.10	−0.079	−2.518	−0.052	3.414
Math/sciences	0.11	0.012	1.234	0.027	3.305
Careers/life skills (all schools)	0.12	0.149	−5.366	−0.122	9.690
Multicultural/international	0.05	−0.064	−0.558	−0.009	4.080
Extended day	0.03	0.010	1.682	0.021	4.578
Constant			42.08		
r^2			0.346		
df			300		

Notes:

[a] A negative sign means less deviation from racial balance, defined as 50 percent white and 50 percent minority.

[b] Significant at .05 or better, level.

[c] The term e−5 or e−4 to the right of the b coefficient means to add 5 or 4 decimal places respectively to the left of the decimal place shown.

means more deviation from racial balance and a negative sign means less. There are five significant predictors of deviation from racial balance, and four of these are school district variables. The higher the percentage of students who are minority in the school district and the higher the median educational level, the more deviation from racial balance. Plans that have been implemented more recently have less deviation from racial balance. Districts with voluntary plans have less deviation from racial balance in their magnet schools than do mandatory plans, although it is not clear why. At the school level, the higher the percentage of pupils who are minority, the more deviation from racial balance. None of the magnet curriculum variables does a better job than the others in predicting deviation from racial balance when all of these variables are controlled. This does not mean that parents do not have preferences for magnet themes, but only that no magnet theme has a clear advantage over another when other factors are taken into account.

The Cost of Magnet Schools

Voluntary plans with magnet schools produce more interracial exposure than mandatory plans, but they also cost more. It would be useful to know the relationship between the level of funding of a magnet school plan and its success. There are, however, no data on this. Moreover, determining the cost of magnet schools above and beyond the normal operating cost of a school system is fraught with difficulty. Indeed, this is the case for any school desegregation plan, regardless of whether it has magnets. A common complaint of the plaintiffs in desegregation trials, for example, has been that the defendants were overestimating the cost of desegregation by including normal operating costs in their calculations.

Fiscally dependent school districts find themselves subjected to another complaint—that they are *under*estimating the costs of desegregation. As a result of annual budgetary battles with the city over the costs of desegregation, the Buffalo school district has consistently refused to identify which costs are attributable to the magnet school plan and which are part of the normal operation of the schools. School administrators maintain that it cannot be done.

Nevertheless, school districts that propose magnet school plans are often asked to identify the cost of the plan and particularly of the magnet programs and they usually do so. The budgets of two successful magnet school plans are shown in Tables 4.11 and 4.12. The costs of the five-year phased-in magnet–voluntary plan for the Savannah–Chatham School District are listed in table 4.11. The figures are for the combined startup and annual operating costs for 11 magnet schools. They do not include renovation or construction costs, which under this plan are substantial, since the two schools at the end of the table, Downtown East and Downtown West, will be constructed in 1990 and 1991. Nor do they include transportation costs, which are typically greater with a voluntary plan than with a mandatory plan. On the other hand, the costs listed do not reflect the reduction in other teachers' salaries. That is, the assumption in this table is that the specialists who are hired will be an addition to the current teaching staff. It is more likely, given the capacity of these schools, that they will displace another teacher rather than supplement one.

This table shows that the average magnet program has operating and startup costs of a little more than $500,000 produced by a combination of additional teachers for the magnet specialty, additional teachers' aides, equipment, supplies, and teacher training. Some of this is duplicative of the regular budget, as suggested above.

These costs can be broken down into annual operating costs and one-time startup costs. Equipment is typically the single biggest item in the budget for each school, and most of this consists of one-time startup costs. Teacher training is largely a one-time startup cost as well. If we subtract out these two components, the annual operating costs are $2,623,197 and the one-time startup costs are $3,134,000 for 11 magnet programs enrolling a projected 3,450 students.

The Savannah magnet school budget can be compared with that of the Yonkers school district in Table 4.12. The data in the first column of figures in Table 4.12 are for the entire plan, including renovations and rehabilitation to the white neighborhood schools that have no magnet programs but are eligible for majority-to-minority transfers. The data in the last column of figures are for the magnet programs alone. The startup cost of the 12 proposed magnet programs is $843,323. The annual operating costs are another $633,658. The total cost of the 12 magnet programs is $1,476,981, in contrast to a projected cost of almost $6 million for the Savannah plan. Part of the difference is attributable to the fact that Savannah simply has more expensive magnet programs and part to the fact that its schools were more in need of equipment than Yonkers'. In addition, Yonkers has not counted its specialist teachers as *additional* teachers, but assumed that they would supplant the current teachers or that the current teachers would be trained.

Table 4.12 also lists almost $9 million in construction costs for the two new magnet schools (probably a low estimate) and $2.3 million in transportation costs for the magnet programs. Of course, any desegregation plan will incur transportation costs, but magnet programs are indeed more expensive in that regard. In a mandatory reassignment plan, entire neighborhoods will be reassigned to another school. Therefore, one bus can be dispatched to several adjoining blocks and be filled by the children from that neighborhood. That bus will then transport the children to a single school. This is not the case for magnet schools. The children enrolled in a magnet school will come from all over the school district. Therefore, bus routes are complicated, and standard-sized buses will typically be underutilized. The use of small buses, vans, and taxis increases the cost of transportation for voluntary plans.

The complexity of the transportation routes is so great that

TABLE 4.11

SAVANNAH–CHATHAM COUNTY: ESTIMATED MAGNET SCHOOL PROGRAM COSTS, 1987–1991

Area	Theme	Personnel	Cost	Number	Subtotal	Estimated 1988 Budget
Gadsden Elementary	Performing and fine arts (enrollment 300)	Drama specialist	$ 25,393	1	$ 25,393	
		Resource specialist	25,393	1	25,393	
		Aides	15,750	4	63,000	
		fringe 24.5%			27,878	
		Equipment	22,000		22,000	
		Supplies	20,000		20,000	
		Teacher training	25,000		25,000	$208,664
Hodge Elementary	Computer science (enrollment 300)	Computer specialist	25,393	1	25,393	
		Aides	15,750	4	63,000	
		fringe 24.5%			21,656	
		Equipment	45,000		45,000	
		Supplies	35,000		35,000	
		Teacher training	25,000		25,000	215,050
Bartow Elementary	Gifted/talented (enrollment 200)	Resource specialists	25,393	2	50,786	
		Aides	15,750	4	63,000	
		fringe 24.5%			27,878	
		Equipment	80,000		80,000	
		Supplies	35,000		35,000	
		Teacher training	25,000		25,000	281,664
Ellis Elementary	Montessori (enrollment 200)	Classroom teachers	25,393	3	76,180	
		Aides	15,750	5	78,750	
		fringe 24.5%			37,958	
		Equipment	60,000		60,000	
		Supplies	80,000		80,000	
		Teacher training	80,000		80,000	412,887

School	Program	Item		No.	Amount	Total
Haven Elementary	Sciences/ mathematics (enrollment 150)	Science specialist	25,393	1	25,393	
		Mathematics specialist	25,393	1	25,393	
		Aides	15,750	4	63,000	
		fringe 24.5%			27,878	
		Equipment	400,000		400,000	
		Supplies	75,000		75,000	
		Teacher training	25,000		25,000	641,664
Spencer Elementary	Honors (enrollment 300)	Resource specialists	25,393	2	50,786	
		Aides	15,750	4	63,000	
		fringe 24.5%			27,878	
		Equipment	75,000		75,000	
		Supplies	25,000		25,000	
		Teacher training	25,000		25,000	266,664
Subtotal				37	$2,026,593	$2,026,593
Beach High	Mathematics/ sciences (enrollment 200)	Mathematics specialist	$ 26,663	1	$ 26,663	
		Science specialist	26,663	1	26,663	
		Aides	16,538	6	99,228	
		fringe 24.5%			37,376	
		Equipment	675,000		675,000	
		Supplies	95,000		95,000	
		Teacher training	28,000		28,000	$987,930
Hubert Middle	Computer science (enrollment 300)	Computer specialist	26,663	1	26,663	
		Aides	16,538	6	99,228	
		fringe 24.5%			30,843	
		Equipment	200,000		200,000	
		Supplies	95,000		95,000	
		Teacher training	28,000		28,000	479,734

[continued]

TABLE 4.11
(continued)

Area	Theme	Personnel	Cost	Number	Subtotal	Estimated 1988 Budget
Savannah High	Business administration Legal professions (enrollment 300)	Business specialists	26,663	3	79,989	
		Legal specialists	26,663	2	53,326	
		Aides	16,538	6	99,228	
		fringe 24.5%			56,973	
		Equipment	200,000		200,000	
		Supplies	95,000		95,000	
		Teacher training	28,000		28,000	612,516
Downtown East	Computer science Extended day (enrollment 600)	Computer specialist	27,996	1	27,996	
		Aides	17,364	4	69,456	
		fringe 24.5%			23,876	
		Afterschool teachers	13,500	3	40,500	
		Equipment	375,000		375,000	
		Supplies	58,000		58,000	
		Teacher training	35,000		35,000	629,828
Downtown West	Mathematics/ sciences Extended day (enrollment 600)	Science specialist	29,396	1	29,396	
		Mathematics specialist	29,396	1	29,396	
		Aides	18,223	4	72,892	
		fringe 24.5%			32,312	
		Afterschool teachers	16,200	3	48,600	
		Equipment	640,000		640,000	
		Supplies	130,000		130,000	
		Teacher training	38,000		38,000	1,020,596
Subtotal	(enrollment 3,450)			43	3,730,603	3,730,603
Total	(enrollment 313)			80	5,757,197	5,757,197
Average				7		523,382

Source: Board of Public Education for the City of Savannah and the County of Chatham (1988), 8–9.

TABLE 4.12

YONKERS SCHOOL DISTRICT: TOTAL ESTIMATED COST OF REMEDY PROPOSAL,
1986–1989

Costs	All Schools	Magnet Schools
CAPITAL IMPROVEMENT		
Rehabilitation	$12,335,500	
Equipment	420,000	
	12,755,500	$ 1,291,000
OPERATING COSTS: STARTUP		
Staff development	377,160	
Instructional equipment	932,000	
Contractual	745,000	
Materials and supplies	627,000	
Textbooks	258,000	
	2,939,160	843,323
OPERATING COSTS: IMPACTED		
Additional staff/fringe	1,598,491	
Salary-related costs	410,000	
Contractual	1,250,000	
	3,258,491	633,658
NEW SCHOOLS		
Construction	12,525,000	
Equipment	750,000	
	13,275,000	8,850,000
FINANCIAL IMPACT ON DISTRICT	32,228,151	11,617,981
TRANSPORTATION COSTS		
Magnet programs	2,368,800	
State standard 1.5-mile costs		
for public school students	1,511,640	
Parochial school students	792,000	
Total transportation costs	4,672,440	

Source: Board of Education, Yonkers, N.Y. (1986), 273–355.

Note:
[a]The Board of Education requested New York State to "hold harmless" the anticipated transportation costs for the first year. The state did so.

it is often beyond the capacity of the school system. The Milwaukee transportation plan simply broke down in the third year, when it became so complex that the school system could not deal with it. Now many school systems simply hire consultants who specialize in transportation programming.

Conclusions

The analysis of the magnet school programs in our sample demonstrates that magnet schools enroll on average one-third of the students in school districts with voluntary plans and 13 percent of the students in school districts with mandatory plans. However, the ceiling on magnet participation seems to be as high as 100 percent in small school districts such as Montclair that have eliminated attendance zones.

These data suggest that Royster, Baltzell, and Simmons (1979:92) and I (1985b) were correct in concluding that magnets in minority neighborhoods have greater difficulty in reaching their racial composition goals and thus desegregating the school system than do magnets in white neighborhoods. The data do not confirm Blank et al.'s (1983:88) conclusion that there is no significant correlation between magnet location and magnet desegregation success. The indications are that their conclusion is an artifact of their measure of success (see note 1). The finding that magnets in minority neighborhoods have difficulty attracting whites means only that they need more resources to attract whites. Authorities can neither exclude all minority schools from desegregation nor simply close them, as the courts have usually maintained that schools cannot be closed solely for "racial" reasons.

I found, as did Royster, Baltzell, and Simmons (1979:92), that one-third of the programs are in white locations. Another 21 percent are in integrated locations, presumably to stabilize the existing racial balance of the school. The largest proportion of magnet programs (46 percent) are in minority locations. But this is still less than is optimal for the most efficient utilization of resources. Because minority parents are willing to transfer their children to white schools solely because of those schools' greater prestige, but whites will transfer to minority schools only if the district puts additional funds and a special curriculum there, most magnets should be located in minority neighborhoods.

All magnet programs seem to be equally attractive to white parents when other variables are controlled. Only the basic skills/individualized magnets stand out as more successful in the multiple regression equations. Thus, the school districts, in general, are doing a good job of selling their magnets, and enough whites enroll their children as a result to desegregate a school system in combination with a majority-to-minority transfer program and negative incentives in the form of racial controls. These data provide further evidence that substantial numbers of whites are able to act in a rational manner on issues of race and, when motivated by positive and negative incentives, to collectively produce a socially desirable outcome.

On the other hand, magnet–voluntary plans are more complex and more expensive than mandatory reassignment plans. They test the capacity of most school systems in a way that mandatory reassignment plans do not. Even if school districts and judges believed that magnet–voluntary plans would produce more interracial exposure, these problems alone might discourage some school systems from adopting such a plan.

5

What Have School Desegregation Plans Accomplished?

ONE OF THE MORE important issues concerning desegregation remedies has been their "reasonableness." The public perception of the behavior of the Warren Court and the federal courts in the early 1970s on school desegregation issues has been that they were "out of control," imposing extreme and radical remedies on an intransigent population. The reality, however, appears to be quite different. Although *Swann* (1971) held that school desegregation remedies could be "administratively awkward, inconvenient, and even bizarre in some situations," they usually were not.[1] Pairing and clustering may cause white flight, but they are not unreasonable per se. The courts have not required children to be bused two to three hours a day in order to achieve racial balance, because that would not be "reasonable." They have not required that every school exactly mirror the school district's racial composition, because that would not be "reasonable." They have not forbidden school districts to close black schools no matter how dilapidated, because that would not be "reasonable." This notion of reasonableness that runs through the court decisions is a relative one based in part on a consideration of what has been required in other cases and what has occurred in other school districts.

Judges consider what is "reasonable" because judicial authority is significantly constrained—the courts cannot guarantee a successful solution. Although legal mandates affect the implementation of court-ordered remedies, the actual outcome depends on mobilizing diverse community resources, including the good will of those affected. In short, the courts depend for the implementation of a remedy on the cooperation of the parties to the dispute. That dependency leads them to structure a political bargaining relationship designed to achieve agreement between the parties and, ultimately, compliance on the part of the defendant. This is not a typical political bargaining relationship, of course, because permissible outcomes are constrained by legal precedent. But that legal precedent is not so clear that only one type of plan is possible. Nor is it so clear that the judge's own opinions will not be reflected in the remedy.

Judges have often seen the remedy as a process. The trial judge in Denver[2] noted that "the purpose of the hearing now is for the most part to receive any suggested remedies that you wish to offer, you know, so that we can enter a final judgment in this case. It won't be too final, I don't think. I think it's going to be temporary final" (Marseille, 1979:47). In Las Vegas, Nevada, the district court approved a one-year experiment with a freedom-of-choice desegregation plan; only after it failed to achieve substantial desegregation was a more extensive plan put into effect.[3] In Yonkers, the district court judge, Leonard B. Sand, issued an "Opinion and Proposed Order" on a school desegregation remedy and ordered some mandatory reassignments that were contrary to the district's proposed choice plan. In labeling his opinion "proposed," Judge Sand appeared to be inviting a response. When the opinion met with strong opposition from the school district and its expert (this author), the court revised it. Judge Sand's subsequent opinion adopted the district's plan with only minor modifications.[4]

Thus, even during the "affirmative action" era from 1968 to 1981, the courts did not mandate wholesale and sweeping changes that had no hope of being effectively implemented. Although such a conclusion is a matter of personal values, of course, I argue that the findings of this chapter suggest a very different notion from the one commonly held of the kind of compliance required in school desegregation cases.

This chapter has three purposes. The first is to convey some idea of what the courts have been allowing in school desegregation plans. The second is to allow us to compare the data for the 20 school districts analyzed in Chapters 3 and 4 with what is occurring in other school districts. The data displayed in this chapter include a northern control group that provides a benchmark against which we can measure the positive and negative impacts of school desegregation. Thus, this group tells us what can be expected if a school district does not adopt a desegregation plan. The data presented in this chapter also include an analysis comparing mandatory and voluntary plans in "big city" school districts. This analysis addresses not only what kinds of plans judges order in school districts with "adverse" demographic conditions but also whether the conclusion that voluntary plans produce more interracial exposure holds for a set of school districts with different demographic conditions.

This presentation of national trends has a third purpose as well—to suggest the direction that school desegregation policy might take in the next decade when school districts take their plans back into court. Courts clearly tailor their orders to the racial composition and enrollment trends in school districts. They order racial balance plans only in districts where such orders are demographically feasible, and they may consider voluntary plans more favorably in districts where demographic trends do not look good. In addition, the type and extent of remedies the courts order are based on the type and extent of remedies that other courts have ordered. Thus, this chapter offers a summary of the extent of past remedies as a guide to future remedies.

In the analyses of national trends in this chapter, the school districts are categorized by region and the source of the desegregation order because this chapter deals with broad policy trends. What are the courts requiring in desegregation plans in the North and in the South? What are school boards adopting? What is happening to school districts without a plan? The difference between school districts with no identifiable plan and the board-ordered districts may in some cases simply be the difference between a school board's formal policy decision and a school administration's informal policy producing the same (typically small) effect; that is, some of the school districts categorized as having no desegregation plan may have a voluntary majority-to-minority transfer policy that is virtually identical to that of some of the school districts categorized as having board-ordered desegregation plans, except that in the latter districts the plan was formally approved by the school board. Thus, there is a "fuzzy" dividing line between the school districts with the least extensive board-ordered plans and the most desegregated school districts with no plans. This problem does not affect conclusions regarding trends in the control group school districts, however, since any voluntary desegregation plan would have to be quite minimal to avoid a formal school board vote. In other words, the control group really is a control group. Error—if there is any— would lie in the fact that some of the school districts with minimal board-ordered plans more properly belong in the control group. This condition would not change the nature of the control group, however, since the school districts with minimal desegregation plans are quite similar to the control group school districts in the quantity and quality of their desegregation transfers.

Enrollment Trends

One of the first ways in which we can get an idea of what is happening to school districts with and without desegregation plans is to compare their enrollment trends. The sample analyzed in this chapter is the entire 119-school-district sample described in Chapter 3. This sample includes most large school districts in the United States. Table 5.1 shows the average desegregation year, enrollment data for 1970 and 1984 (the last year for which I have such data), and percentage of students who are white in four categories of school districts: northern (i.e., nonsouthern) districts with court- or HEW-ordered plans; southern districts with court- or HEW-ordered plans; northern districts with board-ordered plans; and a control group of dis-

TABLE 5.1

ENROLLMENT DATA IN 119 SCHOOL DISTRICTS

Category	Deseg. Year (Avg.)	1970 Enrollment (No.)			1970 % White			1984 Enrollment (No.)			1984 % White		
		Avg.	Min.	Max.	Avg.	Min.	Max.	Avg.	Min.	Max.	Avg.	Min.	Max.
Northern court-ordered	1975	105,311	14,931	642,895	63.3%	19.3%	91.2%	74,796	12,023	563,007	45.8%	10.4%	86.3%
Southern court-ordered	1973	89,091	16,016	241,139	61.4	28.6	85.8	72,904	11,923	228,062	45.8	7.6	80.8
Northern board-ordered	1973	64,708	7,724	1,140,359	69.7	21.4	91.6	48,112	5,429	931,768	54.1	2.2	87.8
Northern control group	1973	39,208	8,524	145,330	47.7	4.5	93.3	28,228	8,050	82,596	33.7	0.3	91.1

tricts with no identifiable plan. There are 39 districts in the northern court/HEW-ordered category; 25 in the southern court/HEW-ordered category; 40 in the northern board-ordered category; and 15 in the control group.[5]

The northern school districts tended to have larger enrollments than the southern school districts in 1970 but are similar in percentage of students who are white. The northern court-ordered school districts had an average 63.3 percent white enrollment in 1970. By 1984 this had declined to 45.8 percent. The southern court-ordered school districts had an average 61.4 percent white enrollment in 1970. By 1984 this had declined to 45.8 percent white. The northern board-ordered school districts were, on average, 69.7 percent white in 1970. By 1984 this had declined to 54.1 percent. In contrast, the northern control group had an average white enrollment of 47.7 percent in 1970 and 33.7 percent in 1984. Thus, any policymaker contemplating new desegregation proposals for these school districts will have to consider the following reality: in the school districts with court-ordered desegregation plans and those with no plans at all, on average, racial minorities outnumber whites. This is also undoubtedly why those with no plans at all have not had a suit filed against them or adopted a plan. Most of these districts do not have enough whites to make their distribution throughout the system worth the effort to many potential plaintiffs.

Table 5.2 shows the percentage change in total enrollment from 1970 to 1984, the change in the percentage of students who are white from 1970 to 1984,[6] the percentage white enrollment change from 1970 to 1980, and the percentage white enrollment change from 1970 to 1984 for the four categories of school districts. The change in the percentage white is a function of two factors—the decline in white enrollment and the increase in minority enrollment. It is calculated by simply subtracting the percentage white in 1984 from the percentage white in 1970. The percentage white enrollment change, on the other hand, reflects only change in white enrollment as a percentage of prior enrollment. The percentage white enrollment change from 1970 to

TABLE 5.2

CHANGE IN ENROLLMENT DATA IN 119 SCHOOL DISTRICTS

Category	Deseg. Year (Avg.)	% Total Enrollment Change, 1970–1984			Change in % White, 1970–1984			% White Enrollment Change, 1970–1980			% White Enrollment Change, 1970–1984		
		Avg.	Min.	Max.	Avg.	Min.	Max.	Avg.	Min.	Max.	Avg.	Min.	Max.
Northern court-ordered	1975	-31.5%	20.1%	-52.2%	-19.1%	-4.9%	-36.0%	-45.7%	43.4%	-73.6%	-53.3%	9.5%	-79.7%
Southern court-ordered	1973	-16.4	6.4	-37.3	-15.6	-0.4	-34.0	-32.7	6.9	-81.6	-38.3	2.9	-84.6
Northern board-ordered	1973	-29.9	-9.4	-48.6	-16.0	-2.1	-29.6	-41.2	-7.7	-87.5	-49.1	-11.6	-92.0
Northern control group	1973	-22.4	4.3	-43.2	-13.9	-0.7	-29.4	-47.7	-15.8	-97.4	-55.3	-17.2	-97.4

1984 is calculated as white enrollment in 1984 minus white enrollment in 1970, divided by white enrollment in 1970 and multiplied by 100 to create a percentage. The percentage white enrollment change from 1970 to 1980 is calculated the same way except that 1980 white enrollment is subtracted from 1970 white enrollment. This reflects only the decline in white enrollment; it is not a function of change in any other group's enrollment as is the change in percentage white and thus it is the preferred measure to assess "white flight."

As shown in the first six columns after the average desegregation year, the northern court-ordered school districts had an average total enrollment decline of almost 32 percent during this period and a decline of 19.1 points in percentage white. These averages obscure a great deal of variation, however, from a 52.2 percent total enrollment decline in St. Louis, Missouri, to a 20.1 percent enrollment increase in Las Vegas. The decline in the percentage white varies from a 36 point decline in Boston to a 4.9 point decline in Evansville, Indiana.[7]

The southern court-ordered school districts had an average total enrollment decline of 16.4 percent during this period and a decline in percentage white of 15.6 percentage points. This suggests either that the northern school districts did not experience as great a decline in percentage white as they should have because they were also experiencing a decline in minority enrollment or that the southern school districts experienced a greater decline in percentage white than they should have because of an increasing minority enrollment. The northern board-ordered school districts had an average total enrollment decline of 29.9 percent and a decline in percentage white of 16 percentage points—almost as large as the northern court-ordered districts. The northern control group, by contrast, had an average total enrollment decline of 22.4 percent and a decline in percentage white of 13.9 points.

The last six columns in Table 5.2 show the percentage white enrollment decline from 1970 to 1980 and from 1970 to 1984. The 1970–1980 figures are included here to enable us to compare the northern control group with the school districts analyzed over a 10-year period in Chapter 3. In Chapter 3 we found that the school districts with minority enrollments above 30 percent and with voluntary plans had a white enrollment decline of 37 percent over a 10-year period and that those with mandatory plans had a decline of 55 percent. The northern control group, by contrast, had a 10-year white enrollment decline of almost 48 percent. The northern court-ordered group in Table 5.2, with a much higher percentage white than the control group in 1970 before all the desegregation began, had a white enrollment decline of 45.7 percent, higher than would have been expected solely from their demographics. The southern school districts with court-ordered plans, by contrast, had the least white enrollment decline—32.7 percent.

The northern control group decline is a baseline white enrollment decline that has nothing to do with school desegregation. This decline is caused by the declining white birth rate and the "normal" city–suburban migration that is caused by a host of "push" factors (crime, congestion, housing costs, racial residential change, etc.) and "pull" factors (lower-cost housing, lower density, more attractive environments, neighborhoods with children, houses with yards, etc. in the suburbs). These factors are also a cause of some portion of the white enrollment decline in the school districts with desegregation plans.

All of the northern school districts, including the control group, had greater white enrollment declines than the southern court-ordered group. This is primarily due to northern white migration to the Sunbelt, but it may also be a function of the nature of southern school districts and southern desegregation plans. Southern school districts tend to be countywide, encompassing the suburban areas that white middle-class families typically migrate or flee to when mandatory reassignment plans are implemented. Northern school districts tend to be coterminous, or nearly coterminous, with the city's boundaries. Thus, the greater white enrollment decline in the North in this sample may be in part a function of the availability of numerous suburbs, which makes fleeing a mandatory reassignment plan, or other adverse conditions in the city, much easier. An analysis of the 20 school districts presented in Chapter 6, however, suggests this may not be an important factor. More important than the availability of suburbs may be the fact that the desegregation plans implemented in the South are less extensive than those implemented in the North. More areas in the school district were excluded from reassignment in the southern plans because of long busing distances. In addition, when resegregation occurred because of white flight and residential change after implementation of the initial mandatory reassignment plan, southern plaintiffs and courts were more likely to allow it to occur and do nothing about achieving racial balance in later years. Thus, it is not uncommon in the South to have plans implemented in the late 1960s and early 1970s so completely undone by white flight and resegregation that parents are no longer aware that the school district has a desegregation plan. The schools are relatively segregated and children attend their neighborhood school. Thus, there may be little postimplementation white flight from desegregation in the southern plans because there are few or no postimplementation reassignments and, as shown below, less desegregation than in the northern plans.

Desegregation Assessment Measures

A number of valid measures can be used by scholars to assess desegregation trends nationwide. Although interracial exposure is the most appropriate measure, given the goals of school desegregation plans, many comparative assessments do not use interracial exposure because of the need to control for the percentage white in the school system. Evaluators who compare interracial exposure figures and fail to control for the "pretreatment" percentage of students who are white in the cities can easily conclude that policymakers are less than willing to desegregate schools. Policy conclusions should not be drawn from descriptive state-by-state or regional data, as, for example, Orfield (1983, 1988) and Orfield and Monfort (1986) have done.[8] Some cities, states, or regions may have less interracial exposure than others, not because they are somehow dragging their feet in the desegregation of their schools, but because they have a lower percentage of students who are white, something policymakers cannot control. Therefore, a variety of desegregation measures should be used in any comparative assessment, particularly when there is no control for predesegregation percentage white. Each of these measures will assess desegregation from a different angle, and each will yield a different image. These, when added together, should result in a more coherent picture.

INTERRACIAL EXPOSURE

The first measure used here is interracial exposure. Table 5.3 shows interracial exposure at three points in time: the year before implementation; the implementation year (the average year for the entire sample is 1973); and 1984, the last year for which data are available. The categories, as before, are northern court-ordered districts, southern court-ordered districts, northern board-ordered districts, and a "control" group of school districts with no identifiable school desegregation plan. Voluntary and mandatory assignment plans are grouped together in each of these categories.

The data in Table 5.3 show considerable variation. Although northern court-ordered districts had, on average, 34.7 percent white students in the average minority child's school before implementation, the minimum interracial exposure was 7.3 in Wilmington, Delaware, and the maximum was 72.6 in Erie, Pennsylvania. In the average implementation year (1975 for the northern court-ordered group), white students made up 45 percent of the enrollment in the average minority child's school, but the minimum interracial exposure was 9.8 in Chicago and the maximum 85.9 in Evansville. By 1984, these figures had declined to an average of 39.6 percent, with a minimum of 8.1 percent in Detroit and a maximum of 82.3 percent in Evansville.

TABLE 5.3

INTERRACIAL EXPOSURE IN 119 SCHOOL DISTRICTS

Category	Deseg. Year (Avg.)	Preimplementation			Implementation Year			1984			% White 1984 (Avg.)
		Avg.	Min.	Max.	Avg.	Min.	Max.	Avg.	Min.	Max.	
Northern court-ordered	1975	34.7	7.3	72.6	44.6	9.8	85.9	39.6	8.1	82.3	46%
Southern court-ordered	1973	23.1	7.2	56.8	37.3	9.5	74.3	36.2	5.2	75.9	46
Northern board-ordered	1973	49.2	10.9	78.6	50.1	9.4	80.1	46.1	1.2	75.7	54
Northern control group	1973	29.6	2.1	77.1	28.3	1.9	76.7	21.4	0.3	77.8	34

TABLE 5.4

CHANGE IN INTERRACIAL EXPOSURE IN 119 SCHOOL DISTRICTS

Category	Deseg. Year (Avg.)	Preimplementation to Implementation			Implementation Year to 1984			% White 1984 (Avg.)
		Avg.	Min.	Max.	Avg.	Min.	Max.	
Northern court-ordered	1975	10.0	-3.7	64.9	-4.9	-30.0	14.5	46%
Southern court-ordered	1973	14.2	-0.3	43.9	-1.0	-12.7	28.4	46
Northern board-ordered	1973	4.2	-2.4	32.6	-3.1	-24.2	11.4	54
Northern control group	1973	-1.4	-4.6	0.3	-4.5	-14.4	1.3	34

In southern court-ordered school districts, there was an average 23.1 percent white enrollment in the average minority child's school before implementation, but figures varied from 7.2 in Birmingham, Alabama, to 56.8 percent in Amarillo, Texas. In the implementation year, the average was 37.3 percent, with a range from 9.5 percent in New Orleans, Louisiana, to 74.3 percent in Lexington, Kentucky. By 1984, interracial exposure had declined to an average 36.2 percent, with a minimum of 5.2 percent in Atlanta, Georgia, and a maximum of 75.9 percent in St. Petersburg, Florida.

The northern board-ordered school districts began with more interracial exposure before desegregation (an average 49.2 percent, with a minimum of 10.9 in Hartford, Connecticut, and a maximum of 78.6 in Montgomery County), and ended with more interracial exposure as well (an average 46.1 percent in 1984, with a minimum of 1.2 in East St. Louis, Illinois, and a maximum of 75.7 in Des Moines).

Contrary to the impression one gets from descriptive national studies that compare all northern school districts to all southern school districts (Farley, 1981; Orfield, 1983; Orfield and Monfort, 1986), these data show large, northern court-ordered school districts to have much greater interracial exposure in the implementation year than large, southern court-ordered school districts, although both groups have the same percentage of students who are white. One reason for this is the higher preimplementation interracial exposure in the northern school districts that resulted from more successful freedom-of-choice plans in the pre-*Keyes* period.

The southern school districts, on the other hand, experienced the greatest *increase* in interracial exposure from the preimplementation period to the implementation year (Table 5.4) as well as from the preimplementation period to 1984. Although there are some cases of a decline in interracial exposure after implementation so large that it eliminated the increase in the implementation year, on average, this does not happen. In northern court-ordered school districts, there was an average increase in interracial exposure of 10.0 percentage points in the implementation year, but a decline of only 4.9 percentage points from the implementation year to 1984. The southern court-ordered school districts had an average increase in interracial exposure of 14.2 percentage points, but a decline of only 1.0 percentage point after implementation. The northern board-ordered school districts show an average increase in interracial exposure of 4.2 percentage points, but a decline of only 3.1 percentage points after implementation. However, a considerable amount of 1984 data for this group were missing because OCR did not sample many of these cities. The control group school districts, by contrast, experienced a decline in interracial exposure of 1.4 percentage points from 1972 to 1973 (the average year of desegregation for the other school districts), and a decline of 4.5 percentage points from 1973 to 1984.

On average, these desegregation plans, which include both voluntary and mandatory plans in districts with high and low percentages of pupils who are minority, produced more interracial exposure with desegregation than they lost in subsequent years as a result of white flight and the declining white birth rate. In short, overall, school desegregation plans are *not* counterproductive. Moreover, the average net gain in interracial exposure of 5 to 13 points for court-ordered school districts represents 8,000 to 15,000 more whites coming into contact with minorities in the average school system than would have if nothing at all had been done.

RACIAL IMBALANCE: THE INDEX OF DISSIMILARITY

The more traditional measure of desegregation effectiveness used by academics is racial imbalance, typically assessed with the index of dissimilarity described in Chapter 2. In descriptive comparative analyses, the index of dissimilarity is more commonly used than interracial exposure because with the former there is no need to control for the predesegregation percentage of students who are white. A racial balance measure adjusts to whatever racial proportions exist in the school district.

Table 5.5 shows the average, minimum, and maximum racial

imbalance in different categories of school districts. The higher the measure, the more racially imbalanced the school district. Again, these data show considerable variation, from a minimum in the implementation year of 11.6, nearly perfect, in Pasadena, California, to a maximum of 76.9 in Philadelphia. There is as much variation in the southern school districts as in the northern districts, from a minimum of 16.6 in Charlotte–Mecklenburg to a maximum of 75.6 in Birmingham.

Again, we see that the southern school districts have a much higher average level of racial imbalance than the northern school districts, in both the implementation year and the postimplementation period. By 1984 both northern board-ordered and northern court-ordered school districts have an average level of racial imbalance of about 33, lower than the southern court-ordered school districts' index of 45.1. The northern control group, by contrast, has more racial imbalance (an index of 54.1), but not a whole lot more than the southern school districts.

These data suggest that the southern courts have not demanded the same amount of racial mixing as the northern courts have, an explanation consistent with the lower level of support for integration in the South during the period in which these plans were being implemented. Interestingly, although southern attitudes became more favorable toward integration, few plans were modified to produce more racial balance in the decade following their implementation. Civil rights groups and the Justice Department seem to have been more interested in implementing new plans than in going back and completing the racial balancing of the old plans, particularly when the remaining racial imbalance was produced by white flight from an otherwise adequate mandatory reassignment plan.

Table 5.6 shows the reduction in racial imbalance from preimplementation to implementation and from implementation to 1984. On average, the court-ordered school districts experienced a reduction in racial imbalance of almost 20 percentage points with desegregation, compared with a reduction of only 9.1 percentage points for the board-ordered school districts. The northern control group, on the other hand, had a negligible in-

TABLE 5.5
RACIAL IMBALANCE IN 119 SCHOOL DISTRICTS

Category	Deseg. Year (Avg.)	Preimplementation			Implementation Year			1984		
		Avg.	Min.	Max.	Avg.	Min.	Max.	Avg.	Min.	Max.
Northern court-ordered	1975	56.7	27.7	83.9	39.0	11.6	76.9	32.7	13.6	69.6
Southern court-ordered	1973	73.0	45.2	90.1	53.1	16.6	75.6	45.1	17.4	75.8
Northern board-ordered	1973	50	12.3	80.0	43.0	8.0	80.9	33.4	3.4	78.5
Northern control group	1973	50.8	0.0	78.4	51.0	0.0	79.1	51.4	0.0	83.7

TABLE 5.6
CHANGE IN RACIAL IMBALANCE IN 119 SCHOOL DISTRICTS

Category	Deseg. Year (Avg.)	Preimplementation to Implementation			Implementation Year to 1984		
		Avg.	Min.	Max.	Avg.	Min.	Max.
Northern court-ordered	1975	-17.9	-65.4	3.4	-6.4	-39.4	15.3
Southern court-ordered	1973	-20.3	-50.8	0.3	-8.0	-38.8	15.6
Northern board-ordered	1973	-9.1	-36.3	1.6	-8.9	-30.0	10.5
Northern control group	1973	0.2	-5.9	7.1	-6.6	-39.2	9.3

crease in racial imbalance of 0.2 percent. All categories of school districts, including the control group, have had an average reduction in racial imbalance during the postimplementation period that varies from 6 to 9 percentage points. In other words, on average, these districts are not resegregating when measured by racial imbalance. As the last column shows, however, some school districts experienced considerable resegregation and this was greatest among the school districts with court-ordered desegregation plans.

THE PERCENTAGE OF STUDENTS IN DESEGREGATED SCHOOLS

While interracial exposure and racial imbalance are useful measures for social scientists, they are rarely used as a standard by the courts. One notable exception to this is the 1984 consent decree in Cincinnati, which approved a "Taeuber Index" (that is, an index of dissimilarity) of "approximately 36 by the 1990–91 school year."[9]

Measures such as the index of dissimilarity are seldom used as a standard for an adopted desegregation remedy because the courts typically want to control racial balance in each school. The index of dissimiliarity does not allow that. In other words, an index of dissimilarity of 36 could be achieved by leaving some schools all black and strictly racially balancing the others, or by having all schools racially balanced with some specified deviation. But this kind of freedom is usually not tolerated by the courts.

There are also problems with interracial exposure that have prevented it from being used by the courts as a standard for an adopted remedy. I have introduced interracial exposure into a dozen court cases[10] to assess the effectiveness of alternative desegregation plans. I have, however, never been able to convert my interracial exposure projections into something the court could use as a goal for the chosen plan. One problem is that interracial exposure is influenced by demographic trends, and thus the courts are understandably reluctant to insist on an interracial exposure goal when the underlying demographics are subject to change. This is not a problem when assessing proposed alternative plans, however, because the underlying demographics are constant.

Interracial exposure is also, like racial balance, an aggregate measure, not a standard for each school. As is true of racial balance, a measure of interracial exposure is a systemwide average that could be achieved by leaving some schools segregated and others perfectly balanced, or by having all schools within a certain specified range of the systemwide interracial exposure.

Thus, the index of dissimilarity has not been used as a standard by the courts because of its obliteration of interschool differences and because of uncertainty over what level of the index should serve as a goal. Interracial exposure has not been used as a standard for all of these reasons, plus uncertainty over future demographics.

The most common court-ordered desegregation standard in predominantly white and 50–50 school districts is that all schools, or some designated percentage of schools (e.g., 75 percent in Milwaukee), come within plus or minus 15 percentage points of the school district's racial proportions. In the 1980s plus or minus 20 percentage points has been accepted as a standard in San Jose, Yonkers, and Savannah, for examples.[11] Standards like this are not used, however, in school districts above 70 percent minority, because doing so would produce racially balanced schools that are overwhelmingly minority, and neither the courts nor white parents have considered that "reasonable." Indeed, Cleveland is one of the few predominantly minority school districts where such an across-the-board standard has been used by a court. Typically, the standard for predominantly minority school districts with mandatory assignment plans is to parcel out all the whites to achieve a ratio of 50 percent white–50 percent minority up to the capacity of each school until the district runs out of whites. The remaining schools are then left racially isolated. This was the principle used in Detroit and St. Louis, for example.[12]

Table 5.7 shows the percentage of students in schools that would be considered desegregated according to either standard (15 or 20 percentage points) in the implementation year and in 1984. Of the 40 northern school districts that desegregated under court order, only Pasadena had 100 percent of its students in schools considered desegregated by either criterion in the year its plan was implemented. By 1984, only one school district—Erie's—had 100 percent of its students in desegregated schools by the plus or minus 20 percentage point criterion. Despite *Pasadena v. Spangler*,[13] in which the Supreme Court said that school attendance zones did not have to be continually redrawn to achieve racial balance once the dual system was eliminated, the Pasadena schools have declined in racial balance only slightly—93 percent of their students are in schools whose enrollment is within 15 percentage points of the district's racial composition, and 99 percent are in schools whose enrollment is within 20 percentage points of it. No court-ordered districts were able to have 100 percent of their students in schools that met the 15 percentage point criterion in 1984.

For the northern court-ordered districts, the year of implementation saw, on average, 55.4 and 70 percent of the students in racially balanced schools under, respectively, the 15 and 20 percentage point standards. By 1984, the average had increased to 68.5 and 81 percent for these respective threshold criteria.

None of the southern court-ordered school districts in this sample ever had 100 percent of their students in racially balanced schools, by either criterion, at any time. On average, these school districts had 38 percent of their students in schools meeting the 15 percentage point standard, and 52 percent in schools meeting the 20 percentage point standard, in the implementation year. The 1984 averages for these districts are 50.1 percent (15 percentage point standard) and 64.9 percent (20 percentage point standard).

Among the northern board-ordered school districts, only two (Montclair and Cambridge) had 100 percent of their students in desegregated schools (under either standard) in the implemen-

TABLE 5.7

STUDENTS IN RACIALLY BALANCED SCHOOLS IN 119 SCHOOL DISTRICTS

Category	Deseg. Year (Avg.)	Implementation Year 15% Criterion Percentage Avg.	Min.	Max.	All Schools Balanced (No.)	20% Criterion Percentage Avg.	Min.	Max.	All Schools Balanced (No.)	1984 15% Criterion Percentage Avg.	Min.	Max.	All Schools Balanced (No.)	20% Criterion Percentage Avg.	Min.	Max.	All Schools Balanced (No.)
Northern court-ordered	1975	55.4%	9.8%	100.0%	1	70.0%	18.5%	100.0%	1	68.5%	10.3%	97.2%	0	81.0%	21.1%	100.0%	1
Southern court-ordered	1973	38.2	8.4	95.2	0	51.9	13.9	97.5	0	50.1	11.3	95.5	0	64.9	19.0	97.9	0
Northern board-ordered	1973	64.0	5.7	100.0	2	74.9	21.1	100.0	2	72.1	19.6	100.0	2	83.3	30.5	100.0	3
Northern control group	1973	51.7	10.0	100.0	1	46.5	16.2	100.0	1	64.6	0.0	100.0	1	70.9	8.9	100.0	2

tation year and in 1984. The respective averages are 64 and 74.9 percent in the implementation year and 72.1 and 83.3 percent in 1984.

The school districts with desegregation plans and 100 percent of their students in desegregated schools have two things in common—they are small, and they are predominantly white. Enrollments range from approximately 5,000 in Montclair to 13,000 in Erie. The percentage of students who are white ranges from 51 percent in Montclair to 72 percent in Erie.

In short, the available evidence suggests that contrary to the implications of most of the school desegregation literature and the holdings of some court orders, the vast majority of school districts do not even come close to achieving the kind of racial mixing that a strict application of the prevailing Supreme Court standard would have required at the time they were implemented. The court opinions of that time could have been interpreted as requiring 100 percent of the schools to be racially balanced unless a school district could demonstrate a compelling reason for excluding a school. This was rarely done. Indeed, judging from the experiences of the school districts in this sample, having three-quarters of the students in desegregated schools (Milwaukee's standard) would be considered an ambitious goal.

Why do some courts insist in their initial orders on having 100 percent of the students in desegregated schools? There are a number of reasons. When desegregation plans are drawn, racial compositions are projected for each school. If anything less than 100 percent desegregation is stated as a goal, the school district or the plaintiffs have to decide which schools are to be left racially isolated. In many school districts, particularly those with mandatory plans, this is an obvious decision (for instance, in the Boston plan the exclusion of the geographically isolated East Boston was disputed by no one), but in other plans, particularly voluntary plans, it is not so obvious. It is one thing to say that "some schools" may not be desegregated because of white flight or the failure of opposite-race students to transfer there voluntarily; it is quite another to specify those schools and thus provoke an argument with the plaintiffs over the reasonableness of that assertion.

The first "choice" plan generated in Yonkers during pretrial negotiations proposed a goal of 90 percent of the students in schools that were racially balanced, plus or minus 20 percentage points. The reaction of the plaintiffs and the plaintiff-interveners was to demand to know which schools were to be left segregated. When several schools were mentioned as possibilities, the merits of leaving school x and school y segregated became the subject of such controversy that the school district reversed itself and proclaimed a goal of 100 percent. The court was more reasonable—the order states only that "the District shall *seek* to achieve" (emphasis added) the placement of 100 percent of the students in racially balanced schools.[14]

Some courts may demand 100 percent desegregation because they are ignorant of the fact that other courts are not requiring it. If one reads only certain cases, one might very well think that all schools must be racially balanced. An interesting question is why there is such variation. Why does one court accept placement of three-fourths of the students in racially balanced schools (e.g., Milwaukee),[15] while another court in a geographically similar school district (e.g., Buffalo)[16] orders mandatory assignments because the school system has not achieved 100 percent desegregation? The diversity of acceptable remedies from one city to another suggests that there are many factors at work in shaping a decision. The judge's own opinions, the alternatives proposed by the parties to the suit, and the dynamics of the political bargaining process in each city all shape the final legal opinion. As a result, anyone looking for consistency and logic in the school desegregation decisions of the mid-1970s and 1980s will be disappointed.

THE PERCENTAGE OF MINORITY STUDENTS IN WHITE AND MINORITY SCHOOLS

The two racial balance measures I have discussed so far—the index of dissimilarity and the percentage of students in desegregated schools, using the plus or minus 15 or 20 percentage point standards—are considered especially problematic in school districts with a high percentage of students who are minority. If a school district is 80 percent minority and every school is balanced at 80 percent minority, it will have an index of dissimilarity of zero—perfect racial balance—and all of its schools within 15 or 20 percentage points of the district's racial composition. Many observers, however, would not consider such schools to be desegregated. Similarly, the same school district could have 100 percent of its students in desegregated schools, plus or minus 20 percentage points, if half the schools were 100 percent black and half were 60 percent black. Yet virtually no one would consider schools that are 100 percent black to be desegregated, even if that figure is within 15 percentage points of the district's racial composition.

Orfield (1983), Orfield and Monfort (1986), and the courts in St. Louis and Detroit have proposed an absolute standard for a desegregated school in predominantly black school districts that is more acceptable to many than the notion that a desegregated school should mirror the district's racial composition. This criterion defines a desegregated school as "at or above 50 percent white." Orfield (1983) and Orfield and Monfort (1986) also define a "highly segregated" school as one at or above 90 percent minority.

These are useful measures, but there is no consensus on the cutoff point of 50 percent or 90 percent. The use of 50 percent or more white students as a standard for a desegregated school in both Detroit and St. Louis has been widely criticized as too strict. While there are good arguments for using it, and it is certainly supported by the literature on the positive effects of school desegregation, such a standard may no longer reflect either white attitudes or changing demographics. For example, the Buffalo school system in 1985 was 56 percent minority, with virtually no district-level white enrollment loss. It has several magnets stably integrated at 45 percent white. By Orfield's standard, however, these schools would be segregated schools. In analyzing the present data, I have therefore used two additional categorical measures. Besides Orfield's measures—the

TABLE 5.8

CATEGORICAL MEASURES OF DESEGREGATION IN 119 SCHOOL DISTRICTS, 1984

Category	Deseg. Year (Avg.)	% of Minorities in Schools >40% White			% of Minorities in Schools >50% White			% of Minorities in Schools >80% Minority			% of Minorities in Schools >90% Minority		
		Avg.	Min.	Max.	Avg.	Min.	Max.	Avg.	Min.	Max.	Avg.	Min.	Max.
Northern court-ordered	1975	45.2	0.0	100.0	31.7	0.0	100.0	27.4	0.0	86.5	18.7	0.0	76.8
Southern court-ordered	1973	43.0	0.0	95.9	33.7	0.0	90.0	39.3	0.0	89.6	31.7	0.0	86.2
Northern board-ordered	1973	59.1	0.0	100.0	47.6	0.0	100.0	27.1	0.0	100.0	22.1	0.0	97.1
Northern control group	1973	21.7	0.0	100.0	20.0	0.0	100.0	69.4	0.0	100.0	58.0	0.0	100.0

percentage of minority students in schools at or above 50 percent white, and the percentage of minority students in schools at or above 90 percent minority—I look at the percentage of minority students in schools at or above 40 percent white and the percentage of minority students in schools at or above 80 percent minority. Both the 80 percent and 90 percent minority standards have been commonly used in court cases[17] and can therefore be useful in assessing national desegregation trends.

Table 5.8 shows these four measures of desegregation for our sample in 1984. In the court-ordered school districts, less than one-third of the minority students are in desegregated schools by Orfield's standard—schools with enrollments 50 percent (or more) white. By contrast, 45.2 percent of minority students are in schools at or above 40 percent white in the North and 43 percent are in schools at or above 40 percent white in the South.

Because they have a higher percentage of students who are white than the school districts in the other categories, the northern board-ordered school districts are at an advantage in comparisons that employ these measures. Fifty-nine percent of minority students in northern board-ordered plans are in schools at or above 40 percent white, and 47.6 percent are in schools at or above 50 percent white.

School districts with plans do substantially better than the control group. The control group has only 20 to 21.7 percent of its students in schools at or above 40 and 50 percent white.

The northern board-ordered school districts also do well in terms of the percentage of students in schools at or above 80 and 90 percent minority. The southern court-ordered districts have 31.7 percent of their minority students in schools at or above 90 percent minority, whereas the northern board-ordered districts have only 22.1 percent of their minority students in such schools, and the northern court-ordered districts have only 18.7 percent of their minority students in them. The northern control group, by contrast, has 58 percent of its minority students in such schools, in part because its percentage of students who are minority is 20 points higher than that of the school districts in the other categories. These data once again show the northern court-ordered school districts being held to a stricter standard than the southern court-ordered school districts.

This sample of school districts with desegregation plans can be compared with the national average and with districts in five regions in the United States, using tables compiled by Orfield (1983) and Orfield and Monfort (1986). Table 5.9 indicates that the school districts in this sample that have court-ordered plans are in some respects not doing as well as the United States as a whole or their regions as a whole. In 1984 the national and regional averages for the percentage of black students in schools with minority enrollments over 50 percent ranged from 56.9 to

TABLE 5.9

RACIAL COMPOSITION OF SCHOOLS, BY MINORITY ENROLLMENT AND REGION

	1968	1972	1976	1980	1984	Change 1968 to 1984
% OF BLACK STUDENTS IN SCHOOLS WITH MORE THAN 50% MINORITY ENROLLMENT						
U.S. average	76.6	63.6	62.4	62.9	63.5	−13.1
South	80.9	55.3	54.9	57.1	56.9	−24.0
Border states	71.6	67.2	60.1	59.2	62.5	−9.1
Northeast	66.8	69.9	72.5	79.9	73.1	6.3
Midwest	77.3	75.3	70.3	69.5	70.7	−6.6
West	72.2	68.1	67.4	66.8	66.9	−5.3
% OF BLACK STUDENTS IN SCHOOLS WITH 90–100% MINORITY ENROLLMENT						
U.S. average	64.3	38.7	35.9	33.2	33.2	−31.1
South	77.8	24.7	22.4	23.0	24.2	−53.6
Border states	60.2	54.7	42.5	37.0	37.4	−22.8
Northeast	42.7	46.9	51.4	48.7	47.4	4.7
Midwest	58.0	57.4	51.1	43.6	43.6	−14.4
West	50.8	42.7	36.3	33.7	29.4	−21.4

Sources: For 1968–1980 data: Gary Orfield (1983), "Public School Desegregation in the United States, 1968–1980" (Washington, D.C.: Joint Center for Political Studies), p. 4; for 1984 data: Gary Orfield and Franklin Monfort (1986), *Are American Schools Resegregating in the Reagan Era? A Statistical Analysis of Segregation Levels from 1980 to 1984*, Working Paper, National School Desegregation Project (Chicago: University of Chicago).

73.1. In the sample analyzed in Table 5.8, the averages for court-ordered districts ranged from 31.7 to 33.7 percent of minorities in schools more than 50 percent white. This is probably due in part to the higher percentage of students who are minority in the school districts in this sample (about 55 percent) than in the United States as a whole (about 25 percent). On the other hand, nationally and regionally the percentage of black students in schools with 90–100 percent minority enrollments ranged from 24.2 percent in the South to 47.4 percent in the Northeast. In the sample analyzed in Table 5.8, the averages range from 18.7 to 31.7 percent for the court-ordered school districts.

These data also indicate that there was no resegregation in the first four years of the Reagan administration. The percentage of black students in schools with enrollments more than 50 percent minority and in schools with enrollments more than 90 percent minority remained essentially the same over this term.

Big City School Desegregation

The voluntary–mandatory comparison in Chapter 4 excludes two highly publicized magnet–voluntary plans in Chicago and Philadelphia because they did not meet the sampling criteria of the original Abt Associates study. Nevertheless, these districts are important enough to examine in some depth. Although the Reagan administration's Justice Department touted the Chicago plan as a success, numerous academics, reporters, and civil rights attorneys that I have spoken to have concluded that the Chicago and Philadelphia plans are failures.[18] Indeed, I cannot recall anyone (outside the Reagan administration) ever saying that they were anything but failures. When school districts have the kind of demographics that Philadelphia and Chicago have— large and more than three-quarters minority—casual observers make an egregious error in comparing them not with school districts with the same demographics, but with predominantly white school systems, as if any well-designed plan could achieve the same desired outcome in districts with completely different demographic characteristics. It is, of course, absurd to think that a desegregation plan could reverse decades of demographic change, but that is the implicit assumption behind the evaluations that are often made. These plans are considered failures because there are many all-black schools remaining in the school system, and it is assumed that this is a function of the plan rather than of the district's demographics.

In this section I compare two big city court-ordered school districts—St. Louis and Detroit—that desegregated under magnet–mandatory reassignment plans with three big city court-ordered school districts that desegregated under magnet–voluntary reassignment plans—Houston, Philadelphia, and Chicago. I define "big city" here as a district having a total enrollment greater than 100,000 in 1970 and a percentage of students who are minority greater than 50 percent. In fact, all but Houston had a minority enrollment greater than 65 percent in 1970. Houston had a much lower percentage minority in 1974, but by 1986 there was no difference. Consequently, averages are presented with and without Houston.

In order to compare the relative utility of voluntary and mandatory desegregation plans in big city school districts, however, an adjustment has to be made in St. Louis' desegregation indices. In 1982 St. Louis began an interdistrict transfer program that in 1986–87 bused approximately 10,000 black children from the city of St. Louis to the surrounding suburbs. These transfers reduced racial imbalance by 6 percentage points from 1982 to 1986 and increased interracial exposure by 3.2 percentage points; they also reduced the percentage minority in the school system from 81 percent in 1986 to 77 percent. The other four school districts have only intradistrict desegregation plans. Thus, if the effect of the interdistrict transfers is not removed, we will confuse the effect of the voluntary metropolitan plan with that of the mandatory reassignment plan within the St. Louis school district. It should be emphasized, however, that the St. Louis interdistrict transfer plan is an integral part of the entire plan, and there is probably no central city school district in the country that could not benefit from such a program.

When observers pronounce the Chicago and Philadelphia magnet school plans "failures" because so many schools are left racially isolated, they are usually unaware that this would have occurred even under a mandatory reassignment plan. As discussed above, when school districts are more than 70 percent minority, the courts do not require racial balance. Having every school in the system racially balanced at 80 percent black simply because the school system is 80 percent black is not viewed as either "reasonable" or "feasible." Therefore, the courts in both Detroit and St. Louis ordered all whites to be reassigned to bring as many schools as possible to a ratio of 50 percent white to 50 percent nonwhite, up to the school's capacity, until the supply of white students was exhausted. The remaining minority schools were left racially isolated but enriched by remedial programs and smaller classes. Thus, because of the "shortage of whites," both mandatory and voluntary plans leave large numbers of schools racially isolated in predominantly minority school systems, yet the mandatory reassignment plans are not considered failures by most school desegregation advocates. The issue should be which type of desegregation plan produces greater interracial exposure and leaves fewer minority students in racially isolated schools. This issue can be resolved empirically, and I attempt to do so here.

Table 5.10 shows the interracial exposure for minorities (Smw), racial imbalance between minorities and whites (Dm), and the percentage of minority students in schools at or above 90 percent minority in 1974 and 1986, subtracting out the effect of the interdistrict transfers from St. Louis' indices. The districts with the voluntary plans have a 1986 percentage white in the average minority child's school (Smw) of 12.0. This is 1.8 points higher than the 10.2 of the districts with mandatory plans. If Houston is excluded from the voluntary plan group, the difference decreases to 1.5.

The plans in these big city, high percentage minority school districts deliberately leave some minority schools racially isolated. Thus, another way to compare voluntary and mandatory plans in these districts is by the percentage of minority students

TABLE 5.10

COMPARISON OF MANDATORY AND VOLUNTARY DESEGREGATION PLANS IN BIG CITIES

City and Plan	Deseg. Year	1974					1986				
		Enroll-ment	% Minority	Inter-racial Exposure (Smw)	Racial Im-balance (Dm)	Racial Isolation (% of Mi-norities in Iso-lated Schools)	Enroll-ment	% Minority	Inter-racial Exposure (Smw)	Racial Im-balance (Dm)	Racial Isolation (% of Mi-norities in Iso-lated Schools)
MANDATORY											
St. Louis[a]	1980	93,320	70.4%	5.3	90.4	90.6%	58,319	80.7%	13.1	68.5	72.2%
Detroit	1975	256,300	73.9	11.9	73.0	70.9	190,679	90.8	7.2	59.3	76.9
Average	1978	174,810	72.2	8.6	81.7	80.8	124,499	85.8	10.2	63.9	74.6
VOLUNTARY											
Chicago	1982	530,191	72.5	9.0	81.1	80.5	431,290	86.5	9.4	68.2	72.7
Houston[b]	1975	211,369	61.5	15.0	72.6	53.2	194,567	83.2	12.6	55.7	44.6
Philadelphia	1978	266,500	66.8	10.2	79.3	75.9	195,552	75.9	14.0	67.8	66.7
Average	1978	336,020	66.9	11.4	77.7	69.9	273,803	81.9	12.0	63.9	61.3
Average without Houston	1980	398,346	69.7	9.6	80.2	78.2	313,421	81.2	11.7	68.0	69.7

Notes:
[a] 1986 data adjusted to eliminate effect of voluntary interdistrict program. Actual 1986 Sbw is 15.9, and Db is 63.3 (including kindergarten).
[b] Indices have been adjusted to remove the effect of the prior mandatory reassignment plan.

in racially isolated schools left in each type. A racially isolated school is defined here as a school at or above 90 percent minority. There is a greater difference between the two plans in racial isolation than with interracial exposure. The voluntary plans have, on average, 61.3 percent of their students in racially isolated schools while the mandatory plans have 74.6 percent. Then, on this measure as well, the voluntary plans do better.

More important, this analysis is the first that I am aware of to substantiate the racial isolation left by mandatory reassignment plans in big city, high percentage minority school systems. Chicago, which has received considerable criticism from academics for leaving large numbers of black schools untouched by its voluntary plan, has only slightly more (a half percent) minority students in racially isolated schools than does St. Louis and it has fewer than Detroit. About three-fourths of the minority students in these two court-ordered, mandatory reassignment plans are in racially isolated schools. Thus, this analysis suggests that the solution to racial isolation in Chicago schools is not, as so many academics have recommended, the adoption of a mandatory reassignment plan.

There is considerable variation within both types of plans, however. The data in Table 5.10 show that, of the mandatory reassignment plans, St. Louis' is the most successful by every criterion except racial balance, despite the fact that the 1980 mandatory plan increased the annual white enrollment loss from 10 to 22 percent in the implementation year alone (1980). On the other hand, from 1975 to 1979 St. Louis' voluntary intradistrict majority-to-minority transfer program increased interracial exposure from 4.7 to 8.2, a gain of 3.5 points, only a little less than the 4.5 point increase with the mandatory plan from 1980 to 1982 before the interdistrict transfer program began. The voluntary plan also reduced racial imbalance by 10 percentage points, the same reduction produced by the mandatory plan prior to the implementation of the voluntary interdistrict transfer program in 1982. We may question the utility of implementing a mandatory reassignment plan that accomplishes little more than the prior voluntary one.

Of the districts with voluntary plans, Philadelphia and Houston appear to be the most successful. They are the equal or better of St. Louis in interracial exposure and they do much better in terms of the percentage of minority students in racially isolated schools. On the face of it, the Chicago plan appears not to be doing as well, since it produces less interracial exposure than St. Louis, Houston, and Philadelphia and has a higher percentage of students in racially isolated schools. But the sheer size of Chicago—it is more than twice as large as Houston, Philadelphia, and Detroit, and seven times larger than St. Louis—would limit the interracial exposure and racial balance achieved under any type of plan. Chicago is certainly in better shape than Detroit, which desegregated in 1975 under a mandatory reassignment plan similar to the plan used in St. Louis, and it is only doing slightly worse than St. Louis in the percentage of minority students in racially isolated schools. Because Chicago's magnet–voluntary plan had only been in effect for four years as of 1984, the least amount of postimplementation time of the five districts, and because voluntary plans show their greatest gains over the long term, it may be premature to pass judgment on Chicago's outcome. One thing is certain: Chicago is not the huge success that the Reagan administration's Justice Department claimed, nor is it the failure that some academics have alleged.

Table 5.11 compares the change in interracial exposure, racial imbalance, and racial isolation between 1974 and 1986 in the cities with voluntary and mandatory plans. The voluntary plans increased interracial exposure more than the mandatory plans, but the differences are small. Interestingly, only one of these school systems—Detroit, with a mandatory reassignment plan—is experiencing a decline in interracial exposure and an increase in racial isolation. Houston has a decline in the interracial exposure of whites and minorities (blacks, Hispanics, Asians, American Indians), but also a decline in racial isolation. The other school districts, St. Louis (mandatory) and Chicago and Philadelphia (voluntary), are all experiencing increases in interracial exposure as their plans continue to expand. In fact, the

TABLE 5.11
CHANGE BETWEEN 1974 AND 1986 UNDER BIG CITY
VOLUNTARY AND MANDATORY PLANS

City	% Enroll-ment Change	Change in % Minority	Interracial Exposure (Smw)	Racial Imbalance (Dm)	Racial Isolation (% of Minorities in Isolated Schools)
MANDATORY					
St. Louis	−37.5%	10.3%	7.8	−21.9	−18.4%
Detroit	−25.6	16.9	−4.7	−13.7	6.0
Average	−31.6	13.6	1.6	−17.8	−6.2
VOLUNTARY					
Chicago	−18.7	14.0	0.4	−12.9	−7.8
Houston	−7.9	21.7	−2.4	−16.9	−8.6
Philadelphia	−26.6	9.1	3.8	−11.5	−9.2
Average	−17.7	14.9	0.6	−13.8	−8.5
Average without Houston	−22.6	11.6	2.1	−12.2	−8.5

St. Louis plan is becoming more and more a choice plan as the number of magnet schools increases and the number of mandatory reassignments decreases each year.

One conclusion that can be drawn from these data is that the voluntary plans in these big cities are not failures, as many academics have alleged, but neither do the data support such a blanket indictment of all mandatory plans. Ultimately, the decision to adopt a voluntary plan with magnets in a big city school system may have to be made on grounds other than its clear superiority in achieving interracial exposure. These data do show the voluntary plans leaving a smaller percentage of minority students in racially isolated schools, but with so small a sample, the difference is not statistically significant. A voluntary plan with magnets may produce more interracial exposure and leave fewer students racially isolated in big city school districts, but it also may do no better than a mandatory plan with magnets, particularly one that resembles St. Louis'. The St. Louis plan, with its large number of magnet schools, its city–suburban busing program, its racial ceilings on desegregated schools, and its minimal mandatory reassignments—approximately 20 percent of white students in 1986—has produced more interracial exposure than the Detroit mandatory plan and as much as or more than the voluntary plans. But a voluntary plan has an added bonus—the reputation of the educational system is better than it is under a mandatory plan, even those with magnets. Ultimately, that can only redound to the benefit of the city as a whole. Moreover, the research suggests that a choice plan may improve more than a school system's reputation; it may also improve the quality of education.

Conclusions

The data presented here, assessing broad policy trends by region and source of desegregation order, show that court-ordered desegregation plans, in general, produce from two to five times as much interracial exposure as is lost in subsequent years as a result of white flight and the declining white birth rate. There are, however, numerous exceptions to these generalizations. Certain court-ordered school districts have had little increase in interracial exposure with desegregation, and numerous board-ordered school districts have experienced large increases in it. The control group, consisting of those with no identifiable desegregation plans, had smaller declines in interracial exposure than the northern court-ordered school districts but greater declines than the southern court-ordered districts in the period after desegregation.

On the other hand, virtually every comparison shows more desegregation in the northern court-ordered districts than in the southern ones. This finding is contrary to most descriptive national studies, which compare all southern school districts to all northern school districts and find the southern districts to be more racially balanced and to have more interracial exposure. The different findings here are a result of the preponderance of large school districts in this southern sample. Large school districts have powerful economic and political interest groups. Because there is less support for integration among these groups in the South than in the North, and thus a greater danger of white flight, the southern courts have simply not demanded the amount of racial balance that the northern courts have demanded.

These data also show that the courts in both the North and South have tolerated desegregation plans that did not achieve the goal of having 100 percent of a district's children in desegregated schools. This is true even in those districts with a low percentage of students who are minority, where it is theoretically possible. The courts clearly are more reasonable than the popular conception of activist courts bent on social engineering would lead us to believe. Indeed, these data suggest that the courts are quite willing to make political compromises.

The demographic realities of this sample suggest that the courts have been right to refrain from further mandatory reassignments when resegregation occurs because of white flight. Indeed, one of the few courts that did not bow to public pressure against mandatory reassignment in the postimplementation period was that of Judge W. Arthur Garrity in Boston. Boston paid dearly for Garrity's strict interpretation of the racial balance principles of *Swann* and *Keyes*. Statistical analyses of white enrollment loss in Boston for every year beginning with the Phase I plan in 1974 through 1978 (Rossell and Ross, 1979:vii) indicate that every time white students were reassigned, whatever the reason, a significant portion left the school system. Among reassigned elementary students 31.3 percent left in the first year of the limited plan; 32.1 percent left the next year when the extensive plan was implemented; 55 percent the following year when reassignments were made to adjust for white flight in the previous years; 35.6 percent the next year for the same reason; and 29.3 percent in the fifth year for the same reason. The rates of white flight among high school and middle school students who were reassigned are similar in most years. As one black leader in Prince George's County, Maryland, suggested when the court was considering additional mandatory reassignments to remedy resegregation caused by white flight, doing so was like "chasing our tails."

Undoubtedly, many of the school districts in the 119-district sample will be going back to court to achieve unitary status, and some of them may consider changing their plans. The data presented here suggest that, with some black support, the courts will approve neighborhood plans that do not include magnet schools in school districts declared unitary, even if those plans are expected to cause some resegregation. In addition, the courts look favorably on choice plans that provide incentives for desegregation. Such plans make citizens happier than mandatory assignment plans *and* usually produce more interracial exposure. Even in large, predominantly minority school systems, the worst outcome is the same interracial exposure achieved under a mandatory plan. If the courts are indeed political compromisers, they cannot go wrong by approving such plans, and evidence indicates that they will if school districts propose them. Only two court-ordered mandatory reassignment plans have been implemented since 1981, and those (in Hattiesburg and Natchez, Mississippi) caused significant white flight. Although there may be one or two others, it is now unlikely that there will be many.

6

Conclusions and Recommendations

THE ISSUE of which model of policymaking—the "command and control" model or the "public choice" model—is more relevant to school desegregation is part of an ongoing philosophical debate among intellectuals. The debate focuses on the nature and causes of the reaction of white Americans to the mandatory reassignment, or "forced busing," of white children to black schools and the legitimacy of providing incentives for socially desirable behavior on "moral" issues.

White reaction to "forced busing" can be understood within the context of two major conflicts involving desegregation and the legal status of black Americans (see also Taylor, 1986). The first dispute is over the difference between civil rights and social equality. Civil rights are the rights to life, liberty, and the pursuit of happiness guaranteed by the Constitution. The *Brown* decision and its pre-*Green* progeny are viewed as civil rights decisions because they ordered the State to refrain from discriminating against black Americans. Americans now wholeheartedly accept these decisions and the nondiscrimination principle on which they rest. School integration falls within this sphere. It is, in the minds of many Americans, legitimate because it will occur naturally when people stop discriminating.

Americans are not united, however, in supporting the doctrine of social equality. Survey research indicates that the majority of white Americans do not see the difference in socioeconomic status between blacks and whites as a problem, because

183

they believe it is caused, not by discrimination, but by a lack of motivation and skills among blacks (Kluegel, 1985). Blacks, it is believed, violate such traditional American values as individualism and self-reliance, the work ethic, obedience, and discipline (Kinder and Sears, 1981:416); thus, it is unfair for equal social interaction to be forced by government. Blacks have to earn this right by changing their behavior and values.

Nor do whites view these attitudes as racist. Morris Abram, the former vice-chairman of the United States Commission on Civil Rights, summarizes the sentiments of many Americans when he writes that favoritism, affirmative action, and other forms of "reverse discrimination" produce unintended negative consequences and are unconstitutional:

> Civil rights have a unique meaning in this country. Elsewhere, in some of those societies where engineering a certain distribution of wealth and goods is part of the state's mission, people have economic rights—the right to housing, health care, and other goods. But civil rights have a different meaning in this country. We live in a constitutional democracy built not on the proposition that each [individual] has a fundamental entitlement to a particular piece of the economic pie, but rather on the concept that it is up to each individual to compete for economic goods, constitutionally protected from interference by guarantees of equal protection under the law, due process, the Bill of Rights and, most fundamentally, the ballot. (Abram, 1984:52)

The second great dispute, involving desegregation and the legal status of black Americans, concerns whether the behavioral changes required of whites to ensure black civil rights should be voluntary or mandatory. This dispute is tied to the first disagreement over civil rights and social equality. There is a general acceptance of the notion that it is legitimate to force whites to stop discriminating but that compliance with affirmative action policies whose goal is social equality should be voluntary. It is thought that whites will naturally and voluntarily participate in equal social interactions when blacks have earned the right by working hard and increasing their income and social class.

Thus, what appears to be a contradiction between overwhelming white support for the principle of integration and overwhelming rejection of forced busing is not a contradiction at all. It follows logically from the fact that Americans support civil rights—for example, integration—but believe that blacks have to earn social equality, not have it forced through busing or affirmative action.

In the area of school desegregation, academics and intellectuals dispute the implications of these attitudes for the direction of school desegregation policy. There is disagreement among intellectuals over the best policy alternative in part because of differing interpretations of the empirical evidence on these attitudes and their effect on behavior and in part because of differing feelings about whether incentives in matters of race are morally right. There are those who believe that social equality *can* be achieved only by government mandates—in the case of school desegregation, by mandatory reassignments—as well as those who believe that it *should* be achieved only by government mandates. For example, when I gave a lecture at Harvard Law School in 1985 and suggested that government ought to provide incentives for people to live integrated lives, several people in the audience objected to this as "bribing whites." They argued that the history of racism in this country demanded a more "moral" response from government, even if it was less effective than "bribery."

On the other hand, there are those who believe that the resentment, alienation, and mistrust of government that is produced by forcing social equality is so great that voluntary alternatives are preferable even if they produce less integration. Indeed, a number of these scholars explicitly state that they assume that voluntary plans will produce less desegregation than forced busing, but they advocate such plans, nevertheless, because they believe they are more consistent with a policy of nondiscrimination. Glazer, for example, (1985a, 1985b) has argued that freedom of choice in education is philosophically superior to mandatory assignment even though freedom of choice might not produce as much desegregation. Abram argues similarly:

It may not be fashionable to counsel patience, but patience is necessary. We must acknowledge the historical fact that the progress of a group, once barriers are removed, does indeed take time. *Of course, we could accomplish more with greater speed if we were willing to take more drastic measures,* turning our backs on the Constitution. But we dare not do that. (Abram, 1984:64; emphasis added)

Some writers on this issue, however, support freedom of choice on philosophical grounds, but reject it on empirical grounds—it does not achieve its goal of integration. Hochschild (1984:70), for example, writes:

The general attractions of voluntary rather than coerced action are so obvious they do not need explication. No sane political actor would prefer to have policy changes forced on citizens rather than chosen by them. . . . who denies that greater good arises from natural integration than from mandatory racial mixing?

She dismisses voluntary plans, however, because "they seldom achieve the basic step of ending racial isolation. . . . the story generally remains that of 1968: voluntary methods do not desegregate school districts" (1984:71). Hawley and Smylie (1986:282) similarly criticize voluntary plans on empirical grounds, describing the supporters of such plans as succumbing to "wishful thinking."

Others claim to be justifying their disapproval of voluntary plans on empirical grounds, but one suspects that the objection is really a philosophical one. Either consciously or subconsciously, many academics believe that matters of civil rights and social equality are too important to be left to the private acts of individuals. Some may even believe, consciously or subconsciously, that whites must be punished—that is, made to do what they do not want to do—in order to compensate blacks for the centuries of injustice they have endured at the hands of whites.

On the other hand, some believe that voluntary desegregation is not only preferable to mandatory desegregation on philosophical grounds but might logically be a more effective desegregation tool as well, if the proper incentives could be found. A professor of economics contends that

> the policy of open enrollment as a means to desegregate the schools still offers a handsome alternative to mandatory busing, which has stirred such intense controversy and perhaps even increased racial tension. What mainly needs to be explored is whether some incentive program that heightens the attractiveness of a transfer plan can accomplish what has not been accomplished by simply offering the option to transfer. (Meadows, 1976:143)

The research presented in this book is really the first evidence that voluntary plans with incentives do indeed produce more desegregation than mandatory plans. Desegregation is operationalized as interracial exposure—the percentage of students who are white in the average minority child's school. Interracial exposure reflects the net benefit of desegregation plans because it goes up with racial balance reassignments, but down with white flight. Racial balance is an inadequate goal because it ignores the question of how many whites are coming into contact with minorities: As noted above, a school district with one white in each school would have perfect racial balance, but very little interracial exposure. Moreover, if one reads the literature on the social and educational benefits of school desegregation, it becomes quite clear that the authors believe these benefits come from interracial exposure, not merely racial balance. The same is true of the court decisions. It is clear from most of these opinions, particularly those involving predominantly black school districts, that the courts see the goal of desegregation as interracial exposure, not merely racial balance.

The voluntary plans with magnet schools produce more desegregation than the mandatory plans in part because the latter are viewed as an illegitimate use of government power to force social equality. For this and other reasons, half of the whites who are reassigned to black schools under such plans will not comply. On the other hand, almost all white Americans support the principle of integration and thus a substantial proportion is willing to enroll its children in integrated schools when those schools have "earned" it. The superior resources in magnet schools and the innovative curricula "earn" the participation of whites.

As a result of these attitudes, the public choice model is now more effective than the command and control model. It is more efficient to try to change the behavior of citizens by restructuring the range of alternatives to choose from and encouraging socially desirable behavior through positive and negative incentives than it is to order the desegregation assignment of specific students to specific schools.

The difference between the interracial exposure produced by the voluntary plans and that produced by the mandatory plans is, however, not so huge that everyone who looks at these data will immediately agree that voluntary plans are clearly superior solely on interracial exposure grounds. Given the greater expense of magnet schools, having 7,000 to 10,000 more whites come into contact with minorities in the average school system as a result of adopting a voluntary rather than a mandatory plan may not be valued highly by everyone. But the case for voluntary choice plans can also be made on the grounds that both whites and minorities prefer them and that they appear to increase educational achievement. Thus, because of these other benefits, all that voluntary plans should have to achieve to be considered superior to mandatory plans is the same interracial exposure. Since, in fact, they produce greater interracial exposure, they should be the preferred desegregation technique. The worst result would be the same interracial exposure that would have been observed under a mandatory plan, but with far less white opposition, far greater minority support (Rossell, 1986a, 1986b), and an improvement in the quality of education.

The analysis presented in this book also shows that mandatory plans can be dismantled with no harm *if* they are replaced with comprehensive voluntary plans whose goal is at least to maintain the prior level of racial balance. Returning to neighborhood schools and relying solely on majority-to-minority transfer programs will probably produce some resegregation in most large, residentially segregated school systems.

The relative success of the public choice model suggests that most citizens are now sufficiently "rational" concerning issues of desegregation to desegregate a school system. The conclusion that opposition to forced busing was just another form of racism (Caditz, 1975, 1976; Erbe, 1977; Gatlin, Giles, and Cataldo, 1978; Jacobson, 1978; Kelley, 1974; Kinder and Rhodebeck, 1982; Kinder and Sears, 1981; McConahay, 1982; Miller, 1981; Sears, Hensler, and Speer, 1979; Sears et al., 1980; Weidman, 1975), and that individuals would, as a result, not enroll their children in even high-quality desegregated schools, may once have been true, but it is no longer.

Collapsing citizen behavior into one of two models involves, of course, some oversimplification. Some of the more interesting questions that these data cannot address are why some parents residing in a school district with a voluntary desegregation plan believe it is in their self-interest to enroll their child in a magnet school and others do not. I suspect that in a school district with a voluntary plan, the motivation to enroll a child in a magnet school may be a combination of "self-interest" and altruism for many parents. For others it may be solely a matter of self-interest or even a belief that magnet schools are the lesser of two evils when the neighborhood school becomes desegregated by majority-to-minority transfers or neighborhood transition. This is certainly the case with magnet–mandatory plans but it may also be true of some parents in districts with voluntary plans.

Whatever the motivation, desegregating a school system with voluntary transfers is not an easy task. School districts spend a lot of time and money promoting magnets so that parents will be motivated to leave their neighborhood schools, and they do this in both the magnet–voluntary and the magnet–mandatory plans. Indeed, there are surprisingly few differences in the procedures for creating and marketing magnet schools in the two types of plans. School districts with each type of plan strategically place magnets with certain themes in certain neigh-borhoods. Magnet schools enroll, on average, one-third of the students in a school district with a voluntary plan and 13 percent of the students in a school district with a mandatory plan. The ceiling on magnet participation, however, seems to be 100 per-cent in small school districts such as Montclair's. Schools in mi-nority locations are the hardest to desegregate, but it is possible to do so by devoting more resources to the task—that is, by providing more incentives.

Approximately one-third of the magnet programs are in white locations. Another 21 percent are in integrated locations, presumably to stabilize the schools' racial balance. The largest proportion of magnet programs—46 percent—are in minority locations, but this is still less than one would expect if magnet schools are being used solely to induce whites to transfer from their neighborhood schools to black schools. The evidence sug-gests that they are also used to induce minority students to transfer to white schools, although such incentives are not nec-essary. Large numbers of minority students, given the option, would transfer to white schools with or without magnets.

The number of white students whom magnets in minority lo-cations are able to attract varies considerably according to the particular theme of the magnet. When all factors are taken into account, however, only the individualized instruction magnet theme is significantly more attractive than the others. The limit-ing factor in any magnet school plan is clearly the number of whites who will transfer to schools in minority neighborhoods. The magnets in white locations, by contrast, are quite successful in attracting minorities.

Analysis of the national data suggests that the courts have been much more reasonable in the amount of racial balance they have demanded than the popular view would suggest. Only one of the 66 court-ordered school districts in the 119-school-district sample has 100 percent of its children in racially balanced schools. Even by the most generous standard—defining a de-segregated school as one whose enrollment is within plus or

minus 20 percentage points of the district's racial composition—
the northern court-ordered districts have only 81 percent of
their students in racially balanced schools, and the southern
court-ordered districts have fewer than two-thirds.

Moreover, 43 to 45 percent of the minority students in the
court-ordered school districts are in schools that are more than
40 percent white. In northern court-ordered school districts, almost 20 percent are in severely racially isolated schools, and in
southern court-ordered school districts almost 32 percent are.
In terms of the percentage of minority students in white schools,
the northern board-ordered school districts achieve greater desegregation than the districts with court-ordered plans. They
are also the least extensive plans in terms of mandatory white
reassignments (Rossell, 1978a, 1978b).

In virtually every comparison in our sample, we find more
desegregation in the northern court-ordered districts than in
the southern court-ordered districts, contrary, as noted in Chapter 5, to descriptive national studies that compare *all* southern
school districts with *all* northern ones. By contrast, this sample
is primarily composed of large school districts, which southern
judges have treated differently from the way they have treated
small and medium-sized southern districts and differently from
the way northern judges have treated similar northern districts.

The evidence also suggests that, on average, voluntary plans
produce slightly more interracial exposure than do mandatory
plans in big city school districts with a high proportion of students who are minority. The difference is small, however, and
thus for some people, the case for magnet–choice plans will have
to be made on other grounds. The argument can be made that
unlike mandatory reassignment plans, voluntary–magnet school
plans improve the quality of education in a school system for all
children. If one thinks of an educational system as similar to a
market system, the competition among schools that emerges in
a choice plan provides all the right incentives to both consumers
and producers. For the producers, competition provides the
incentive to produce high-quality education in order to attract

students. Because schools are competing against each other to attract students, consumers feel empowered to demand a high-quality education in return for enrolling their children. This dynamic may have produced the achievement gains in Buffalo and Cambridge after the implementation of their choice plans (see Rossell, 1987; Rossell and Glenn, 1988). It is certainly the underlying theory of the voucher systems proposed over the last two decades for public and private education.

Metropolitan Plans

One type of plan that is recommended by virtually every academic writing in the area of school desegregation is a metropolitan plan that combines the (typically) predominantly minority central city with the (typically) predominantly white suburbs. The data presented in this book, however, do not support countywide mandatory reassignment plans. Table 6.1 shows the amount of interracial exposure in five groups of school districts at $T + 1$ (the second year of the plan and the highest point) and $T + 9$, the change in interracial exposure from $T + 1$ to $T + 9$, and the decline in white enrollment from $T - 2$ (the year before the plan and the highest point), to $T + 9$.

The groups are as follows:

1. Countywide mandatory plans in districts with minority enrollment below 30 percent
2. Citywide voluntary plans in districts with minority enrollment below 30 percent
3. Citywide mandatory plans in districts with minority enrollment below 30 percent
4. Citywide mandatory plans in districts with minority enrollment above 30 percent
5. Citywide voluntary plans in school districts with minority enrollment above 30 percent.

Table 6.1 shows the countywide mandatory plans have the greatest interracial exposure at $T + 1$. These data show, however, that the countywide school districts have the *greatest* de-

TABLE 6.1
INTERRACIAL EXPOSURE AND WHITE ENROLLMENT CHANGE
IN COUNTYWIDE PLANS WITH MANDATORY REASSIGNMENT
COMPARED WITH OTHER TYPES OF PLANS

| Plans | % Minority | % Interracial Exposure | | Change in Interracial Exposure | % Change in White Enrollment |
	T − 1	T + 1	T + 9	T + 1 to T + 9	T − 2 to T + 9
<30% MINORITY					
Countywide Mandatory[a]	82.7%	73.0%	63.7%	−9.3	−44.8%
Citywide Mandatory[b]	84.6	68.9	63.6	−5.3	−43.6
Citywide Voluntary[c]	88.6	68.2	70.7	2.5	−34.4
>30% MINORITY					
Citywide Mandatory[d]	56.5	38.3	29.4	−8.9	−60.6
Citywide Voluntary[e]	54.9	37.7	35.0	−2.7	−47.0

Notes:
[a] Louisville–Jefferson County and Montgomery County.
[b] Des Moines, Racine, St. Paul, and Tulsa.
[c] Portland and Tacoma.
[d] Boston, Dallas, Dayton, Springfield, Mass., and Stockton.
[e] Buffalo, Cincinnati, Houston, Milwaukee, Montclair, San Bernardino, and San Diego.

cline in interracial exposure from T + 1 to T + 9. They also show
that the only school districts that do not have a decline in interracial exposure over this time period are the *city* school districts
with lower minority enrollment and voluntary plans. The school
districts with the next-smallest decline in interracial exposure
are those with voluntary plans in school districts with greater
minority enrollment. By T + 9, the countywide mandatory desegregation plans produce substantially *less* interracial exposure than the *citywide* voluntary plans and virtually the same
interracial exposure as citywide mandatory plans in school dis-

tricts with similar minority enrollment. Thus, there is apparently no advantage to having a countywide plan in terms of interracial exposure.

These data suggest two conclusions. First, in terms of the *absolute level* of interracial exposure, the most important factor is the school district's proportion of minority students, not the type of plan. Although the mandatory plans experience more white flight than the voluntary plans, those that begin with a high level of interracial exposure and/or a high percentage of white students will typically end with a relatively high level of interracial exposure. Second, in terms of the postdesegregation *trends* in interracial exposure, the most important factor is the nature of the reassignment plan, not whether it is citywide or countywide. As shown in the last column of Table 6.1, mandatory plans experience more white enrollment decline than voluntary plans, not only in the implementation year but in subsequent years as well, and countywide plans have no advantage over citywide plans. The countywide and citywide mandatory plans experienced virtually the same white enrollment loss with desegregation.

The difference between the 9.3 percentage point decline in interracial exposure in the countywide plans and the 2.5 increase in the voluntary plans in districts with lower minority enrollment represents almost 18,000 fewer whites coming into contact with minorities in a hypothetical school system that began with 40,000 whites. Louisville–Jefferson County and Montgomery County began, however, with an average white enrollment of 116,000. In these school systems, the 11.8 point difference in interracial exposure represents 51,000 fewer whites. This is a substantial loss of interracial exposure.

The decline in interracial exposure in countywide plans is caused by white flight or "non-entrance" as well as residential change. Contrary to popular opinion, countywide plans experience a degree of *school*-level white flight that is similar to that of citywide plans. Because busing distance and the percentage of blacks at the receiving school are causes of white flight, countywide mandatory reassignment plans experience the same

school "no-show" rates as the citywide plans when whites are reassigned to black schools some distance from their neighborhood
school (Board of Education, 1986; Rossell, 1988). The major advantage that countywide plans appear to have is that, because of
the higher percentage of students who are white in the school
system, there are fewer black schools relative to white schools.
Thus, the same school loss rates add up to a smaller district-
level effect because there are fewer schools with big losses. But
citywide plans in districts with low minority enrollment enjoy
the same advantage. Indeed, the similar white enrollment loss
rates of the citywide and countywide plans suggest that the advantage of including the suburbs in a plan and thus incorporat-
ing areas where whites may flee may be offset by the greater
busing distance between the city and suburbs, a significant
cause of white flight (Rossell, 1988).

Thus, Table 6.1 indicates no advantage to having a countywide plan. It does indicate, however, that a voluntary plan has
an advantage over a mandatory plan and a low-percentage-mi-
nority school district has an advantage over a high-percentage-
minority school district, all other things being equal. This analysis suggests that the greatest interracial exposure and the least
white flight are produced by school districts less than 30 percent
minority under a citywide, voluntary plan. Among school districts with a minority enrollment greater than 30 percent, however, a voluntary plan also produces the greatest interracial exposure for that category of school districts.

Policy Recommendations

Any proposed voluntary desegregation plan should be
examined critically to ensure that it is both equitable and comprehensive. The following components of a voluntary plan are
necessary for maximizing interracial exposure:

1. Negative incentives in the form of racial controls on schools so
   that transfers that promote the greatest desegregation are most
   likely to be approved
2. Placement of magnet school programs almost entirely in minor-

ity or integrated neighborhoods to serve as positive incentives
for white transferring

3. A majority-to-minority transfer program in which any student
   can transfer from any school in which his or her race is in a majority to any school in which his or her race is in a minority, with
   transportation provided and annual reenrollment guaranteed
4. A variety of magnet programs, with a heavy emphasis on individualized, child-centered programs, math/science, and computers. Extended day programs by themselves are among the least
   popular and therefore they should always be combined with another magnet theme if they are to be successful.
5. Retention of neighborhood schools and attendance zones
6. Expensive and aggressive publicity and recruitment, including
   phone calls to prospective parents where necessary
7. Ambitious, districtwide desegregation goals. There is no standard applicable to every school district—what would be ambitious for Racine would be impossible for Chicago—but in each
   situation most of the parties involved should be able to agree on
   the definition of such a goal.
8. Ample time to achieve these goals. It takes considerable time to
   build the reputation of magnets. Five years would be a reasonable amount of time in most school districts. In very small school
   districts, a shorter period might be possible; in big city school districts, a longer time frame might be justified. The goal is to
   avoid mandatory reassignments and thus maximize interracial
   exposure and enhance the reputation of the public schools. Ultimately, this will produce a greater benefit for minority children
   than a counterproductive plan implemented immediately.

I recommend that all or nearly all magnet programs be placed
in minority schools for both reasons of efficiency and reasons of
equity. With regard to *efficiency*, it makes no sense to waste
scarce resources by placing magnet programs in white schools.
We know from the research, as well as the successful magnet–
voluntary plans implemented in Yonkers and San Jose in the
fall of 1986, that minority students will transfer to most white
schools even if they have no special magnet programs. Indeed,
virtually all the white schools in these districts were desegregated by means of majority-to-minority transfers. On the other

hand, that does not mean that nothing should be done for these schools. I recommend extensive use of techniques such as cooperative learning to improve race relations (Slavin, 1978, 1979, 1983) in *all* the schools in a desegregation plan. There is no school that could not benefit from interventions aimed at improving race relations—probably the most neglected aspect of school desegregation.

With regard to *equity*, it makes sense to place magnet programs almost entirely in minority schools because magnet programs raise the status of a school. To raise the status of already high-prestige white schools seems unfair and unnecessary. To raise the status of minority schools seems just. Of course, a school district may have low-status white schools, or white schools with reputations as being inhospitable to minorities, and in such cases a magnet program is justified. The ultimate goal of a voluntary–magnet school plan is that of any desegregation plan—"a system without a 'white' school and a 'Negro' school, but just schools."[1]

Controlled Choice

A variation on the magnet–voluntary plan described above is "controlled choice," popularized by Alves and Willie (1987). Controlled choice, as Alves and Willie propound it, and as it is practiced in Cambridge, differs from the magnet–voluntary plan described above in two important ways. First, Alves and Willie do not believe in incentives, such as magnet programs and additional expenditures, in minority schools. Second, their controlled choice plans have no school attendance zones. They argue that magnet schools are elitist and that whites will voluntarily choose minority schools if they lose their "property right" to their neighborhood school through the elimination of attendance zones. Their conclusion appears to be based entirely, however, on the experience of Cambridge, Massachusetts—at 6 square miles one of the smallest urban school systems in the nation and one of the most residentially integrated. If every student simply chose the school closest to his or her home, the Cambridge school system would still be one of the most integrated in the country.

Moreover, eliminating attendance zones and reassigning all new students may not be too difficult in a school system like Cambridge, with 8,000 students spread over 6 square miles, but it could be a logistical nightmare in a school system of 80,000. In order to make this process more manageable, Alves and Willie recommend that large school systems be divided into subdistricts with no transfers allowed across subdistrict lines. Unfortunately, this limits the choices of individuals. It also increases the likelihood of mandatory reassignments because if a minority school cannot draw from the entire school system's pool of whites, it may not get enough of them to desegregate the school voluntarily.

Indeed, controlled choice probably could not work at all as a "voluntary transfer" desegregation plan for a segregated school system in which whites are accustomed to attending their neighborhood school. There is no evidence that whites will willingly transfer their children out of their neighborhood school and into a minority school across town without some incentives. Under controlled choice, however, if whites (and minorities) do not choose schools that produce a desegregated school district, they are simply reassigned. In Cambridge, this results in few reassignments because choosing one's neighborhood school would substantially desegregate the school system. But in most segregated school districts, the adoption of such a plan would be a complete failure if the goal were both desegregation and little or no mandatory reassignments.

As a result, controlled choice has only been implemented in four school systems, all with previous mandatory reassignment plans. Two of these, Montclair, New Jersey, and Cambridge, Massachusetts, are tiny. Nor is Montclair a good example of controlled choice since it has magnet programs in every school (but has eliminated attendance zones). Controlled choice has not worked very well in the two large, desegregated school systems—Little Rock, Arkansas, and Seattle, Washington—in which it has been implemented. Little Rock tried controlled choice for the 1987–88 school year, but found that it was "too costly and too confusing" (Snider, 1988) despite the fact that the school system was divided into subdistricts. Moreover, too few whites were willing to transfer to minority schools even though the school system had previously been under a court-ordered, mandatory reassignment plan. As a result, large numbers of students had to be mandatorily reassigned, which action produced dissatisfaction among both white and black parents. Under the new "incentives" plan to be implemented in the fall of 1989, magnet programs are placed in schools located in minority neighborhoods along the lines of the model I recommend above.

Controlled choice was implemented in Seattle, Washington (also divided into subdistricts and then into clusters), in the fall of 1989. The plan has experienced problems similar to those of Little Rock (Lalonde, 1989; Scigliano, 1989). Because there are no neighborhood schools, there is a good deal of uncertainty and dissatisfaction. Although the school administration claims that 88 percent of parents are getting their first-choice school, that choice is so limited that large numbers are still dissatisfied. Moreover, without school attendance zones, there is a fear that, as with a mandatory reassignment plan, parents are at the mercy of the school administration and its desegregation goals. As a result, the nonbinding Initiative 34 was passed by Seattle voters in November 1989 to dismantle controlled choice and adopt a neighborhood school system with magnet schools in minority neighborhoods in order to "preserve and enhance system-wide integration" (Save Our Schools, 1989).

The Boston School Committee also voted to adopt a controlled choice plan designed by Alves and Willie. The plan, implemented in fall 1989, is probably an improvement over the previous mandatory reassignment plan for the parents who are still in the school system. But the elimination of school attendance zones and the fact that magnet programs and other resources are not concentrated in minority neighborhoods means that the new plan has not only resulted in mandatory desegregation reassignments (an estimated 40 percent of whites did not get their first choice), but more important, has not attracted whites back into the school system. Moreover, it appears to have severe logistical problems.

In short, controlled choice is an improvement over a mandatory desegregation plan, but not over a magnet–voluntary plan. Parents must feel they have some control over their children's school assignment or they will not come back into the school system, and controlled choice does not provide this. Parents must also believe there is something good at the end of the bus ride or they will not voluntarily transfer their children to minority schools, and controlled choice does not provide this. The evidence suggests that the greatest interracial exposure and parental satisfaction are produced by a neighborhood school plan with magnet programs in minority schools and a majority-to-minority transfer program to desegregate white schools—not by controlled choice. Although controlled choice may be cheaper than a magnet–voluntary plan, this could be a case of "penny wise and pound foolish."

Costs

There are some valid and some less-valid objections to magnet school plans. The criticism that magnet schools do not desegregate is not valid, but other criticisms are not so easily dismissed.

Hochschild (1984) objects to the expense of magnet schools. Voluntary plans that desegregate with magnet schools cost substantially more than mandatory plans with fewer magnet schools. Levine and Campbell (1977:249–50) state that approximately $4 million was spent in Houston to initiate magnet programs at 31 campuses during the 1975–76 school year. In 1976 the average per pupil expenditures for St. Louis' magnet schools were roughly double those for its regular schools (Levine and Campbell, 1977).

In Boston in the same year, magnet schools cost $844 per pupil for regular teachers and $221 per pupil for special instruction, compared with $715 and $184, respectively, for regular schools. The average per pupil expenditure for instructional supplies was $65 in magnet schools and $50 in regular schools. The average age of the facility and pupil–teacher ratio similarly favored magnet schools (Massachusetts Research Center, 1976: 56). The cost of transportation is also, as noted in Chapter 4, much greater in voluntary plans (in which students have to be picked up at locations all over the school district and delivered to locations all over the school district) than in mandatory plans, in which entire neighborhoods are reassigned to the same school.

For most school districts, however, it is the up-front implementation costs of magnet schools that decimate the budget. As discussed in Chapter 4, the Savannah school administration estimated the operating costs for 11 magnets to be $5.7 million (Board of Public Education, 1988), and in Yonkers the estimated bill was $11.6 million, which included renovation and new construction but not transportation.

As Hochschild points out, this is a financial drain on the rest of the school system. She argues that it is a psychological drain as well because magnet schools siphon off commitment and diminish morale in the rest of the system (Hochschild, 1984:77). The principals, teachers, and students in the regular schools may feel as if they are the stepchildren of the school system. What she misses, however, is the fact that this is much less likely to occur in the voluntary plans with magnet schools than it is in the mandatory plans with magnet schools. In the voluntary plans, the regular neighborhood school is still valued because it is the school that parents chose by moving into that neighborhood. If this is a big city voluntary plan, which leaves some minority schools racially isolated, the courts have protected such schools by ordering "Milliken II relief"—that is, additional expenditures and smaller pupil–teacher ratios.[2] In a mandatory plan, however, there are no neighborhood schools, and so a dual

202   Conclusions and Recommendations

system is created consisting of the desegregated schools that the school administration assigns students to and the superior magnet schools that are chosen.

There is certainly a dual system in Boston. I know of no middle-class person in the city of Boston with children in the public schools, unless they are in one of the elite magnet schools, and that includes the chairman of the Massachusetts Commission Against Discrimination. Thus, although magnet schools can create a dual system in any district, this is less likely to happen under the voluntary plans.

Nevertheless, the elitism generated by magnet schools with superior resources is a problem that policymakers must address, and it is the reason I recommend putting magnets in minority neighborhoods. But elitism is not so great a problem as to dissuade the courts from approving voluntary plans with magnet schools or keep the public from supporting them (see Rossell, 1987). It is surprising, however, how few school districts propose magnet–voluntary plans. Most administrators in districts that currently have mandatory reassignment plans appear to be resigned to their "Ford" desegregation models and are not interested in the expensive "Mercedes" plan; nor do they care much about public sentiment concerning the legitimacy of forced busing or the value of choice. For these administrators, it is more important to keep the cost of desegregation to a minimum than to produce more interracial exposure.

School districts that do not already have mandatory reassignment plans appear to be the primary constituency for adopting voluntary–magnet school plans. Indeed, since 1980 every school district convicted of intentional segregation has proposed a voluntary–magnet school plan rather than a mandatory plan. Moreover, I know of only two instances (Hattiesburg, in 1987, and Natchez, in 1989) in which that was not the plan implemented. Magnet school plans thus appear to be the wave of the future. Bell offers an explanation for the current preference for voluntary plans: "The interest of blacks in achieving racial equality will be accommodated only when it converges with the interests of whites" (Bell, 1980:95). Thus, voluntary–magnet school plans may be more effective desegregation tools than mandatory plans because they structure the environment so that the white interest in a superior education converges with the interest of blacks in achieving racial equality.

Moreover, for increasing numbers of black and other minority parents, school desegregation has been transformed from a symbolic issue to a substantive one. The white protest and flight in response to mandatory desegregation diminishes its attractiveness. Plans that engender intense white hostility would seem to offer little to black parents contemplating putting their children into the schools affected by such plans. Black parents want to know how school desegregation can benefit their child, and an environment of white hostility does not seem to offer much hope of any benefit.

Equity, Efficiency, and Effectiveness

One of the enduring issues in the public policy literature is the relative weight that should be given to the goal of equity in the delivery of public services and to the often competing goals of efficiency and effectiveness. Frequently, a policy does better than alternatives on one criterion, but worse on another. In such instances, the relative value of each criterion and the proper tradeoff among criteria must be weighed.

As with other policies, school desegregation alternatives have been evaluated, at least implicitly, in terms of the criteria of equity, efficiency, and effectiveness. What follows, however, is perhaps the first *explicit* comparison of school desegregation policies on these three criteria.

EQUITY

Equity is synonymous with social justice in most policy debates. In theory, equity means that similarly situated people should be treated equally. In reality, to measure how fairly a service is distributed, one must consider how much of a *needed* service the individuals in each recipient group receive. Because the needs of individuals and groups differ, equity does not mean that equal amounts of a good or service be provided to each group or individual. Indeed, the notion of equity is probably best embodied in Marx's dictum—from each according to his ability and to each according to his needs. Equity really means fairness rather than equality in the sense of equal amounts.

In school desegregation policy, equity claims are made by civil rights leaders and attorneys for equal treatment of blacks and whites. This translates into demands for equal school closings, equal access to and participation in educational programs, equal disciplinary action and outcome, and equal "busing burden." The pre-1968 freedom-of-choice desegregation plans were considered inequitable by civil rights leaders not only because they did not desegregate black schools, but because only blacks did the transferring. Equity then was defined as equal proportions of whites and blacks being "burdened" by taking away their choice and mandatorily reassigning them. Thus, in school desegregation policy, equity became synonymous with equality rather than fairness, even when this occasionally led to absurd demands. Civil rights leaders, for example, often demanded that mandatory desegregation plans reassign equal proportions of each race even when, because of very different racial proportions in the student population, it was statistically impossible to do so and still have racially balanced schools.

Magnet–voluntary plans have encountered criticisms similar to those leveled at the freedom-of-choice plans, as well as criticisms unique to magnet school plans. The danger of creating a two-tiered or "dual" system of schools, discussed above, is unique to magnet schools. This problem can be largely alleviated by putting magnet programs only in the low-status, usually minority, schools. If this is done, magnet programs become a way of redressing prior inequities.

A criticism similar to that leveled at freedom-of-choice plans is that more minorities than whites typically will choose to leave their home school for another school in a magnet–voluntary plan and thus, it is argued, the minority students are "burdened." The evidence, however, suggests the differences in transfers by race are relatively small, on average, particularly when most of the magnet programs have been placed in minority neighborhoods. Moreover, after one controls for differences in the size of each student population—something that is rarely done—differential participation may disappear altogether. For example, in San Jose the monitor's report (Arias, 1986) claims that 59 percent of the out-of-attendance-area students are minority. Since 55 percent of the district's students are minority, the disparity is reduced from 10 to 5 percentage points when racial proportions are controlled.

Even if the differences in voluntary transfers do not disappear, I find the argument that minorities are burdened by their choices reasonable only if one assumes that black and Hispanic and Asian parents do not know their own minds. This implicit, and perhaps racist, assumption underlies several court decisions of the 1980s, most recently *U.S. and Nichols v. Natchez Municipal Separate School District* (1989),[3] in which, despite evidence of a black preference for a voluntary transfer remedy, the white plaintiff attorneys[4] and the white judge supported a mandatory reassignment plan. Similarly, the white judge in Boston denied the black plaintiffs' request for a dismantling of the mandatory reassignment plan (Cooper, 1982) for five years, only granting this in 1989 when almost all of the whites had left the school system. In Buffalo in 1982, the black parents of students in the majority-to-minority program asked to intervene in the court suit in order to defend the voluntary transfer program. The judge denied their request. The program was drastically curtailed and replaced by mandatory reassignments. The same parents who once had a choice as to the schools their children attended now saw them mandatorily reassigned, a decision thought to be "equitable" because whites were also "burdened" by being mandatorily reassigned. Although this may make sense to intellectuals and to judges, it makes no sense at all to large numbers of minority parents. Surveys indicate that both black and white parents prefer a magnet school desegregation plan relying on voluntary transfers to a mandatory reassignment plan (Armor, 1989; Rossell, 1986a, 1986b). In a situation in which black parents prefer voluntary plans over mandatory plans, a consideration of equity would suggest the voluntary plan be adopted.

Even where the voluntary plans involve unequal reassignments as a result of the closing of more black than white schools and the consequent rezoning of more black than white students, the choice plans are still more equitable. For one thing, most mandatory reassignment plans also close black schools disproportionately since these buildings are typically the oldest and most inefficient schools in a school system and the hardest to desegregate. For another thing, although both black and white parents prefer voluntary plans over mandatory reassignment plans, almost five times the percentage of black parents support mandatory reassignment as do white parents. Thus, the old notion that equity means equal reassignments does not make sense in light of vastly differing values for mandatory reassignment.

Moreover, if mandatory reassignments are a burden for minorities, the evidence is that a mandatory reassignment plan produces as much, and usually more, minority burden than a voluntary plan, even if the latter has some mandatory reassignment of minorities to contiguous schools. When whites leave the school system in disproportionate numbers, as occurs from a mandatory plan, blacks and Hispanics inevitably assume the busing burden. There is every indication that this has occurred in Boston, and other districts, and that black parents, as a result, feel that a mandatory reassignment plan is inequitable (*Boston Globe*, 1987; Cooper, 1982).

Perhaps the most important reason voluntary plans are more equitable than mandatory plans is that they empower black parents. In a mandatory reassignment plan, both black and white parents are effectively powerless, for they have no choice about the schools their children are assigned to unless they have the resources to move or to choose private schools. A mandatory reassignment plan therefore offers choice only to the affluent, who can leave the school system, not to the poor who must remain behind. Voluntary plans with magnet schools, in contrast, offer choice to people who would otherwise be powerless—those who cannot afford private schools. So long as there are differences in the preferences of whites and minorities, minorities may be expected to transfer more than whites, but if they have chosen to do so freely, it stands logic on its head to call this a "burden."

Moreover, the whole "burden" issue has to be placed in the context of the goals of school desegregation. School desegregation is not a punishment that is to be evenly handed out. It is a benefit to minorities—its paramount goal is to improve *minority*, not white, life chances. In that context, a magnet–voluntary plan that gives minority children choice is an opportunity, not a burden, regardless of the relative number of whites and minorities that transfer. Bennett (1986) also argues that the only "burden" in a choice process is the assignment of students to schools that are not the first choice of their parents. Parents who receive their first-choice school are not burdened so long as there are a considerable number of schools to choose from.

It is important, nevertheless, that school administrators do everything humanly possible to avoid the appearance of disproportionate burden, while also trying to maximize interracial exposure. Some policymakers may understandably be willing to trade off less interracial exposure for more symbolic equity. But it is important to understand also that, although the magnet–voluntary plans have their problems, mandatory reassignment plans are not the answer, for these plans are less, not more, equitable than magnet–voluntary plans.

EFFICIENCY

Efficiency is the other criterion that is used to evaluate public policies. Efficiency is the ratio of inputs to outputs. Inputs are resources transformed through activities into outputs. Policies that achieve more of a desired goal at less cost are more efficient than those that achieve the same goal at greater cost or less of a goal at the same cost.

"Cost" is usually defined in an economic sense. For school desegregation policy, cost can also be defined in a human resource sense, and this definition is actually more important to the courts than the economic one (see Rossell, 1986a). Thus, efficiency in school desegregation can be defined as the ratio of students reassigned to those who actually enroll. Using this definition, the least efficient desegregation alternative is a mandatory reassignment plan. For every 100 white students who are reassigned to a school formerly above 90 percent minority, approximately 55 will not show up at the school they are assigned to. Overall, across all reassignments to minority schools, almost half the white students will not show up at the school they are reassigned to (Rossell, 1988). It is hard to imagine a business operating for long with such inefficiency.

The pre-1968 freedom-of-choice plans were probably more efficient than the mandatory plans that followed them, although this may not have been the case in the early years of freedom of choice. Although there are few data, undoubtedly some—and perhaps many—of the black students who applied for a transfer in the 1950s were intimidated during the interim period between their application and the opening of school and did not actually enroll at the school they had requested a transfer to. By the late 1960s, however, when these plans had become fairly routine and acceptable, it is probable that most of the students who requested a transfer and were assigned to an opposite-race school actually did enroll at that school the following fall. This can be inferred from *Green v. County School Board of New Kent County* (1968),[5] in which 15 percent of the black students were taking advantage of the freedom-of-choice plan. Since this figure is quite close to current black willingness to transfer to white schools (Rossell, 1986a, 1986b), it is likely that almost all of the students who wanted to transfer actually did so.

The magnet–voluntary plans of the mid-1970s appear to be the most efficient plans in terms of the ratio of students assigned to students enrolled. Conversations with school administrators indicate that most of the students assigned to their first-choice schools do indeed show up at that school. There is probably some white loss from second- and third-choice school assignments, but since that typically represents less than 10 percent of the assignments, and since there are magnet programs at even the second- and third-choice schools, magnet–voluntary plans are still much more efficient than mandatory reassignment plans and somewhat more efficient than pre-1968 freedom-of-choice plans.

EFFECTIVENESS

Effectiveness is another criterion used in the evaluation of policy alternatives. Effectiveness is a measure of the extent to which a policy achieves its goals. In technical terms, it is the ratio of actual output to planned output over a particular time period. It differs from efficiency in that it measures ultimate attainment whereas efficiency is concerned only with how much of a given outcome unit is achieved for a given input unit. Thus, the late 1960s freedom-of-choice plans were very efficient in that the ratio of students assigned to students enrolled was close to 1. However, these plans were rather ineffective—at most, 15 percent of the black students transferred and none of the whites did so. In a 50 percent white and 50 percent black school system, that meant that only 7.5 percent of the students made desegregation transfers—not enough to dismantle the dual school system.

Court recognition of this outcome began the era of mandatory reassignment in the 1970s. These plans were usually more effective than the old freedom-of-choice plans in terms of the extent of racial balance and interracial exposure produced. The level of racial balance was about 30 to 40 points greater under the mandatory reassignment plans than under freedom-of-choice plans (Rossell, 1978a; Welch and Light, 1987). In addition, the level of interracial exposure was initially about 15 points higher and about 10 points higher after five years under the mandatory plans than under the old voluntary plans (Rossell, 1978a). Finally, the mandatory reassignment plans were always more effective in desegregating *black* schools than the earlier voluntary plans because under the latter no whites ever volunteered for black schools.

Thus, the conventional wisdom of the 1970s, based on empirical observation, was that mandatory reassignment plans were more effective than voluntary plans in desegregating school systems. However, the advent of comprehensive, court-ordered, magnet–voluntary plans in 1976 changed all this. As the research presented here indicates, magnet–voluntary plans desegregate a school system more effectively than either mandatory reassignment plans or the pre-1968 freedom-of-choice plans. Moreover, unlike the pre-1968 freedom-of-choice plans, magnet–voluntary plans are able to desegregate black schools through the use of incentives.

RANKING BY THREE CRITERIA

A ranking of the three types of desegregation plans used in the three decades since *Brown* in terms of the criteria discussed above yields the following order (Table 6.2):

Thus, as the table indicates, although conflict between equity and either the efficiency or effectiveness criterion is found in most policy areas, that is no longer the case with school desegregation policy. Currently, the most effective plan—a magnet–voluntary plan—is also the most efficient and the most equitable. It is the most effective plan because it produces the greatest interracial exposure, and the most efficient type of plan because the ratio of students assigned to students enrolled is the highest

TABLE 6.2
A RANKING OF DESEGREGATION PLANS BY EQUITY,
EFFECTIVENESS, AND EFFICIENCY

Equity	*Effectiveness*	*Efficiency*
Magnet–voluntary	Magnet–voluntary	Magnet–voluntary
Mandatory reassignment	Mandatory reassignment	Freedom-of-choice
Freedom-of-choice	Freedom-of-choice	Mandatory reassignment

of all the plans. It is the most equitable because it empowers both black and white parents and is preferred by both races. In this sense, a magnet–voluntary plan is the "new civil rights alternative" because it is the choice of the group whose civil rights have been violated, and it is the plan that will restore them to the position they would have occupied were it not for the violation—a situation in which they can freely choose to, and actually do, attend desegregated schools.

Models of Policymaking

School desegregation is not the only policy area in which it is argued that the public choice model is more efficient than the command and control model. "Market" incentives have been demonstrated on paper to be more efficient than mandates in other areas of education, as well as in such disparate policymaking areas as energy, pollution, welfare, health, and occupational safety. Why then is the command and control model so pervasive? Why are market incentives not adopted more widely by governments?

For one thing, there are extraordinary economic and technical problems to be worked out in devising the structure of incentives to be offered. For another, there are important moral objections to market incentives. Kelman has summarized the moral objections to the use of economic incentives in environmental policy. The objections are that economic incentives (1) make a social statement of indifference toward the motives of polluters, (2) fail to stigmatize polluting, and (3) bring environmental quality "into a system of markets and prices of which it previously has not been a part" (Kelman, 1981:27–28).

Thus, in many policy areas, not just school desegregation, market incentives are rejected because they are amoral (indifferent about the motives of those participating in socially undesirable behavior) or, worse, immoral ("bribing" the people responsible for the problem to act in a socially desirable manner). For all of these reasons—the technical and the philosophical—

marketplace incentives are seldom used, and the command and control model dominates policymaking.

Indeed, there may be no area of public policy in this country that relies as much on incentives to motivate socially appropriate behavior as does school desegregation. There are fewer than 20 voluntary desegregation plans with magnet schools in this country, but they represent a good deal more reliance on the market or public choice model than exists in any other policy area. Why would school desegregation, with its history of moralism, be the one policy area in which incentives have been used by policymakers?

There are probably two reasons. The first is technical. The solution is technically simpler in school desegregation than in other areas such as pollution or welfare. No one knows at what rate an effluent tax would have to be set to diminish pollution or how to monitor emissions so that polluters can be accurately charged. The guaranteed income experiments tried several income tax rates and guaranteed income levels to determine their relationship to participants' willingness to work, but economists still do not understand the relationships. Magnet school plans, by contrast, are much simpler. Although there are a few technical details to be worked out regarding the lottery process and other issues, problems are relatively easy to solve, and school districts have been able to learn from each other. The most important task of school administrators under a magnet–voluntary plan is simple—to "sell" the schools and hope for the best.

The second reason policymakers in the area of school desegregation have experimented with the market incentive model more than policymakers in other areas is probably that the moral issues are more conflicting and less clear here than in other areas. There are two contradictory moral positions in school desegregation, one supporting the command and control model and the other the public choice model. For a significant number of white Americans, the moral position in school desegregation policy is to support freedom of choice with incentives, because "forcing" equality involves favoritism. In no other policy area is it the case that the market incentive alternative is considered morally superior—in these areas market incentives are supported on grounds of efficiency.

The public choice model of school desegregation is compatible with the decisionmaking theory of disjointed incrementalism propounded by Braybrooke and Lindblom (1970). Incrementalism is a strategy of continual policy readjustments in pursuit of marginally redefined policy goals. Long-range plans are rejected in favor of short-range politically expedient plans as a result of disagreement over values and policy objectives and the difficulty of obtaining the information needed to evaluate all possible alternatives and produce a long-range plan.

The voluntary school desegregation plans in this study are more incremental than the mandatory plans. Mandatory plans are legally carved in stone; every student receives a desegregation assignment as a function of his or her race and residence, and this is fixed for the life of that plan. Although parents may subvert the plan with individual decisions to withdraw their children from the school system, this rarely results in a change in the legal document describing the plan. Voluntary plans with magnet schools, by contrast, have no student assignment other than to the neighborhood school, and no one knows who will transfer to the magnet schools. As a result, the plan is constantly in flux.

This can be seen in the court decisions. The decisions approving mandatory plans never acknowledge the possibility that some schools, although included in the plan, might not become desegregated. Court opinions approving voluntary plans, by contrast, are rife with language noting the uncertainties and dynamic nature of such plans. In *Diaz v. the San Jose Unified School District*, the court noted, "If the District exhausts the potential for voluntary transfers *without meeting desegregation goals*, it will place ethnic enrollment caps . . . on segregated schools *until* they become desegregated" (emphasis added).[6] In the Savannah desegregation case, the court rejected a specific mandatory backup *"in case* the voluntary techniques fail to desegregate completely the public schools" (emphasis added), because

> such a back-up plan . . . fails to take into account the particular problems and circumstances which might exist in three years at a particular school; moreover, it fails to recognize that some other measure may be more appropriate and more effective under circumstances which no one can today foresee. This Court refuses to recognize the validity of a "one size fits all," knee-jerk remedy under the circumstances of this case.[7]

Similarly, the district court in the Yonkers case stated:

> Should sufficient majority race students not voluntarily transfer from identifiably white schools and/or sufficient minority students not transfer to identifiably white schools, the Board shall propose its plan for accomplishing the desegregation of all its schools. . . . Those schools which do not meet the district's integration goals and which remain predominantly minority during the transition period shall provide supplemental educational services.[8]

The provision of supplemental educational services (or "Milliken II" relief) to racially isolated schools referred to in the Yonkers decision superficially resembles the courts' approval of such remedies for racially isolated schools in mandatory reassignment plans in largely black, big city school systems (e.g., St. Louis and Detroit). There is one important difference, however. In the mandatory reassignment plans, the schools that would remain racially isolated would be known and named in the opinion because they would be intentionally excluded. In Yonkers, the schools are not named, because no one knows which ones, if any, will remain racially isolated.

Thus, a fundamental difference between a mandatory and a voluntary plan is that in the latter, uncertainty about the exact characteristics and outcome of the plan is explicitly noted and approved in the court opinion. In the mandatory plans, uncertainty regarding white compliance and its effect on the plan's characteristics is completely ignored. Voluntary desegregation plans with magnet schools are thus explicitly incremental and serial and, as Braybrooke and Lindblom (1970) would have predicted, usually more successful than the mandatory plans.

On the other hand, the magnet–voluntary plans also differ among themselves in the extent to which they are incremental and serial. Plans that use mandatory components such as enrollment caps and forced choices because of short timetables and overly ambitious annual goals may have more white flight than those with no mandatory elements. Though data on this issue are sparse, it is quite possible that the more serial and incremental the voluntary plan, the more interracial exposure it ultimately produces.

Thus, Hochschild's conclusion that incremental policymaking works poorly to desegregate schools and that "race relations worsen, minority self-esteem declines, black achievement declines absolutely or relatively, white flight and citizen resentment increase" (Hochschild, 1984:91) is simply not supported by the data. Indeed, the evidence presented in this book suggests exactly the opposite—more incremental policymaking works better than less incremental policymaking to desegregate schools because it causes less white flight and less citizen resentment. Since the benefits of desegregation flow from interracial exposure and, all other things being equal, there is greater interracial exposure with less white flight and resentment, it follows that the benefits to minorities will be greater with incremental approaches.

In a sense, voluntary plans, because they resort to the "invisible hand" of the market, produce less conflict than a government mandate and ultimately more interracial exposure. Hence, Braybrooke and Lindblom (1970) may be right when they defend the strategy of disjointed incrementalism against the charge that it is inherently conservative, arguing that it is more likely to result in real policy change than a more synoptic or comprehensive policymaking process.

Hochschild ends her book with the conclusion that racism is not an anomaly within liberal democracy—that the history of school desegregation provides much more support for the symbiosis thesis. She argues that racism and its psychological, structural, and behavioral consequences are so deeply embedded in American society that the standard practices of incrementalism and popular control will not eradicate it (Hochschild, 1984:203–4).

The data presented in this analysis refute this conclusion. Racism is not so deeply embedded in American society that substantial proportions of Americans cannot be persuaded to enroll their children voluntarily in desegregated magnet schools with superior resources. Furthermore, the public choice model and the theory of disjointed incrementalism, as adapted to school desegregation policy, have a moral quality despite the notion that parents are acting in their self-interest. If deliberation and the exercise of choice are the essence of what it means to be human, a policy that allows choice and also achieves a socially desirable goal is the morally superior alternative.

Notes

CHAPTER 1
The Past and Future of Desegregation Remedies

1. *Brown v. Board of Education of Topeka*, 347 U.S. 483 (1954).

2. See *Bush v. Orleans Parish School Board*, 308 F. 2d 491 (1962); *Northcross v. Board of Education*, 302 F. 2d 818, 370 U.S. 944 (1962).

3. *Green v. County School Board of New Kent County* [Virginia], 391 U.S. 430 (1968).

4. *Alexander v. Holmes County Board of Education*, 396 U.S. 19 (1969).

5. *Swann v. Charlotte–Mecklenburg Board of Education*, 402 U.S. 1 (1971).

6. Ibid., pp. 24, 25.

7. Ibid., p. 26.

8. Ibid., p. 28.

9. Ibid., pp. 29–31.

10. *Northcross v. Board of Education*, 489 F. 2d 15, 16–17 (1973).

11. *Thompson v. School Board*, 363 F. Supp. 458, 461–62 (1973).

12. *Keyes v. School District No. 1, Denver, Colorado*, 413 U.S. 189 (1973).

13. Data in Figure 1.1 are from two different studies: Taylor, Sheatsley, and Greeley (1978:42–49) and Farley and Wurdock (1977). To make the measures used by the two studies comparable, the Treiman scale of racial tolerance is reversed so that it measures racial intolerance—that is, the failure to give a pro-integration response to the five questions or statements used in the scale. This makes it comparable to the index of dissimilarity (racial imbalance) in that the higher the number, the more unfavorable or pejorative a condition reflected by the measure. The five questions or statements in the Treiman scale are as follows: (1) "Do you think white students and Negro students should go to the same schools or to separate schools?" (2) "How strongly

would you object if a member of your family wanted to bring a Negro friend home to dinner?" (3) "White people have a right to keep Negroes out of their neighborhoods if they want to and Negroes should respect that right." (4) "Do you think there should be laws against marriages between Negroes and whites?" (5) "Negroes shouldn't push themselves where they're not wanted."

14. White enrollment loss is calculated as follows: white enrollment in one year is subtracted from white enrollment the previous year, and the difference is divided by white enrollment the previous year. This figure is then multiplied by 100 to produce a percentage. This is a standard and widely accepted method of calculating annual white enrollment loss.

15. Of course, assuming that the increase in white enrollment loss that occurs with the implementation of a plan results from desegregation is controversial. I have used here the most common method of estimating white flight. Step one of this method involves estimating a predesegregation trend by averaging annual percentage losses over several years or by fitting a straight line to the annual percentage losses in those years. Then one calculates the difference between pre- and postdesegregation annual losses. The difference is assumed to be due to desegregation. Although this is the most common method, it is reasonably reliable only for a short period after the implementation of desegregation because the underlying demographic trends will change after a few years of desegregation and the predesegregation trend will not be an accurate reflection of the "true" postdesegregation demographic trend.

16. A Harris Poll found that the proportion had declined to 57 percent by 1986 (Harris Poll, 1987), but most analysts do not believe this poll, since it contrasts so sharply with every other poll.

17. Although the Appeals Court was not very sanguine about the success of the magnet programs in desegregating two black schools, Jones and Walthall, it overturned the federal district court decision on grounds that the voluntary magnet school plan, "even if the magnet schools come up to expectations, is fatally flawed, because it leaves virtually untouched two historically black schools, Bethune and Eureka, each having almost a totally black student body" (*United States v. Pittman, v. The State of Mississippi and Hattiesburg Municipal Separate School District*, 808 F. 2d 385 [1987] 390). Thus, the fatal flaw was the *lack* of magnet programs in Bethune and Eureka. Unfortunately,

the mandatory reassignment plan that was implemented in place of the magnet–voluntary plan caused almost a 30 percent white enrollment loss at the elementary level over two years, only slightly more than the 28 percent loss that I predicted (Rossell, 1985c) for a similar mandatory reassignment plan on the basis of the school loss rates, described above, in Baton Rouge and Los Angeles.

18. *Arthur v. Nyquist*, 415 F. Supp. 904 (1976).

19. *Amos v. Board of Directors of the City of Milwaukee*, 408 F. Supp. 765 (1976).

20. *Armstrong v. O'Connell*, 416 F. Supp. 1377 (1977); *Armstrong v. Board of School Directors*, 471 F. Supp. 800 (1979).

21. *Stell and U.S. v. The Board of Public Education for the City of Savannah and the County of Chatham et al.* (C.A. 1316, June 5, 1988, Edenfield, J.), (1988) p. 3.

22. Ibid., p. 7.

23. Ibid., p. 41. The court cited *Davis v. Board of Commissioners*, 402 U.S. 33, 37 (1971), and *Calhoun v. Cook*, 522 F. 2d 717, 525 F. 2d 1203 (1975).

24. 391 U.S. at 440.

25. 402 U.S. at 26.

CHAPTER 2

Defining Desegregation and Its Goal

1. The 15 percentage point deviation was once part of the California Administrative Code for defining a segregated school.

2. *Diaz v. San Jose Unified School District*, 633 F. Supp. 808 (1985); *United States and NAACP v. Yonkers Board of Education, et al.* 635 F. Supp. 1538 (1986); *Stell and United States v. The Board of Public Education for the City of Savannah and the County of Chatham et al.* (C.A. 1316, June 5, 1988).

3. Cooperative learning is an instructional technique that produces achievement gains among low-achieving children and cooperative interracial contact among children of different races by restructuring the classroom into heterogeneous academic teams of students who compete against one another. It thus substitutes the incentives of the athletic team for the anomie of the individualist classroom. See Slavin (1978, 1979, 1983).

4. The index of dissimilarity originates with Duncan and Duncan (1955) but it has been most closely associated with Taeuber and Taeuber (1965). It has been used in numerous other studies of school and residential racial imbalance, including Farley (1981); Farley, Wurdock, and Richards (1980); Smylie (1983); and Van Valey, Roof, and Wilcox (1977). Coulter (1989:44) argues, however, that the denominator 2 is correct only for large systems. The denominator should actually be

$$2\left(1 - \min \frac{W_i}{W}\right) \quad \text{where} \quad \min \frac{W_i}{W}$$

is the smallest proportion white in any school in the district.

5. The measure of interracial exposure has been used in several more recent studies of school desegregation to estimate the outcome of a plan: for example, Farley (1981), Orfield (1982, 1988), Orfield and Monfort (1986), Ross (1983), and Rossell (1978a, 1979, 1986a).

6. This score is derived by dividing the number of minorities in each school by the school district total of minorities (in this case, 300), dividing the number of whites in the same school by the school district total of whites (6), subtracting the two amounts for a given school from each other (ignoring minus signs), summing this calculation across all the schools and dividing by two or corrected two (see note 4). Thus, it is a standardized measure whose criteria—racial balance—change as the school district's racial proportions change.

7. *Diaz v. San Jose Unified School District,* 633 F. Supp. 808 (1986); *United States and NAACP v. Yonkers Board of Education, et al.,* 635 F. Supp. 1538 (1986); *Stell and United States v. The Board of Public Education for the City of Savannah and the County of Chatham et al.* (C.A. 1316, June 5, 1988, Edenfield, J.).

8. *United States and Pittman v. The State of Mississippi and Hattiesburg Municipal Separate School District,* 622 F. Supp. 622 (1985).

9. *United States v. Pittman v. The State of Mississippi and Hattiesburg Municipal Separate School District,* 808 F. 2d 385 (5th Cir. 1987).

10. *U.S. and Nichols v. Natchez Municipal Separate School District* (C.A. 1120-W, June 24, 1989, unpublished opinion).

11. An example of how not to use interracial exposure can be seen in a study by Orfield (1988:28), where he lists for 24 "cities" the percentage of students who are white in the school of the average black student in 1980 and whether there was a mandatory busing plan.

There is no control for the student percentage white before desegregation. The "cities" with a high percentage white in the average black
child's school tend to be those with mandatory plans. They are also
largely countywide southern school districts that were about 80 to 90
percent white before desegregation. The cities with a low percentage
white in the average black child's school tend to be those with voluntary plans. They are also, with one exception, big cities whose school
districts were about 30 to 45 percent white before desegregation.
Needless to say, a comparative "analysis" without an adjustment for
the predesegregation percentage white is incomplete and misleading.

CHAPTER 3
Comparison of Voluntary and Mandatory Plans

Acknowledgment. Parts of the analysis presented in this chapter were
first published in "The Carrot or the Stick for School Desegregation
Policy?" *Urban Affairs Quarterly* 25, no. 3 (1990):477–502; and in
"How Effective Are Voluntary Plans with Magnet Schools?" *Educational Evaluation and Policy Analysis* 10 (1989):325–42.

1. Fourteen of the 18 school districts chosen by Abt Associates
were in the sample of 113 school districts I have analyzed and written
about since 1978. The 4 school districts that were added to the original
113-school-district sample because they are in the Abt Associates
study are Dallas, Texas; Montclair, New Jersey; Montgomery County,
Maryland; and Stockton, California. (Two other school districts, Port
Arthur, Texas, and Tucson, Arizona, were also added to the original
113 school districts because researchers reported they had magnet–voluntary plans.) The total of school districts in the larger study is
now 119.

2. *Arthur v. Nyquist*, 566 F. Supp. 511 (1983) at 515.

3. See, for example, *Tasby v. Estes (Wright) (Dallas Independent
School District)*, 342 F. Supp. 945 (1971); 517 F. 2d 92 (1975); 412 F.
Supp. 1192 (1976); 412 F. Supp. 1185 (1976); 572 F. 2d 1010 (1978); 444
U.S. 437 (1980); 520 F. Supp. 683 (1981); 542 F. Supp. 134 (1981); 559 F.
Supp. 9 (1982); 713 F. 2d 90 (1983); 585 F. Supp. 453 (1984); 771 F. 2d
849 (1985); 630 F. Supp. 597 (1986); and numerous unpublished opin-
ions, which can be obtained directly from the court.

4. Chicago and Philadelphia, two districts with nationally known magnet–voluntary plans, could not be included in the sample instead of Cincinnati and San Bernardino, because that would have made the voluntary plan sample even less comparable to the mandatory plan sample than it is now and would have violated the original Abt Associates sampling criterion that district enrollments be between 10 and 60 percent minority. (The Chicago and Philadelphia plans are, however, analyzed in Chapter 5.)

5. Two of the school districts in this sample (Montgomery County and Jefferson County) are countywide, and therefore the population characteristics given for them are for the county, not the city.

6. *Stell and United States v. The Board of Public Education for the City of Savannah and the County of Chatham et al.* (C.A. 1316, June 5, 1988, Edenfield, J.).

7. Since the time of this study, however, San Diego has converted all of its elementary magnet programs to dedicated magnets, even though the change has had the effect of producing many magnet schools, and thus magnet programs, that are 75 to 80 percent minority.

8. Of course, it should be noted that the 1970 mandatory plan was limited. It reassigned between 3 and 6 percent of the white students and reduced racial balance by only 9 percentage points between 1970 and 1974. In terms of change, the 1968 plan was the most successful of all—it reduced racial imbalance by 11 percentage points between 1968 and 1969.

9. *NAACP v. San Bernardino City Unified School District et al.*, 17 C. 3d 311 (1976); 130 Cal. Rptr. 744.551 p. 2d 48 at 325–26.

10. *Bronson et al. v. Board of Education of the City School District of the City of Cincinnati*, 604 F. Supp. 68 (1984) at 76 approved a "Taeuber Index" (i.e., index of dissimilarity) of "approximately 36 by the 1990–91 school year."

11. As noted above, this is measured as white enrollment in one year minus white enrollment the previous year, divided by white enrollment the previous year and multiplied by 100 to create a percentage.

12. Data were estimated for all measures for San Bernardino T + 8 and T + 9, and for San Diego and Des Moines T + 9, by averaging the change in the last two years for which there were data. For white enrollment change in Cincinnati, Portland, and Dallas, T − 3 data were based on the T − 2 data. A hard copy of the summary data for each school district for all analyses presented in this chapter can be ob-

tained from the author, Political Science Department, Boston University, Boston, MA 02215; phone: 617-353-2973.

13. This comparison, however, is less reliable than that for school districts above 30 percent minority, since only two school districts below 30 percent minority have voluntary plans. They are Portland and Tacoma.

14. This analysis shows findings contrary to those of Willie and Fultz's (1984) chapter comparing white flight in Boston and Milwaukee. There are numerous problems with that analysis, including data that are simply erroneous. See my review (1985a) of the book in which it appeared (Willie, 1984).

15. In general, the changing demographics of the metropolitan area will already be reflected in the predesegregation white enrollment decline. Nevertheless, given the controversy surrounding these issues, it probably pays to be somewhat redundant.

16. Bennett (1986) the former deputy superintendent of Milwaukee, offers a counterargument regarding the burden issue in a voluntary plan.

17. As noted above, although technically the post-1981 trend should have been adjusted for the effect of the mandatory reassignments, that would have increased interracial exposure rather than reducing it, enhancing the superiority of the voluntary plans. (The addition of mandatory reassignments increased interracial exposure by only 2.8 points—less than the annual gains under the voluntary plan.)

18. The first column represents the average for that variable in this sample. The r represents the simple correlation between interracial exposure (the percentage white in the average black child's school) and each of the independent variables on the left. The b represents the change in interracial exposure for a one-unit change in each of the variables listed on the left, holding all the other variables constant. The Beta is a standardized regression coefficient that tells us the relative strength of each of these variables in predicting interracial exposure, in standard deviation units, holding all other variables constant. The larger the Beta, the stronger the relationship. The standard error of the b (SE b) is the variability in b regression coefficients that might be found in subsequent samples drawn from the same population. If the standard error of the b is larger than the b, we can have no confidence in the sign of the coefficient—that is, we will not know whether it is a positive or a negative relationship.

19. The b coefficient for "voluntary plan" is −1.061 and for "time" times "voluntary" .947.

20. The b coefficient for "voluntary plan" is −3.434 and for "time" times "voluntary" .979.

21. With Buffalo's interracial exposure set at the 1980 level beginning with 1981, the b coefficient for "voluntary" is −4.359 and for "time" times "voluntary" is .879.

22. The 1982 average white enrollment loss for the districts with mandatory plans was 6 percent. For the districts with voluntary plans it was 2.6 percent.

CHAPTER 4
What Is Attractive About Magnet Schools?

1. One exception to this is found in the Lowry and Associates study that concludes, in apparent contradiction of twenty years of research as well as common sense, that there is no significant correlation between magnet location and desegregation success within magnets themselves (Blank et al., 1983:88). Its measure of desegregation success (pp. IV-3, IV-4), however, is so strange as to render the entire chapter IV, "Desegregating Public School Systems," written by Robert Dentler, unintelligible. Rather than using any of the precise mathematical measures of racial balance or interracial contact developed in the last two decades, Dentler constructs magnet desegregation success from the sum of interviewer ratings from 0 to 100 on four factors, only one of which measures student desegregation. These factors are the following:

1. Magnet school desegregation success: 100 = three sites fully desegregated (defined as "equalized access" and "substantial mix," p. 78); 0 = none of three sites desegregated
2. Voluntariness: 100 = three sites' students are there by parent preferences; 0 = no sites have students there by parent preference
3. Extent of staff desegregation: 100 = three sites' staffs desegregated; 0 = none desegregated
4. Quality of integration scale, composed of interviewer ratings of 10 items of equal status contact.

The four measures of district desegregation and the role of magnets are composed in the same way—as a function of interviewer ratings from 0 to 100 of the "vigorousness" of the effort and the "singular role" of magnets. As one might expect, the conclusions drawn from the statistical analyses of such variables make no sense and, in some cases, run counter to all previous research. This review will therefore simply ignore the Blank et al., findings on desegregation.

2. This is the percentage who express a willingness to send a child to a magnet school with a given theme prior to questions regarding the racial composition and location of the school.

3. There were no interaction effects between "voluntary plan" and the school district and school variables, and so these variables were not included in this final equation.

4. The coefficient for a high school magnet can be interpreted only by adding it to the coefficient for the interaction variable, "careers" times "high school." The net effect is $-.01$ for high school careers magnets and a positive, significant $.08$ coefficient for the 17 percent of high schools that are not vocational or careers magnets.

5. Given the success of all magnets in attaining their predesegregation enrollment and the success of magnets in white locations in attaining the desired minority enrollment, these goals are not analyzed further.

CHAPTER 5
What Have Desegregation Plans Accomplished?

1. *Swann v. Charlotte-Mecklenburg Board of Education*, 402 U.S. 1 (1971).

2. *Keyes v. School District No. 1, Denver, Colorado*, 474 F. Supp. 1265 (1979).

3. *Kelly v. Guinn (Clark County, Las Vegas, School District)*, 456 F. 2d 100 (9th Cir. 1972).

4. *U.S. and NAACP v. Yonkers Board of Education*, 635 F. Supp. 1538 (1980).

5. A hard copy of the individual district data for each of the tables presented in this chapter may be obtained by writing or telephoning the author at Political Science Department, Boston University, Boston, MA 02215; phone: 617-353-2973.

6. This is calculated as total enrollment in 1984 minus total enrollment in 1970, divided by total enrollment in 1970 and multiplied by 100 to create a percentage.

7. Wilmington, Delaware, is excluded from this change analysis because of the misleading and dramatic increase in the percentage of pupils who are white due solely to its merger with 10 other suburban school districts into one school district—New Castle County. This was then divided into four school districts in 1980.

8. See note 11 in Chapter 2.

9. *Bronson et al. v. Board of Education of the City School District of the City of Cincinnati*, 604 F. Supp. 68 (1984) at 76.

10. In reverse chronological order, these cases are *United States and Nichols v. Natchez Special Municipal Separate School District*, 1989; *Stell and United States v. the Board of Public Education for the City of Savannah and the County of Chatham*, 1988; *Pitts v. Freeman*, 1987; *United States and NAACP v. Yonkers Board of Education, City of Yonkers and Yonkers Community Development Agency*, 1986; *Diaz v. San Jose Unified School District*, 1986; *United States and Pittman v. The State of Mississippi and Hattiesburg Municipal Separate School District*, 1986; *United States v. Texas Education Agency (Lubbock Independent School District)*, 1985; *Vaughns v. Board of Education of Prince George's County*, 1985; *United States v. Marion County*, 1984; *Davis and United States v. East Baton Rouge Parish School District*, 1983; *United States v. Texas Education Agency (Port Arthur Independent School District)*, 1980; *Seattle School District No. 1 v. State of Washington*, 1979; *Carlin v. San Diego Unified School District*, 1979.

11. *Stell and United States v. the Board of Public Education for the City of Savannah and the County of Chatham* (C.A. 1316, June 5, 1988, Edenfield, J.); *United States and NAACP v. Yonkers Board of Education, City of Yonkers and Yonkers Community Development Agency*, 635 F. Supp. 1538 (1986); *Diaz v. San Jose Unified School District*, 633 F. Supp. 808 (1986). The U.S. Department of Education has also used plus or minus 20 percentage points as a criterion. This was approved by a district court in *Adams v. Richardson*, 356 F. Supp. 92 (1973). Other court decisions have approved an absolute range (i.e., all schools should be 30 to 70 percent minority) that contains a 35 to 40 point range (or greater) as with the plus or minus 20 percentage point criterion. Some of these decisions are *Armstrong v. Board of School Directors* (Milwaukee), 471 F. Supp. 800 (1979); *Arthur v. Nyquist* (Buffalo), 573 F. 2d 134 (1978); *Arthur v. Nyquist* (Buffalo), 429 F. Supp. 206 (1977); *Arthur v. Nyquist* (Buffalo), 415 F. Supp. 904 (1976);

Calhoun v. Cook (Atlanta), 362 F. Supp. 1249 (1973); *Vaughns v. Board of Education of Prince George's County*, 355 F. Supp. 1044 (1972); *Vaughns v. Board of Education of Prince George's County*, 574 F. Supp. 1280 (1983).

12. *Bradley v. Milliken*, 402 F. Supp. 1096 (1975); *Liddell v. Board of Education of the City of St. Louis*, 469 F. Supp. 1304 (1979); *Liddell v. Board of Education of the City of St. Louis*, 491 F. Supp. 351 (1980).

13. *Pasadena City Board of Education et al. v. Spangler et al.*, 427 U.S. 424 (1976).

14. *United States and NAACP v. Yonkers Board of Education*, 635 F. Supp. 1538 (1986) at 1543.

15. *Armstrong v. Board of School Directors* (Milwaukee), 471 F. Supp. 800 (1979).

16. *Arthur v. Nyquist* (Buffalo), 514 F. Supp. 1133 (1981).

17. The 80 percent, or less, minority definition of a desegregated school was used in Prince George's County, Maryland, in *Vaughns v. Board of Education of Prince George's County*, 574 F. Supp. 1280 (1983). The 90 percent, or more, minority definition of a segregated school was used in Houston in *Ross and United States v. Houston Independent School District*, unpublished opinion, July 18, 1975. There are numerous others.

18. On the other hand, Robert Crain, a well-known and highly regarded supporter of school desegregation, testified on behalf of the Philadelphia magnet school plan in *Pennsylvania Human Relations Commission v. School District of Philadelphia*, 443 A. 2d 1343 (1982).

CHAPTER 6
Conclusions and Recommendations

1. *Green v. County School Board of New Kent County*, 391 U.S. 430 (1968) at 442.

2. The term "Milliken II relief" refers to special compensatory education programs placed in racially isolated minority schools as a substitute for desegregation. It comes from the U.S. district court decision, *Bradley v. Milliken*, 402 F. Supp. 1096 (1975), in which whites in the Detroit school system were assigned to formerly black schools at up to a 50 percent white ratio, while the remaining racially isolated mi-

nority schools were given special compensatory education programs. This was the second phase of litigation (hence the designation "II") necessitated by the Supreme Court decision in *Milliken v. Bradley*, 418 U.S. 717 (1974), overturning the earlier district court decision (*Bradley v. Milliken*, 345 F. Supp. 914 [1972]) requiring cross-district desegregation transfers between the city of Detroit and 53 suburban school districts so as to desegregate all schools in the city at a predominantly white racial composition.

3. *U.S. and Nichols v. Natchez Special Municipal Separate School District*, C.A. 1120-W, U.S. District Court for the Southern District of Mississippi, Western Division, unpublished opinion June 24, 1989.

4. Three of the four plaintiff and plaintiff–intervenors were white; the most junior member was black.

5. *Green v. County School Board of New Kent County*, 391 U.S. 430 (1968).

6. *Diaz v. San Jose Unified School District*, 633 F. Supp. 808 (1986) at 813.

7. *Stell and United States v. The Board of Public Education for the City of Savannah and the County of Chatham*, Civil Action No. 1316, June 3, 1988, at 50.

8. *United States and NAACP v. Yonkers Board of Education et al.*, 635 F. Supp. 1538 at 1544.

References

Abram, Morris B. (1984). "What Constitutes a Civil Right?" *New York Times Magazine*, June 10, pp. 52–64.

Alkin, Marvin C. (1983). "Magnet School Programs Evaluation: Assessing a Desegregation Effort." Paper presented at the annual meeting of the American Educational Research Association, Montreal, April.

Almond, Gabriel, and Sydney Verba (1963). *The Civic Culture: Political Attitudes and Democracy in Five Nations*. Princeton: Princeton University Press.

Alves, Michael J., and Charles V. Willie (1987). "Controlled Choice Assignments: A New And More Effective Approach to School Desegregation," *Urban Review* 19, no. 2:67–86.

Arias, Beatrice (1986). "Compliance Monitor's First Semi-annual Report: *Vasquez v. San Jose Unified School District*." San Francisco: U.S. District Court.

Armor, David J. (1980). "White Flight and the Future of School Desegregation." In Walter G. Stephan and Joseph R. Feagin (eds.), *School Desegregation: Past, Present, and Future*. New York: Plenum Press.

———(1989). "Survey of Natchez-Adams School District Public School Parents, Desegregation Concepts," Exhibit D-18, *U.S. and Nichols v. Natchez Municipal Separate School District*, Federal District Court, Jackson, Mississippi.

Barndt, Michael; Rick Janka; and Harold Rose (1981). "The West and Midwest, Milwaukee, Wisconsin: Mobilization for School and Community Cooperation." In Charles V. Willie and Susan L. Greenblatt (eds.), *Community Politics and Educational Change: Ten School Systems Under Court Order*. New York: Longman.

Bednarek, David I. (1977). "Milwaukee." *Integrated Education* 15, no. 6: 36–37.

Bell, Derrick (1980). "Brown and the Interest-Convergence Dilemma."

In Derrick Bell (ed.), *Shades of Brown: New Perspectives on School Desegregation*. New York: Teachers College Press.

Bennett, David A. (1986). "The School Desegregation Plan: Elements of the Architecture." Working Paper, National School Desegregation Project. Chicago: University of Chicago.

Blank, Rolf K. (1989). "Educational Effects of Magnet School." Paper presented at the Conference on Choice and Control in American Education, University of Wisconsin, Madison, May 17–19, 1989.

Blank, Rolf K.; Robert A. Dentler; D. Catherine Baltzell; and Kent Chabotar (1983). *Survey of Magnet Schools: Analyzing a Model for Quality Integrated Education*. Chicago: James H. Lowry and Associates.

Board of Education, Yonkers, N.Y. (1986). "Educational Improvement Plan for the Yonkers Public Schools." Yonkers: Board of Education.

Board of Public Education for the City of Savannah and the County of Chatham (1986). *Long Range Plan*. Savannah, Ga.: Board of Education.

Board of Public Education for the City of Savannah and the County of Chatham (1988). *Revised Plan*. Savannah, Ga.: Board of Education.

Bortin, Barbara H. (1982). "Magnet School Program: Evaluation Report, 1980–1981, Milwaukee ESAA Title IV." Milwaukee: Milwaukee Public Schools, Department of Educational Research and Program Assessment.

Boston Globe (1987). "Keeping Boston Whole." September 25:20.

Boston Public Schools (1987–88). "Student Assignment Information." Boston: Boston Public Schools.

Braddock, II, Jomills Henry; Robert Crain; and James McPartland (1984). "A Long-Term View of School Desegregation: Some Recent Studies of Graduates as Adults." *Phi Delta Kappan* 66:259–64.

Braybrooke, David, and Charles E. Lindblom (1970). *A Strategy of Decision*. New York: Free Press.

Buchanan, James M., and Robert D. Tollison (eds.) (1984). *The Theory of Public Choice—II*. Ann Arbor: University of Michigan Press.

Buchanan, James M., and Gordon Tullock (1962). *The Calculus of Consent*. Ann Arbor: University of Michigan Press.

Buffalo Public Schools (1987–88). "Magnet Schools." Buffalo, N.Y.: Buffalo Public Schools.

Bullock, Charles S. (1976). "Desegregating Urban Areas: Is It Worth It?" In Florence Levinsohn and Benjamin Wright (eds.), *School Desegregation: Shadow and Substance*. Chicago: University of Chicago Press.

Caditz, Judith (1975). "Dilemmas Over Racial Integration: Status Consciousness vs. Direct Threat." *Sociological Inquiry* 45:51–58.

——— (1976). *White Liberals in Transition*. New York: Spectrum Press.

Cataldo, Everett (1982). "Enrollment Decline and School Desegregation in Cleveland: An Analysis of Trends and Causes." Cleveland: Office of School Monitoring and Community Relations, Cleveland Public Schools.

Charpentier, Roland (1984). "Worcester's Extended-Day Kindergarten Program: Equity Initiatives Lead to Program Improvement." *Equity and Choice* 1, no. 1: 25–30.

Citywide Educational Coalition (1978). "Survey of Magnet School Parents in Three Cities." Report to the Massachusetts Department of Education, Boston.

Clotfelter, Charles T. (1981). "Statement to the Senate Judiciary Committee, Subcommittee on the Separation of Powers" (J-97-29), 97th Congress, 1st Session, September 30.

Coleman, James S. (1977). "Population Stability and Equal Rights." *Society* 14:34–36.

Coleman, James S.; Sara D. Kelly; and John A. Moore (1975a). "Recent Trends in School Integration." Paper presented at the annual meeting of the American Educational Research Association, Washington, D.C., April.

——— (1975b). *Trends in School Segregation, 1968–1973*. Washington, D.C.: Urban Institute.

Comerford, James P. (1980). "Parent Perceptions and Pupil Characteristics of a Senior Magnet School Program." *Integrated Education* 18 (Sept.–Dec.):50–54.

Cooper, Kenneth J. (1982). "Parents Take New Busing Tack." *Boston Globe*, February 21:107.

Coulter, Philip B. (1989). *Measuring Inequality*. Boulder, Colo.: Westview Press.

Crain, Robert, and Jack Strauss (1985). "School Desegregation and Black Occupational Attainments: Results from a Long-Term

Experiment." Baltimore: Johns Hopkins University, Center for Social Organization of Schools.

Cunningham, George K., and William L. Husk (1979). "A Metropolitan Desegregation Plan: Where the White Students Went." Paper presented at the annual meeting of the American Educational Research Association, San Francisco, April.

Dennis, Jack (1973). *Socialization in Politics*. New York: Wiley.

Downs, Anthony (1957). *An Economic Theory of Democracy*. New York: Harper & Row.

Duncan, Otis D., and Beverly Duncan (1955). "A Methodological Analysis of Segregation Indexes." *American Sociological Review* 20 (March):210–17.

Easton, David A. (1965). *A Systems Analysis of Political Life*. New York: Wiley.

Erbe, Brigette M. (1977). "The Politics of School Busing." *Public Opinion Quarterly* 41:113–17.

Estabrook, Leigh S. (1980). "The Effect of Desegregation on Parents' Evaluation of Schools." Ph.D. dissertation, Boston University.

Farley, Reynolds (1975). "Racial Integration in the Public Schools, 1967–1972: Assessing the Effects of Government Policies." *Sociological Focus* 8:3–26.

———— (1981). "Final Report, NIE Grant #G-79-0151." Ann Arbor: University of Michigan, Population Studies Center.

Farley, Reynolds, and Clarence Wurdock (1977). "Integrating Schools in the Nation's Largest Cities: What Has Been Accomplished and What Is Yet to Be Done?" Manuscript. Ann Arbor, Mich.

Farley, Reynolds; Clarence Wurdock; and Toni Richards (1980). "School Desegregation and White Flight: An Investigation of Competing Models and Their Discrepant Findings." *Sociology of Education* 53:123–39.

Fleming, Patricia S.; Rolf K. Blank; Robert A. Dentler; and D. Catherine Baltzell (1982). *Survey of Magnet Schools: Interim Report*. Chicago: James H. Lowry and Associates.

Flood, Dudley E. (1978). "The Magnet School Concept in North Carolina." Paper presented at the International Magnet School Conference, New Orleans, January.

Foushee, Raymond, and Douglas Hamilton (1977). "Housing Desegregation Increases as Schools Desegregate in Jefferson County." Louisville: Kentucky Commission on Human Rights.

Frey, William H. (1977). "Central City White Flight: Racial and Nonracial Causes." Paper presented at the annual meeting of the American Sociological Association, Chicago, September.

Friedman, Milton (1962). *Capitalism and Freedom*. Chicago: University of Chicago Press.

Friedman, Milton, and Rose Friedman (1981). *Free to Choose*. New York: Avon.

Gaines, Margie L. (1987). "Evaluating Magnet Schools Effectively: Challenges and Cautions." Austin, Tex.: Austin Independent School District, Office of Research and Evaluation.

Gallup Poll (1972). *The Gallup Poll, 1959–1971*, vol. 3. Princeton, N.J.: Gallup Poll.

——— (1976). *Gallup Opinion Index*. No. 127, February.

——— (1980). "Whites and Blacks in Sharp Disagreement on Busing: White Parents' Acceptance of Integrated Schools Has Grown Since 1958." No. 30, December 5–8.

——— (1982). *Survey* 202–G, Q. 7. No. 9, September 17–20.

Gatlin, Douglas; Micheal Giles; and Everett Cataldo (1978). "Policy Support Within a Target Group: The Case of School Desegregation." *American Political Science Review* 72:985–95.

Giles, Micheal; Everett Cataldo; and Douglas Gatlin (1975). "White Flight and Percent Black: The Tipping Point Reexamined." *Social Science Quarterly* 56:85–92.

Giles, Micheal; Douglas Gatlin; and Everett Cataldo (1976). *Determinants of Resegregation: Compliance/Rejection Behavior and Policy Alternatives*. Report to the National Science Foundation. Boca Raton: Florida Atlantic University.

Glazer, Nathan (1985a). "Freedom of Choice." Paper presented at Alternative or Supplemental Avenues for Reform, conference on the Law, Theory, and Reality of Equal Education, Harvard Law School, Cambridge, Mass., April.

——— (1985b). "The Future Under Tuition Tax Credits." In Thomas James and Henry M. Levin (eds.), *Public Dollars for Private Schools: The Case of Tuition Tax Credits*. Philadelphia: Temple University Press.

Greenwood, Noel (1972). "School Desegregation—Successes, Failures, Surprises." *Los Angeles Times*, May 21:C1.

Harris, Ian M. (1983). "The Inequities of Milwaukee's Plan." *Integrated Education* 21, nos. 1–6:173–77.

Harris Survey (1987). "Number Opposed to Busing for Racial Purposes Drops 25 Points Over 10-Year Period." January 5. New York: Harris Survey.

Hawley, Willis D. (ed.) (1981). *Effective School Desegregation.* Beverly Hills, Calif.: Sage.

Hawley, Willis D.; Robert L. Crain; Christine H. Rossell; et al. (1983). *Strategies for Effective Desegregation.* Lexington, Mass.: Lexington Books.

Hawley, Willis D., and Mark A. Smylie (1986). "The Contribution of School Desegregation to Academic Achievement and Racial Integration." In P. A. Katz and D. G. Taylor (eds.), *Eliminating Racism: Fears and Controversies.* New York: Pergamon.

Hochschild, Jennifer (1984). *The New American Dilemma.* New Haven, Conn.: Yale University Press.

Hula, Richard C. (1984). "Housing Market Effects of Public School Desegregation: The Case of Dallas, Texas." *Urban Affairs Quarterly* 19:409–23.

Husk, William L. (1980). *"School Desegregation in Jefferson County, Kentucky, Five Years Later: Where Are the Students?"* Paper presented at the annual meeting of the American Educational Research Association, Boston, March.

Jacobson, Cardell K. (1978). "Desegregation Rulings and Public Attitude Changes: White Resistance or Resignation?" *American Journal of Sociology* 84:698–705.

Jud, G. Donald (1982). "School Quality and Intra-Metropolitan Mobility: A Further Test of the Tiebout Hypothesis." Greensboro: North Carolina University, Center for Applied Research.

Kelley, Jonathan (1974). "The Politics of School Busing." *Public Opinion Quarterly* 38:23–39.

Kelman, Steven (1981). *What Price Incentives? Economists and the Environment.* Boston: Auburn House.

Kentucky Commission on Human Rights (1975). "Six Ways to Avoid Busing." Louisville: Kentucky Commission on Human Rights.

——— (1980a). "Blacks Moving to Suburban Apartments." Louisville: Kentucky Commission on Human Rights.

——— (1980b). "Housing and School Desegregation Increased by Section 8 Moves: Under Public Housing Program Most Black Families Chose Jefferson County Suburbs." Louisville: Kentucky Commission on Human Rights.

Kinder, Donald R., and Laurie A. Rhodebeck (1982). "Continuities in

Support for Racial Equality, 1972 to 1976." *Public Opinion Quarterly* 46:195–215.

Kinder, Donald R., and David O. Sears (1981). "Prejudice and Politics: Symbolic Racism vs. Racial Threats to the 'Good Life.'" *Journal of Personality and Social Psychology* 40:414–31.

Kirby, David J.; Robert T. Harris; Robert L. Crain; and Christine H. Rossell (1973). *Political Strategies in Northern School Desegregation.* Lexington, Mass.: D. C. Heath.

Kluegel, James R. (1985). "If There Isn't a Problem, You Don't Need a Solution." *American Behavioral Scientist* 28:761–84.

Kohn, Melvin L. (1976). "Occupational Structure and Alienation." *American Journal of Sociology* 82:111–30.

Lalonde, James E. (1989). "District's Controlled-Choice Plan is Careening Toward Chaos." *Seattle Times,* June 12.

Larson, John C. (1980). "Takoma Park Magnet School Evaluation, Part 1." Rockville, Md.: Montgomery County Public Schools.

————— (1981). "Takoma Park Magnet School Evaluation, Part 2." Rockville, Md.: Montgomery County Public Schools.

Larson, John C., and Barbara A. Allen (1988). "A Microscope on Magnet Schools, 1983–1986. Vol. 2: Pupil and Parent Outcomes." Rockville, Md.: Department of Educational Accountability, Montgomery County Public Schools. January.

Levine, Daniel U., and Connie Campbell (1977). "Developing and Implementing Big-City Magnet School Programs." In Daniel U. Levine and Robert Havighurst (eds.), *The Future of Big-City Schools.* Berkeley, Calif.: McCutchan.

Levine, Daniel U., and Eugene F. Eubanks (1980). "Attracting Nonminority Students to Magnet Schools in Minority Neighborhoods." *Integrated Education* 18:52–58.

Levine, Daniel U.; Eugene F. Eubanks; Connie Campbell; and Lois S. Roskoski (1980). "A Study of Selected Issues Involving Magnet Schools in Big-City School Districts." Report to the National Institute of Education, Washington, D.C., June.

Lord, Dennis J. (1975). "School Busing and White Abandonment of Public Schools." *Southeastern Geographer* 15:81–92.

Los Angeles Monitoring Committee (1979). "Proposed Expanded and New Magnet Programs, 1979–1980." Report to the Superior Court of the State of California for the County of Los Angeles, April.

Mahard, Rita, and Robert L. Crain (1983). "Research on Minority

Achievement in Desegregated Schools." In C. H. Rossell and W. D. Hawley (eds.), *The Consequences of School Desegregation*. Philadelphia: Temple University Press.

Marseille, Elliott (1979). "Denver." In David Kirp et al., "Judicial Management of School Desegregation Cases." Report prepared for the National Institute of Education, Washington, D.C.

Massachusetts Research Center (1976). "Education and Enrollment: Boston During Phase II." Boston: Massachusetts Research Center.

Mayesky, Mary E. (1980). "Phillips Extended Day Magnet: A Successful Blend of Day Care and Academics." *Educational Horizons*, Summer, pp. 179–82.

McClendon, McKee J., and Fred P. Pestello (1982). "White Opposition: To Busing or to Desegregation?" *Social Science Quarterly* 63:70–82.

McConahay, John B. (1982). "Self-Interest Versus Racial Attitudes as Correlates of Anti-Busing Attitudes in Louisville." *Journal of Politics* 44:692–720.

McConahay, John B., and Willis D. Hawley (1977). "Attitudes of Louisville and Jefferson County Citizens Toward Busing for Public School Desegregation: Results from the Second Year." Durham, N.C.: Duke University, Institute of Policy Sciences and Public Affairs.

Meadows, George R. (1976). "Open Enrollment and Fiscal Incentives." In Florence Levinsohn and Benjamin Wright (eds.), *School Desegregation: Shadow and Substance*. Chicago: University of Chicago Press.

Miller, Steven (1981). "Conflict: The Nature of White Opposition to Mandatory Busing." Ph.D. dissertation, University of California, Los Angeles.

Milwaukee Public Schools (1985). "Catalog of Educational Opportunities for September." Milwaukee: Milwaukee Public Schools.

Montclair Public Schools (1985). "Watchung." Montclair, N.J.: Montclair Public Schools.

Morgan, David R., and Robert E. England (1981). "Assessing the Progress of Large City School Desegregation: A Case Survey Approach." Report to the National Institute of Education. Norman, Okla.: University of Oklahoma.

—— (1982). "Large District School Desegregation: A Preliminary

Assessment of Techniques." *Social Science Quarterly* 63:688–700.

Myrdal, Gunnar (1944). *An American Dilemma: The Negro Problem and Modern Democracy.* New York: Random House.

National Opinion Research Center (1985). "General Social Surveys, 1972–85: Cumulative Codebook," pp. 148–61. Chicago: NORC.

——— (1988). *1988 General Social Surveys.* Chicago: NORC.

Nicoletti, John A., and Tom W. Patterson (1974). "Attitudes Toward Busing as a Means of Desegregation." *Psychological Reports* 35:371–76.

Olson, Mancur (1965). *The Logic of Collective Action.* Cambridge, Mass.: Harvard University Press.

Orfield, Gary (1969). *The Reconstruction of Southern Education: The Schools and the 1964 Civil Rights Act.* New York: Wiley.

——— (1976). *Desegregation and the Cities, the Trends, and the Policy Choices.* Washington, D.C.: Brookings Institution.

——— (1978). "Report to the Court: Crawford v. Los Angeles." Los Angeles: U.S. Superior Court.

——— (1982). "Desegregation of Black and Hispanic Students from 1968 to 1980." Washington, D.C.: Joint Center for Political Studies.

——— (1983). "Public School Desegregation in the United States, 1968–1980." Washington, D.C.: Joint Center for Political Studies.

——— (1988). "School Desegregation in the 1980s." *Equity and Choice* 4 (February Special Issue):25–28.

Orfield, Gary, and Franklin Monfort (1986). "Are American Schools Resegregating in the Reagan Era? A Statistical Analysis of Segregation Levels from 1980 to 1984." Working Paper, National School Desegregation Project. Chicago: University of Chicago.

Page, Benjamin J. (1977). "Elections and Social Choice: The State of the Evidence." *American Journal of Political Science* 21:639–68.

Pearce, Diana (1980). "Breaking Down Barriers: New Evidence on the Impact of Metropolitan School Desegregation on Housing Patterns." Washington, D.C.: National Institute of Education.

Pride, Richard A. (1980). "Patterns of White Flight: 1971–1979."

Nashville, Tenn.: Vanderbilt University, Political Science Department.

Pride, Richard A., and J. David Woodard (1978). "Busing Plans, Media Agenda, and White Flight." Paper presented at the annual meeting of the Southwestern Political Science Association, Houston, April.

—— (1985). *The Burden of Busing: The Politics of Desegregation in Nashville, Tennessee.* Nashville, Tenn.: Vanderbilt University.

Rosenbaum, James E., and Stefan Presser (1978). "Voluntary Racial Integration in a Magnet School." *School Review* 86:156–87.

Ross, J. Michael (1981). Statement to the Senate Judiciary Committee, Subcommittee on the Separation of Powers (J-97-29), 97th Congress, 1st Session, September 30.

—— (1983). "The Effectiveness of Alternative Desegregation Strategies: The Issue of Voluntary Versus Mandatory Policies in Los Angeles." Boston: Boston University.

Ross, J. Michael; Brian Gratton; and Ruth Clarke (1982). "School Desegregation and White Flight Reexamined: Is the Issue Different Statistical Models?" Boston: Boston University.

Rossell, Christine H. (1975–1976). "School Desegregation and White Flight." *Political Science Quarterly* 92:675–96.

—— (1978a). "Assessing the Unintended Impacts of Public Policy: School Desegregation and Resegregation." Report to the National Institute of Education. Boston: Boston University.

—— (1978b). "The Effect of School Integration on Community Integration." *Journal of Education* 160 (May):46–62.

—— (1978c). "White Flight: Pros and Cons." *Social Policy* 9 (Nov.–Dec.):46–51.

—— (1979). "Magnet Schools as a Desegregation Tool: The Importance of Contextual Factors in Explaining Their Success." *Urban Education* 14:303.

—— (1983). "Applied Social Science Research: What Does It Say About the Effectiveness of School Desegregation Plans?" *Journal of Legal Studies* 12:69–107.

—— (1985a). Review of Charles Willie (ed.), *School Desegregation Plans That Work* (1984). *Contemporary Sociology* 14:392–94.

—— (1985b). "What Is Attractive About Magnet Schools?" *Urban Education* 20:7–22.

—— (1985c). "The Effectiveness of Alternative Desegregation Plans

For Hattiesburg, Mississippi." A Report to the U.S. Department of Justice, Exhibit G-2, *United States v. Pittman*, 622 F. Supp. 622 (1985).

———— (1986a). "Estimating the Net Benefit of School Desegregation Reassignments." *Educational Evaluation and Policy Analysis* 7:217–27.

———— (1986b). *Estimating the Effectiveness of a Magnet School Desegregation Plan for the Yonkers School District*. Report prepared for the U.S. District Court in the case of *United States and NAACP v. Yonkers Board of Education et al.*, March 17.

———— (1986c). *Estimating the Effectiveness of a Magnet School Desegregation Plan for the Savannah–Chatham County School District*. Report prepared for the U.S. District Court in the case of *Stell and United States v. The Board of Public Education for the City of Savannah and the County of Chatham*, September 23.

———— (1987). "The Buffalo Controlled Choice Plan." *Urban Education* 22, no. 3:328–54.

———— (1988). "Is It the Busing or the Blacks?" *Urban Affairs Quarterly* 24, no. 1:138–48.

Rossell, Christine H., and Charles L. Glenn (1988). "The Cambridge Controlled Choice Plan." *Urban Review* 20, no. 2:75–94.

Rossell, Christine H., and Willis D. Hawley (1982). "Policy Alternatives for Minimizing White Flight." *Educational Evaluation and Policy Analysis* 4, no. 2:205–22.

———— (eds.) (1983). *The Consequences of School Desegregation*. Philadelphia: Temple University Press.

Rossell, Christine H., and J. Michael Ross (1979). *The Long Term Effect of Court-Ordered Desegregation on Student Enrollment in Central City Public School Systems: The Case of Boston, 1974–1979*. Report prepared for the Boston School Department.

Royster, Eugene C.; D. Catherine Baltzell; and Frances C. Simmons (1979). *Study of the Emergency School Aid Act Magnet School Program*. Cambridge, Mass.: Abt Associates.

Salamon, Lester (1979). "The Time Dimension in Policy Evaluation: The Case of the New Deal Land-Reform Experiments." *Public Policy* 27:129–83.

Salem, Richard G., and William J. Bowers (1972). "Severity of Formal

Sanctions as a Deterrent to Deviant Behavior." In Samuel Krislov et al. (eds.), *Compliance and the Law.* Beverly Hills, Calif.: Sage.

San Diego City Schools (1988–89). "Magnet Programs." San Diego, Calif.: San Diego City Schools.

Save Our Schools (1989). "Initiative 34 Petition." Seattle, Wash.: Save Our Schools.

Schwartz, Michael (1976). *Radical Protest and Social Structure.* New York: Academic.

Scigliano, Eric (1989). "The Plan Hits the Fan." *Seattle Weekly,* June 21:25.

Sears, David O., and Harris M. Allen, Jr. (1984). "The Trajectory of Local Desegregation Controversies and Whites' Opposition to Busing." In N. Miller and M. Brewer (eds.), *Groups in Contact: The Psychology of Desegregation.* New York: Academic Press.

Sears, David O.; Carl P. Hensler; and Leslie K. Speer (1979). "Whites' Opposition to 'Busing': Self-Interest or Symbolic Politics?" *American Political Science Review* 73:369–84.

Sears, David O.; Richard R. Lau; Tom R. Tyler; and Harris M. Allen, Jr. (1980). "Self-Interest vs. Symbolic Politics in Policy Attitudes and Presidential Votings." *American Political Science Review* 74:670–84.

Sears, David O.; Tom R. Tyler; Jack Citrin; and Donald R. Kinder (1978). "Political System Support and Public Response to the Energy Crisis." *American Journal of Political Science* 22:56–82.

Sieber, Samuel D., and David E. Wilder (1973). *The School in Society.* New York: Free Press.

Slavin, Robert E. (1978). "Student Teams and Comparison Among Equals: Effects on Academic Performance and Student Attitudes." *Journal of Educational Psychology* 70:532–38.

——— (1979). "Effects of Biracial Learning Teams on Cross-racial Friendships." *Journal of Educational Psychology* 71:381–87.

——— (1983). *Cooperative Learning.* New York: Longman.

Smith, Vernon H. (1978). "Do Optional Alternative Public Schools Work?" *Childhood Education* 54:211–14.

Smylie, Mark A. (1983). "Reducing Racial Isolation in Large School Districts: The Comparative Effectiveness of Mandatory and

Voluntary Desegregation Strategies." *Urban Education* 17: 477–502.

Snider, William (1988). "Little Rock Rejects 'Controlled Choice,' Seeks New Plan." *Education Week*, October 19:15.

Stancill, Nancy (1981). "Houston's Strongest Little Magnet." *American Education* 17:19–22.

Stanley, Cheryl (1982). "Parent and Student Attitudes Toward Magnet Schools: Do the Decision Makers Care?" Paper presented at the annual meeting of the Southwest Educational Research Association, Austin, Tex., February.

Stinchcombe, Arthur L., and D. Garth Taylor (1980). "On Democracy and School Integration." In Walter G. Stephan and Joe R. Feagin (eds.), *School Desegregation: Past, Present, and Future*. New York: Plenum Press.

Stover, Robert V., and Don W. Brown (1975). "Understanding Compliance and Noncompliance with Law: The Contributions of Utility Theory." *Social Science Quarterly* 56:362–75.

Taeuber, Karl, E. and Alma Taeuber (1965). *Negroes in Cities*. Chicago: Aldine.

Taeuber, Karl E., and Franklin D. Wilson (1978). "The Demographic Impact of School Desegregation Policy." In M. E. Draft and M. Schneider (eds.), *Population Policy Analysis*. Lexington, Mass.: Lexington Books.

Taylor, D. Garth (1986). *Public Opinion and Collective Action*. Chicago: University of Chicago Press.

Taylor, D. Garth; Paul Sheatsley; and Andrew Greeley (1978). "Attitudes Toward Racial Integration." *Scientific American* 238, June, pp. 42–49.

Tiebout, Charles M. (1956). "A Pure Theory of Local Government Expenditures." *Journal of Political Economy* 64:416–24.

U.S. Commission on Civil Rights (1962). *Civil Rights U.S.A.: Public Schools, Southern States*. Staff reports. Washington, D.C.: Government Printing Office.

Van Valey, Thomas L.; Wade C. Roof; and Jerome E. Wilcox (1977). "Trends in Residential Segregation: 1960–1970." *American Journal of Sociology* 82:826–44.

Weaver, Roy A. (1979). "Magnet School Curricula: Distinctly Different?" Paper presented at the annual meeting of the American Educational Research Association, San Francisco, April.

Weber, Larry J.; Janice K. McBee; and Joseph H. Lyles (1983). "An Evaluation of Fundamental Schools." Paper presented at the annual meeting of the American Educational Research Association, Montreal, April.

Wegmann, Robert G. (1980). "School Impact on Neighborhood Composition." Paper presented at the annual meeting of the American Educational Research Association, Boston, April.

Weidman, John C. (1975). "Resistance of White Adults to the Busing of School Children." *Journal of Research and Development in Education* 9 (Fall): 123–29.

Welch, Finis, and Audrey Light (1987). *New Evidence on School Desegregation.* Washington, D.C.: U.S. Commission on Civil Rights.

Wilkinson, III, J. Harvie (1979). *From Brown to Bakke: The Supreme Court and School Integration.* New York: Oxford University Press.

Willie, Charles V. (ed.) (1984). *School Desegregation Plans That Work.* Westport, Conn.: Greenwood Press.

Willie, Charles V., and Fultz, M. (1984). "Do Mandatory School Desegregation Plans Work?" In Charles V. Willie (ed.), *School Desegregation Plans That Work.* Westport, Conn.: Greenwood Press.

Wilson, Franklin D. (1985). "The Impact of School Desegregation Programs on White Public School Enrollment, 1968–1976." *Sociology of Education* 58: 137–53.

Index

Index of Court Cases

259